THE ART OF DRAMA

THE
ART OF
DRAMA

BY

Ronald Peacock

GREENWOOD PRESS, PUBLISHERS
WESTPORT, CONNECTICUT

Library of Congress Cataloging in Publication Data

Peacock, Ronald, 1907-
   The art of drama.

   Reprint of the 1957 ed. published by Routledge &
K. Paul, London.
   Bibliography: p.
   1. Drama. 2. Arts. I. Title.
[PN1631.P37 1974]   808.2   73-3026
ISBN 0-8371-6825-2

28.816.

First published in 1957 by Routledge & Kegan Paul,
London

Reprinted with the permission of Routledge & Kegan
Paul Ltd.

Reprinted in 1974 by Greenwood Press,
a division of Congressional Information Service, Inc.
88 Post Road West, Westport, Connecticut 06881

Library of Congress catalog card number 73-3026
ISBN 0-8371-6825-2

Printed in the United States of America

10 9 8 7 6 5 4 3 2

CONTENTS

CONTENTS

CHAPTER ONE

INTRODUCTION

ONE OF THE MOST challenging problems of criticism is to define in a satisfactory way the nature of drama as an art-form, because, as we well know, it belongs both to literature and the theatre. It is a composite form, using different "arts" to one end. The dramatist, the author, the scene and costume designer, each with their own materials, contribute expressive forms that harmonize and create a single unified effect. This process suggests very forcibly the kinship of the arts; if they had not something in common they could scarcely interfuse so smoothly and effectively. And it lays on us the obligation to find, if we wish to account adequately for dramatic form, either a single aesthetic principle for all the arts, or at least a principle that accounts for their effective association in composite forms. Only in this way can a theory be worked out to explain the variety of drama, the main types of play, the relation between acting, scene and dialogue, the varying use of verse and prose, and the creation of style and poetic effect. A "theory of literature" in itself is not enough. We need a theory that links literature and poetry with the other arts, a theory that reaches further than those conceived with reference only to words or to literary forms for reading.

Amidst a large number of suggestive ideas about art there are two, " form" and "expression", that still exert the greatest attraction and prove more generally useful even though their meaning is complicated and difficult to define. Neither gives the help needed, however, for our particular problem. So I shall base my argument on a view of *images* and *imagery*, which in due course will be related to both form and expression. As a first step I shall try to establish certain principles of imagery in relation to all art, including the arts of language, and it may as well be said at once that this will mean liberating the term imagery from its over-narrow connotation, for figures of speech, in English literary criticism. A characteristic use of images in aesthetic contexts will be focused and related to other kinds of imagery and thought, and the significance of metaphor will be discussed.

The next step will be to examine the implicit imagery in language whether in written or spoken form, after which it will be possible to suggest a comprehensive definition of art. The problem of the literary forms and kinds has then to be squarely faced and I shall re-state it, as far as its aesthetic aspects are concerned, in terms of imagery, but with a reference to psychological and social influences to account for the genesis of such forms and kinds. I shall devote a chapter to music in its relation to poetry, in order to view the whole problem afresh, including the idea of music as the perfect art-form, from the point of view of the new principles of imagery. This section will explore the meaning of such notions as "the music of poetry", the nature of the overlapping between the two arts, the relation between auditory imagery in language and in music, and also the historical influence of the musical ideal cultivated by romantic and symbolist poets, and its effect particularly on modern views of "the poetic" in all the arts. It will also include a comment on the relation between drama and opera. I have gone into this whole subject with particular care for the further reason that the epithet "musical" is too often used loosely and imprecisely; we tend to fall back on it to indicate with finality an element in poetry that defies analysis. This has the effect of making a quite inordinate mystery of music and obscuring the real relationship of the latter with life and experience, a relationship which I believe it shares with poetry and the other arts. Finally, with the ground thus prepared in many directions, the problems of dramatic form will be reviewed.

I look upon my definition of art, given in chapter seven, as tenta-tive because I do not pretend to the kind of statement a professional philosopher would wish to make. It is put forward because it helps my main argument along. Insofar as this essay is a study in aesthetics it is limited to one aspect, the problem of inter-related art-forms, which it attempts to illumine by a theory of *intertextures* of imagery in which the characteristic feature is the *functioning* of images in a unified structure. This puts me nearer to criticism than aesthetic; a philosopher or a psychologist would give a much more elaborate account of images, for example. There are in any case innumerable theories about the mental event or phenomenon known as "image" and it could not be claimed that agreement has yet by any means been reached upon a generally satisfactory hypothesis. If we first tried to solve absolutely the problem of what images are we should probably never reach our own particular problem. In general, however, I have found the middle section of Collingwood's *Principles of Art*, and Sartre's *Psychology of Imagination*, very illuminating, though this does not mean that I have made either of their theories my particular starting point. I have thrown the emphasis myself on the way images are constructively modified through their function in certain contexts. Given this circumscribed purpose I hope my language is precise enough to mean something useful.

It must, however, be a language of generality, since the essence of my inquiry is not the analysis of particular arts in unique examples but the search for generalizations that account for kinship, unity in variety, overlap, and forms of synthesis. Scholars in the various arts, specializing in a period, a genre, one single artist, or any other limited subject, have an enormous wealth of specialized terminology at their disposal, the effect of which, as it clarifies detail, is to make broader generalization appear vapid. Some may feel that the ideas of this essay are sometimes presented in a generalized form that involves an over-simplification. I can only hope that the argument as a whole has its own kind of precision and particularity. If I had used the technical languages and detailed procedures of various specialisms at every stage, supposing that possible for one person, my main purpose of suggesting a theory of inter-relationship could not have been executed. But a theory of this kind is indispensable to the elucidation of a composite form like drama.

In the text I have avoided polemical diversions and even, to a large extent, references to the many theories of art, poetry, and drama put forward in the past. I aimed to keep my argument within decent limits and as simple and unencumbered as possible. A select bibliography and the notes indicate part of my debt to scholarship. I say part because it is nowadays impossible to list all the aesthetic and critical writings which one reads. My interest in the aesthetic aspects of the subject reaches back to my student days in England and France, and afterwards in Germany, where one of my early studies was about the musical aspects of Thomas Mann's work.

Some of the material of chapters IX and X appeared, in somewhat different form, in an article entitled "Probleme des Musikalischen in der Sprache", in *Weltliteratur*, Festschrift für Fritz Strich (Francke, Bern, 1950); and in a Rylands Lecture, "Public and Private Problems in Modern Drama", published in the *Bulletin of the John Rylands Library*, Vol. 36, No. 1, 1953. My thanks are due to the Editors of these publications for permission to use the material.

CHAPTER TWO

IMAGES AND REPRESENTATION

i. IMAGES AND ACTUAL OBJECTS

IN PAINTING AND SCULPTURE, in drama, narrative, and descriptive poetry, we are accustomed to find pictures of the external world. We are aware, at the same time, that our apprehension of these images of art is not the same thing as that of seeing the real world in front of us. When we view a man, and his portrait, we see two different things. The one is a living, moving object, the other an image fixed in paint on canvas. But the appearances of nature can be captured so faithfully in art that we recognize likeness, and we then speak of "representation". What applies to portraits is also true of landscapes, interiors, and genre pictures.

The processes involved in seeing an original person or scene, seeing a representation, and recognizing the resemblance between them are extraordinarily complex. To realize this we need only remind outselves that there are many ways of securing in paint a likeness of the same scene, many ways of rendering a portrait of the same sitter, all with truth and resemblance. It is not part of my intention to go into the problems of theory of knowledge, or to analyse in detail the psychological processes by which we apprehend the outside world. I want simply to find a convenient way of distinguishing the images of art from other kinds, or, putting it another way, of focussing attention on the features of *aesthetic contexts* of imagery in contrast to other contexts in which images play a part. The percepts, sensations, and impressions (or "impression-images") I have in response to the external world are part of a constant stream amidst which I perform certain actions; either I use them for my activities or they are a background accompaniment. The remembered images of objects, on the other hand, form part of contexts of

5

thought, either as the subjects of simple recollection, or of studied analysis, or of information, and so on; but they too belong to an incessant process of change. The first mark of the aesthetic context, say in a painting or a descriptive poem, is that the images are fixed in a medium. Viewing a sunset I may in aesthetic enthusiasm form a beautiful picture for myself; but the scene changes, the sun sets, and I am helpless to prevent it. Turner's suns, always setting, never set. They are a formula of paint, a construction with a special kind of meaning and made with its own kind of purpose.

What those meanings and purposes are will be touched upon gradually in this inquiry, but one of them faces us at the outset because it is concerned with the question of resemblance, of the similitude between a description of art and an original in nature. Art is not simple imitation, but some resemblance is often part of the artist's purpose. No doubt he will say that his picture is "his" view, or his "impression", of the scene, that it differs from another artist's (and from yours and mine), and that he sets store by the difference, which marks his originality. It is, nevertheless, in some measure a depiction, and *of* something. It has some sort of a link with an original. And the question is, what are the limits of such resemblance? Can they be so close that they cease to be art?

It will make for clarity if we concentrate at this point on visual art, since the problem of representation appears here in its most striking form, and also because drama, with which we shall later be concerned, involves a visual representation of persons and milieu. We can best start from the question: what do we mean when we speak of what a thing "actually" looks like. Can this be reproduced in a drawing? And is such a drawing "art"?

In order to have a point of reference I shall use the notion of "naive realism", assuming a commonsense world by virtue of which we can speak of different views or "interpretations" of things observed. If two people sit in a park they will see objects before them, a group of trees, a shrubbery, a lake, lawns, flower-beds, old men on benches, young women with prams, boys playing cricket, houses overlooking the park, and so on. They can talk about these things and understand each other's references. If they were to choose a house and draw it from where they were sitting their drawings, given a modicum of ability, would probably reveal something in common, for instance its outline, colour, and the arrangement of doors, windows, and gables. This content of common perception denotes the agreed external world. Apart from the common content there are the variable elements, due to the fact that we each see differently, each noticing some things at the expense of others, some of us more susceptible to shape, others to colour, and so on.

The agreed world of common perception is in one sense a steady, secure world; it is reassuring to feel that the park, lawns, lake, trees, houses are solidly there and won't run away. But it is also in another sense, and from the visual point of view, an imprecise world, since it is always changing with the time of day, the atmosphere, the seasons, and the years, and since two people never, even at the same moment, see the identical visual scene, nor do they necessarily scrutinize or absorb it. This is what makes the question as to what things "actually" look like so difficult. Normally, what we actually see is a mass of approximately perceived or visualized objects. When, on the other hand, we try to find out what things "actually look like" we interrupt what we are doing in order to pursue a special purpose. We enter an inquiry; we find ourselves looking closer, focusing our attention, considering and thinking, and in fact conducting a scrutiny. And this scrutiny may be of a kind leading through analysis to conceptual and scientific precision or it may be of another kind leading through images to aesthetic precision. The first contributes to a public world of scientific knowledge, whilst the second remains our private, individual experience.

The problem is well seen in the approach of some present-day physiologists and neurologists. They distinguish between a "physical world" and a "perceptual world". The one is a common world scientifically established by evidence and inference, and agreed upon as the source of the perceptual world. The perceptual world is private to each individual, determined by all the factors of his own physiological constitution and situation in the physical world at any given moment. This perceptual world has been described as a "symbolic representation of the physical world".[1] It is a representation, and a set of symbols, because its contents are neither identical nor contemporaneous with something in the physical world, but *correspond* to the latter, their own seat being in the mind that generates the representation.

Drawings that attempt to achieve as close a likeness as possible to physical objects are animated in principle by a scientific purpose; they avoid studiously the impressionistic, subjective, partial view; they seek a truth of "normal" appearances. Think, for instance, of a

7

complicated road-crossing with double roundabout, traffic islands and signals, illuminated with lamps of various shape and colour. In such a place one usually has a vague general impression of road channels, kerbstones, concrete stands and posts, islands, mounds, and other shapes. But an attempted drawing of the "actual" scene would be an elaborate blue-print showing the precise lay-out of the roadways, traffic signals, and so on, all spaced—from one chosen position in space of course—proportionately according to their actual positions and with their particular shapes and colours. Such a drawing still lacks in the strictest sense precision, but it has eliminated the element of impression and eschews also any feeling about the scene. It is a pictorial reconstruction based on analysis. So-called faithful depictions are always like this, carried through to the last detail. We go over and round the objects, isolating and inspecting their details one by one, marking off one small area and then another for attention, and eliminating accidental features. Examination by microscope, telescope, X-ray, and all the other instruments of analysis, follows as the natural and logical prolongation of the process. The drawing of what a hand actually looks like is supplemented by what a patch of skin looks like under the microscope, or the bone structure under X-ray. A realistic copy from nature is an image in which every detail of the object receives *isolated* attention, the only co-ordination of all the pieces being one of spatial measurement. Botanical and anatomical illustrations are proper examples of analytical drawing. Depictions of this sort certainly constitute a kind of imagery; I propose to call them scientific copy-images. Of course no graphical reproduction can attain perfect precision; the perfect representational image does not exist. They are most accurate in the proportions of measurement, which are easier to deal with than colour or light. Otherwise they are very decidedly approximations. Monochrome photographic likeness is also based on measurement, for which reason this word is often used to convey the sense of the realistic. It is worth noting, however, that monochrome photographs, except for their measurable exactitude, and certain effects of light and shade, are unrealistic. (Eisenstein recognized in this feature the potentiality of the film as an art-form, black-and-white in itself being a convention or formalization.)

Scientific copy-images, belonging as illustrations to contexts of thought and theory, are devoted to "objects", whilst aesthetic images are concerned with appearances. It cannot be maintained that they are absolutely separated from each other. We can see this from a type of image that is intermediate and might function equally well either as a scientific illustration or as an aesthetic image. A perfectly representational painting of an apple which had been positioned so as to emphasize its "apple-ness", its character of being a representative of its class, wherein would lie a preliminary normalizing process, would be both a scientific, analytical copy-image and an aesthetic image of one possible mode of appearance. I think it must also be admitted that an exact representation of any one of the innumerable possible "appearances" of an apple, alone or in juxtaposition with other objects, as a matter of light, colour and visual form, bears a scientific character, but with a change of direction; the object of representation is then not the common object "apple " but the forms of colour and light themselves. Works of art, either in part or as wholes, might easily bear the exactness of scientific illustrations, as may be seen for instance in much Flemish and Dutch art, or in the topographical water-colours of Dürer, or in the desire of Leonardo da Vinci to be true to an exact vision of objects as at least part of his purpose.[2] Impressionism, too, developed from realistic beginnings as an attempt to capture precise instantaneous visual images under the fleeting effects of light.

Acknowledging the overlap between scientific copy-images and art-images helps towards understanding their divergence, which is due to the motive for their use and the function given them. The former belong to a context of analytic seeing and scientific, or conceptual, truth. The latter belong to a context of aesthetic, or imaginal, seeing. They are both "constructions" in the sense that they are actively incorporated into processes of thought, the one with a conceptual aim, the other with an imaginative one. But further elements enter into the latter context, such as the natural interests, desires, tastes, and feelings of the artist, all of which, whilst helping to create an aesthetic context, tend to prevent a scientific or conceptual one. To these we now turn.

ii. THE GENESIS OF REPRESENTATIONAL ART-IMAGES

If the scientific copy-image attempts to answer the question as to what things *actually* look like, which involves a rational sense of the normal and the average, the aesthetic image shows what they *look* like, admitting a multiplicity of possible visual appearances. This carries with it the suggestion of a certain mode of attention from which results a certain kind of context for images.

Schopenhauer classed the aesthetic state as one in which we cease to be involved in interested action (the mainspring of life) and become contemplative. In this condition the aspect of things, to which our fretfully purposive activity otherwise blinds us, is revealed. This idea, though in some ways over-simple, is still one of the most helpful pointers to the aesthetic experience, because it indicates clearly a frame within which it occurs. One kind of activity ceases and another begins. The first is vital, physical; thought is involved only insofar as the mental faculties, the use of intelligence and knowledge and so on, support the aims of the activity, as in walking, cooking, playing cricket, catching a bus, earning one's living, or whatever, which we can do better for a little application. The second kind of activity is purely mental.[3]

Our ordinary habit is thus to treat objects in a practical way, concentrating attention on them only to the extent that suits our purpose. When going to a station to catch a train we are vaguely aware of our surroundings as a flux of sensations amidst which we perceive in a somewhat more stabilized or concretized form our route to the train. We then see the train standing at a platform. Since we wish to catch it we register "our train" and assume that it is an object of many aspects but with two or three attributes pre-eminently important to us at this moment, the faculty of locomotion, of transporting passengers, and being the train we want. Whatever it looks like, or, with more complication, whatever range of images it might present to a disinterested eye, it is useful for us at the moment to overlook them and act on the sense of the conventional object "train". Otherwise we may allow the images to hold our attention, enter in consequence an aesthetic trance, and miss the train, which is what artists often do. The assumption that an object before us corresponds to a conventional type makes possible innumerable daily actions which fall into a pattern of automatic and time-saving habits.

These habits ingrained by practical necessity make us impervious to what things look like. Sometimes, by accident, the phenomenal nature of a scene is forced upon us, as when in a landscape of high mountains and lakes with the sun shimmering unevenly through banks of clouds it is often impossible to distinguish between water, sky, cloud, and mountains; each appears as the others and only the recollection of our geographical situation in a commonsense world persuades us that there is anything before us but a composition of shifting gleams in varying hues of grey. Normally, however, if we wish to seek a high visual awareness of something we have to dispose ourselves first. To pause for a moment and secure an impression of a scene for its own sake is an elementary form of incipient aesthetic experience. We see, for example, in a vague sort of way, this small-town main street along which we must pass to reach a proposed destination and we do not observe more than our purpose requires. But if we attend to the street as a varied content of visible things we experience a state of visual awareness and concentration which may become in various ways exclusive and establish a certain kind of completeness framed off from the rest of things. Where before there were blurred or at least neglected appearances of no value to an inattentive mind a picture forms with pictorial coherence and meaning. Not that there is one meaning only in the scene. Different minds or sensibilities, the same mind in different moods, or with changing attention, will see variations of the visual picture, but the experience, however modified, is of a recognizable type. The impressions of sense have been organized into an order, so that we may say : what a riot of life and colour! Or, how quiet the street and how beautiful and still the low white houses and over-arching trees under the blue sky! Or, with a more recherché intention, what an impressive pattern of lines, masses, surfaces, textures and colours! If, going beyond this aesthetic situation, we wanted to make art by painting a picture of the scene, we should do so in such a way as to make our main impression or feeling apparent, by selecting some, and modifying others, of the various visual elements of the scene. In other words we should construct in paint the imagery that incorporated our centralizing idea or feeling.[4]

This is what we mean by aesthetic contexts, which are contexts of imaginative thought, and they are the basis of the images of art in their simpler representational aspects. A picture is a total image of this kind, and by total image we mean a unified image-pattern, in which all the elements of the scene are adjusted and assimilated to each other within one predominant visual purpose. Analytically we distinguish in a painting its composition, colour, light, tone, perspective, the objects and their design, etc., but all these cohere inseparably in an imagery carrying one visual interpretation of a scene.

Contexts of imaginative awareness, as distinct from perceptual or conceptual awareness, enable us to make visual discoveries about the world. Many painters have explored nature in this sense. They set out to study its appearances and they felt always that their painting discovered aspects of nature which were in no way a "subjective" matter but were essentially there to be seen and, once displayed, to command assent from others. Constable, a prominent example, sought by close observation qualities in nature not portrayed before; he spoke of the "art of seeing nature", to be learnt by humble application.[5] A remark of Cézanne illustrates how the artist tries to put himself into the closest touch with circumjacent nature: "So I was obliged to give up my project of doing Poussin again entirely from nature, and not constructed piecemeal from notes, drawings and fragments of study; in short of painting a living Poussin in the open air with colour and light, instead of one of those works imagined in a studio, where everything has the brown colouring of feeble daylight without reflections from the sky and the sun.[6] "*Instead of one of those works imagined in a studio*—Cézanne here places the imagination in direct contact with colour and light, so that his painting, in its turn, may reflect this intimacy. He sees; and then he paints.

As we said above, however, in connexion with the street scene, different aspects of the scene may be focused, and you cannot have them all together, but only successively. You must choose which visual meaning you are at the moment most interested in or impressed by or emotionally responsive to and wish to establish. So that although the aesthetic experience produces a "discovery" in the sense just discussed, it is always a selective imagery abstracted from all the possible imagery of the scene. When Constable wishes to represent something in nature not discovered before he must presumably stress that at the expense of what had in fact before been known; so that his discovery is not of "reality" in the absolute but of a new aspect of reality presented as imagery. Not a wilful imagery concocted solely by his own imagination and not corresponding to what others might experience; but nevertheless an imagery that constitutes a selective interpretation. Thus we may say that the representational aspect of art shows a progressive discovery of visual truth in all its variety, set against habit perception, which is practical, and against mechanical processes which determine prominence for some features over others in our ordinary perceptual experience.

When the imagination interprets the external world in the way suggested we admit a factor of construction in the process, since selection, or emphasis, are constructive processes. And as we said earlier, interest itself, the pre-rational element, as for instance Constable's interest in landscape, constitutes an initial direction of the imaginative process. But the constructive factor is important in connexion with composition and the unity of effect achieved by it. For the unity of art-imagery is constructive by contrast with the analytic disunity of scientific copy-imagery. In the latter the only unified features are the simple outlines or shapes of natural objects, or their parts, taken separately. There is mathematical co-ordination, of course, but apart from that such images serve a unity not in but outside themselves, the implied conceptual unity of scientific theory. In art-imagery the unity derives from the focusing of a meaning in visual terms (I avoid complications at this stage) and the accompanying centripetal character of all the elements of the composition.

Up to this point we have been trying to understand a representational quality or function of images for the simple reason that art often includes depiction and portraiture as part of its purpose. We have already mentioned, however, that varied motives, most of them passionate rather than rational or scientific, influence the making of art, so that " pure representation " is rarely, if ever, its single purpose. The artist gives us a picture of a landscape, but he also expresses his feelings. Visual interpretation, which we associate with the aesthetic type of imagery, is itself influenced profoundly by the feelings, which speak to us with great eloquence from the images of art. The artist's picture shows us nature, as seen by him, in his own way, to the making of which his temperament and feelings have made a contribution whether small or large. What a painter paints, or a poet writes about, the subjects they choose, the ideas they have, are governed both by the immediate stimulus, a given subject or scene, and also by their whole mental and emotional habit, which determines the direction of their interest. Everyone is at the mercy of this pre-intellectual and pre-moral power, which extends its influence into the very manner of conceiving and treating the problems that we are always consciously having to face. There is a non-representational and subjective significance in any picture or poem if for no other reason than that it has *this* content, *this* subject, *these* situations, when it might have had so many others; and this applies to the most devotedly " objective " picture ever attempted. Raphael chooses one subject, Rembrandt another, according to the compulsion of their interest.

The true position is that representation and expressive feeling intermingle constantly and it is an error to wish to confine the purpose of art, when it does in fact show the external world, to either one or the other. The question of the complete "distortion" of natural forms, and the related one of abstraction, will be dealt with later. Here we are considering the element of deliberate representation and its place in art, and we wish, in opposition to a strong contemporary tendency to dissipate its importance in favour of extreme theories of symbolism or expressionism, to defend its rights, but on proper aesthetic grounds. The best way of putting the matter is that, according to these, the representational in art includes expression, as in the nature of individual vision; and expression in its turn may include the representational since some of our feelings are a direct response to the visual world. Their interfusion takes innumerable forms, as may be observed in the landscapes of such varied artists as Constable, Ruysdael, Turner, Corot, and the Impressionists. All the characterizing terms of art criticism reflect the process, as we see when, in connexion with landscape painting, there is room for epithets like ideal, neo-Platonic, literary, pious, heroic, dramatic, sentimental, Arcadian, serene, nostalgic, and so on. This language of criticism, indicating both nature and its treatment, an impression together with a response, reality and an adherent feeling, does justice to the great variety of emotional tone with which the external world may be pictured. Sir Kenneth Clark's *Landscape into Art* is a brilliantly sustained analysis of the involutions of the representational and the expressive in the depiction of nature. But in all this the essential point is that the interest lies not naively in the natural scene, and not in the feelings only, with the scene degraded to a mere titillating agent, but simultaneously in both ; in the emotional response and the scene that occasions it. An example of a similar aesthetic process in poetry is found in Wordsworth where human and emotional meanings flow from the lakes, fells, crags, flowers, birds and beasts of Wordsworth's nature but are only real so long as the nature itself is real. They are indissolubly linked with the *presence* of nature.

The limit of representational art is reached when the imagery loses all its possible literal significance and becomes purely "symbolic" or abstractly "expressive". Obvious cases are allegorical or dream landscapes, as in Bosch and the surrealists. A less obvious one would be for instance Claude, whose landscapes often present a scene recognizably possible in nature, but with its elements so selected and composed, and generally related in a serene recession to a distant expanse of light, that it is suffused with nostalgic aspiration for Paradise, for a guiltless and beatific world. The natural scene, voided of its significance as either representation or nature, tends to become a vehicle of feeling alone, or at least of an idealization springing from feeling.

This completes our survey of the possibilities of "representational" images. At one end of the scale we have scientific copy-imagery, near to which we distinguish a simple aesthetic image of representational function, that is, a faithful descriptive image. Then we observe a range of images, the most customary in representational art, in which expressive function is co-existent with the representational. And, finally, at the end of the scale we observe images losing their natural meaning and functioning as symbols in an allegorical or emotionally expressive scheme.

iii. THE AMBIVALENCE OF ART-IMAGERY IN RELATION TO REALITY

We have adopted the view that an aesthetic situation is initiated when the mind interrupts the continuum of sensations and impressions and transfixes a selection from it; the eye ceases to be in receptive contact with the flux of the visible world and is absorbed into a stabilized pattern of vision-thought. At this point "reality" —the physical world—is strictly speaking no longer relevant except as the inferred source of the imaginative construction, though the latter is, as we say, an interpretation of that reality. The symptom of this in the finished work of art is that its imagery has a compulsive sway over the spectator. Before nature you are free to make your own selection of features, to make your own picture, in short, and to replace it with another a moment afterwards, and still another after that. But a work of art guides your eye in the maze of its own imagery; the artist has chosen the images and distributed the emphasis and you cannot escape them. For this reason the onlooker must see the artist's images as exactly as he possibly can ; the canvas, the text, is sacred. Our mode of looking at pictures differs therefore from our mode of looking at nature. The artist, in a process partly unconscious and partly conscious, selects his images and constructs his own vision. The onlooker has to yield to the artist and construct for himself the precise imagery of the picture given him. The artist doesn't copy nature, but the onlooker has in a sense to "copy" the work of the artist with his own eyes. This unprejudiced seeing is the basis of appreciation and criticism, which, without it, are capricious.

We may conveniently recall at this stage our earlier observation that we need the world of naive realism as a point of reference. For we are only aware of the particular nature of imagination and its products because we know of other kinds of experience, thought, and awareness. We only recognize an imaginative structure of thought by contrast with other kinds. We perceive approach to or withdrawal from "reality" in a painting by recalling other kinds of contact with reality. For example, we refer representations of the human figure to our own perceptual and scientific knowledge of it. In this sense painters have often been criticized for not knowing their "anatomy". Such scientific and perceptual knowledge provides a reference that is *constant*. In short there is nearly always implicit in art a reference, by way of contradistinction, to the commonsense perceptual world, a reference which is in consequence a constituent of the imaginative experience. When looking at pictures, for instance, or seeing a play, we always at one moment or another realize that we have left the ordinary world, just as we know at once when we return to it from our temporary trance. Or, to look at it from another angle, those who are bewildered by art are so because they fail to find there the world of naive realism, the only one they know; whilst those who like art do so precisely because the world looks different and new.[7]

iv. REPRESENTATION, REALISM, AND FAULTY ART

Associated with the question of representation is that of "realism" in art. The approach from imagery puts us in a position to deal sensibly with this problem. Representational art must obviously be in some degree realistic. But as there are a thousand forms of realism the word has no value in criticism except as a relative term. This, in fact, is how it began its career round about 1830, and the historical view helps to clarify its use. At that time many artists and literary writers, surfeited by romanticism, had just begun to discover a new interest in what could be called the "real" world by contrast with the romantic world of nostalgia, fantasy, dreams, fairy-tale, subjective lyricism, and various forms of transcendental-ism. "Realism" was a useful word to point the counter-tendency; and of course it often has the sense of facing *unpleasant* reality as against buoyant wish-fulfilment or escape. We complain now that the word is too general; but in this historical context it has at least one sufficiently particular meaning.

Representational style must not be confused with bad art or art that appeals to popular taste. The average conventional portrait, for instance, pleases ordinary people because it is a fair "likeness"; by which is usually meant that only the naturally most prominent features (white hair, a fleshy nose, high colour, thick lips, etc.) are obviously repeated. It displeases those of trained taste because it lacks artistic interest or style. The displeasure does not arise, how-ever, because the portrait is too "representational" or "realistic'; after all, a portrait that eliminates the sitter is no longer a portrait, and many portraits by great painters have been highly faithful in the sense of "very like". The conventional portrait is unsatis-factory either because it is lazy in conception or crude in execution. By its intention to portray it is really by way of being a scientific drawing, a copy-imagery of the kind referred to above; and even artistically good portraits have something of this character.[8] The accusation of laziness or muddle may be brought when the painting stops short of this essential purpose, failing to be exact enough. The failure may be one of sensuous observation, or of psychological insight, or it may be due to technical inability to do justice to these. In the good portrait, on the other hand, either the painter disposes of a representational technique so exact and delicate that it equals in tone and colour the exquisite forms of nature, as in the art of the Van Eycks, and therefore suggests, like nature itself, the soul in the forms, which makes it humanly interesting; or, having psycho-logical power, he states an interpretation of character in adequate sensuous terms. This, of course, entails selection and emphasis on some features at the expense of others. It may also involve modi-fication, or "distortion", of the natural images, in order to bring to the surface what is hidden from the cursory glance. And of course, as soon as 'interpretation of character' is involved, the artist's own temperament and interest, including the motive of idealization (as in Titian), are in play, with a consequent element of self-expression mingling with the portraiture. But this only shows that portraits come under the same laws as all representational art.[9]

V. REPRESENTATION IN LITERARY ART

Having defined the problem of the representational image where it is most obvious, in the graphic arts, we turn now first to literary art, and later to drama. In literary art the problem is modified to a considerable degree by two things. First, the process of representing is an evocation; we see things only by means of words. A description of a person or scene in a poem or novel works with the images one can summon up in the imagination, and though these may sometimes be very vivid and faithful, they are so in a different way from the visual images of the graphic arts. And secondly, the writer does not represent directly from models so frequently as the painter, except in connexion with places used as the settings of stories. He makes a fragmentary use of real models, building up a fiction that is a generalized picture of life. But representation, in the sense of descriptive evocation, is certainly aimed at and the principles governing it are the same as for graphic art though the details vary.

When we speak of representation in literary works we mean that something more is intended than the simple reporting of information. The story-teller, whether he writes verse or prose, evokes the setting of his scenes, suggests the appearance of his characters and the places, houses, and rooms in which they live and work, expending all his art on making these things vivid for the sensuous imagination. Above all he makes his characters "live", as we say, indicating that he bodies forth the stuff of life itself, making us accept his fiction on equal terms with a real story. Clearly the meaning of "representation" extends beyond the visual aspects of people and their lives, and indeed most good novelists avoid too much straight description, which retards the narrative; they are satisfied with a light envelope of visual life within which they depict all the more powerfully the stream of events and dialogue.

Literary representational art in all its complexity is obviously beyond the scope of this chapter. For our present purpose it will be sufficient to look at one or two simpler kinds of description in which images play a part.

The law holds, no less in literary than in graphic art, that representations are always an imagery embodying an interpretation. They do not aim to put real objects or scenes before us with total exactitude but give a selected imagery which is true to those *aspects* of the subject which the artist requires for his immediate effects. The possibilities are of course infinite. Every author, poet, novelist, essayist, historian, has his own methods. But two passages, one prose, the other verse, will indicate salient features of the problem. First, the prose extract, from D. H. Lawrence's *The Ladybird*:

> A tall, beautifully-built girl, she had the fine stature of her father. Her shoulders were still straight. But how thin her white throat! She wore a simple black frock stitched with coloured wool round the top, and held in a loose coloured girdle: otherwise no ornaments. And her face was lovely, fair, with a soft exotic white complexion and delicate pink cheeks. Her hair was soft and heavy, of a lovely pallid gold colour, ash-blond. Her hair, her complexion were so perfectly cared for as to be almost artificial, like a hot-house flower.
>
> But alas, her beauty was a failure. She was threatened with phthisis, and was far too thin. Her eyes were the saddest part of her. They had slightly reddened rims, nerve-worn, with heavy, veined lids that seemed as if they did not want to keep up. The eyes themselves were large and of a beautiful green-blue colour. But they were dull, languid, almost glaucous.

Lawrence's descriptions of people, places, animals, and objects witness to his intense interest in the visual aspects of things. This passage is certainly not just a vague evocation, or a merely adequate indication of the appearance of one of his characters. It describes with insistence; it invites the reader to visualize, or rather it forces him to the effort, and piles up details. And yet they are governed by a central idea, and a melancholy feeling, that the girl ought to have been beautiful but wasn't, the failure being detected and traced in all the contradictions of the detail.

The verse passage will illustrate a different but very noticeable feature of descriptive writing, namely, that a predominant impression is conveyed with a great sense of clarity and sensuous impact by the use of many images which in themselves may be entirely undefined. *The Eve of St. Agnes* opens for instance thus :—

St. Agnes' Eve—Ah, bitter chill it was !
The owl, for all his feathers, was a-cold ;
The hare limp'd trembling through the frozen grass,
And silent was the flock in woolly fold :
Numb were the Beadsman's fingers, while he told
His rosary, and while his frosted breath,
Like pious incense from a censer old,
Seem'd taking flight for heaven, without a death,
Past the sweet Virgin's picture, while his prayer he saith.

The poet, by reference to fragments of a scene, here evokes an image
of a cold winter's night, and every reference to things is as general
as the total image is complete, vivid, precise, and particular. What
does the owl look like? We do not know; it is *an* owl, any owl. The
hare limps trembling through the grass; but there are many ways,
even for a hare, of limping through grass. Numb were the beadsman's fingers; but apart from numbness what was their physical
conformation? Were they fat or thin, wrinkled or smooth, dirty or
clean? The sweet Virgin's picture is equally general; we supply any
we may know of or care to imagine on the spur of the moment.
But from all these objects referred to in so unparticularized a manner,
and to which we each respond with images fetched from our own
recollection, and with varying vividness, there arises something very
particular, a vivid, unified impression or idea of a cold St. Agnes'
Eve which the poet prescribes to us and which we all agree about on
the basis of his presentation. It is the sort of description that evokes
in early exercises in appreciation the exclamation: the poet makes us
feel the cold!—though if he really did we might be less pleased.

This give-and-take between generality and precision in the use of
images is a most fundamental feature of literary art. Without it,
description of persons or scenes fails. One thinks of Wordsworth's
'host of golden daffodils', where the precision of the image arises
not from adding together three separate words or images but from
the contextual relation between them. A passage in Giraudoux
illustrates the point. In the *Fin de Siegfried* he describes a man as
"grand, mince, triste", and adds: 'Ces mots vagues font de lui un
portrait si précis que tu le reconnaîtras entre mille.' It is true; the
three words are separately vague, but coalescing impose a vivid
image. Descriptive passages aim always, when they are successful,
not to accumulate details with an equal degree of visual quality,

but to produce a visual impression the unity and precision of which lie in the relations created by a governing idea.

Literary description rests entirely for its visual or otherwise sensuous reality on our previous knowledge and experience of things in nature. It relies implicitly on references to our memories of sense-experience and is ineffective where these are absent.[10] I know, for instance, what sapphires, diamonds and rubies look like and their mention brings an appropriate image to my mind. But I am much less sure of onyx and agate. To these words I respond with a thought, not an image, the thought of "precious stones"; or at most I have a very tentative, fluid, rather sham image of coloured gems which is probably a pure invention. On the other hand we can have images—of exotic unknown flowers, for instance —to which we cannot put names.

Our dependence on sensational memory entails obstacles of varying force to our understanding of descriptive writing. Many descriptions occurring in novels, history, biography, and travel books, are not concerned with the sort of scene found in the Keats example, but seek a closer fidelity to the actual details of a local scene or of a person's appearance. The more this kind of fidelity is sought the more does it depend on the reader's own previous experience of similar local features. Simple examples are descriptions of scenes in foreign countries or in periods of time remote from our own. What does a " stage-coach " signify to people who have only seen automobiles? Or a samovar to a Frenchman who only drinks coffee? Or a vast secretive German "Wald" to Englishmen who have only strolled through a "wood"? One recalls the pathetic ignorance of slum children in great cities, who, never having seen trees, cannot conceive what the word means. The attempt to convey in words a sensuous image of unexperienced scenes or objects is mostly doomed to failure. All a writer can hope to do is to convey an "idea" of his subject by adroitly using analogies that do come within the experience of his reader.

This procedure is exploited to extreme lengths by journalists and radio commentators even for the description of familiar things, the reason being that it secures vividness instantaneously so long as the reference is known. Any well-known public figure, for instance, serves very well for this trick of description. To say that someone had a " Churchill look" or a "Charlie Chaplin walk", which is high-speed analogical portraiture, means that the writer relies, not on a common language, but on a common image-reference. Such a method pays for its momentary effectiveness with rapid mortality, since as soon as the particular set of references used has been replaced by another more topical, people cease to understand.

A further illustration of the same principle, but from another point of view, is found in the common experience of reading a verbal description of a person's appearance in conjunction with a portrait, as often happens in connexion with biographical or historical books. As we check the words against the reproduced portrait we feel that they are apt or penetrating. But what should we visualize for ourselves if we only had the words?

In view of these difficulties we have to accept the fact of enormous variation in vividness (or visual understanding) in connexion with descriptive writing. In the most favourable circumstances there is a high degree of sensuous realization; in the most unfavourable we are left with nothing more than a scheme of information or uncretized knowledge. As such we can of course "understand" it in some degree; but its aesthetic meaning is impaired for us.

It is not easy to make judgements as to the value of descriptions generally since so many such factors and complications are involved. But we must certainly distinguish between a description that is adequate merely because it evokes places or persons already known to us (e.g. a description of part of the town we live in or of a familiar part of London) and one that brings before our imagination a fictive setting for part of a story. The latter kind has to be an imaginative creation. The former need only be an adequate reminder; but it can also be a creation if it is conceived with equal vividness for a reader unfamiliar with the original scene. In general we can lay down that the greatest vividness, and the most forceful poetic style, are found where, as in the Keats passage, a sharp predominant impression is achieved by means of images which separately may be general, but contribute to a single meaning. In this process the poet enlists the reader's own imagination in his service, leaving it freedom in detail but guiding it irrevocably towards his main idea, his commanding total image.

This factor of the predominating idea is, as Coleridge noted, all-important, and it makes clear to us that the representational purpose in literary art follows a similar law as in the graphic arts in spite of the peculiarities of language referred to. For here, too, representation is not a copy-imagery but a selection and transposition of images that secures a particular vision or interpretation of the external world or of a world like it. The cumulative exactitude of all the possible detail of a given real scene or object is abandoned for a more purposeful selection, the result of which is a vivid imagery incorporating the sense of reality all the more persuasively in chosen aspects.

As with the graphic arts, however, quite simple descriptions are rare. The images are usually assimilated to a context in which they function not only pictorially but also as expressions of feeling. Of this more complex process, in which the dual function is maintained, Tennyson's poem CXV from *In Memoriam*, on the theme of the return of spring, is a good example :—

> Now fades the last long streak of snow,
>   Now burgeons every maze of quick
>   About the flowering squares, and thick
> By ashen roots the violets blow.
>
> Now rings the woodland loud and long,
>   The distance takes a lovelier hue,
>   And drown'd in yonder living blue
> The lark becomes a sightless song.
>
> Now dance the lights on lawn and lea,
>   The flocks are whiter down the vale,
>   And milkier every milky sail
> On winding stream or distant sea ;
>
> Where now the seamew pipes, or dives
>   In yonder greening gleam, and fly
>   The happy birds, that change their sky
> To build and brood, that live their lives
>
> From land to land; and in my breast
>   Spring wakens too, and my regret
>   Becomes an April violet,
> And buds and blossoms like the rest.

To express the passing of the numbness of sorrow and the rebirth of life the poet here incorporates himself into the cycle of nature and pictures the coming of springtime by evoking a few of its characteristic features—the unfreezing of earth, the first flowers in sheltered places, the awakening of the birds, the return of light and recovery of sparkling colour. The beautiful sensuousness of the picture is vivid with the pulse of renascent life and joy, so that if the picture leads to the feeling—"in my breast Spring wakens too"—the feeling has already surged through the picture.

Going a step further we may illustrate from drama another relationship between a poet's descriptive image and the reality of nature or people, a relationship always dependent on a context and the refraction of images as they function within it. Descriptions in the dialogue of drama show a double functional relation between reality and image, first in the description itself, and secondly in the overlapping function of the description in the dramatic economy. Take for example the famous description of Cleopatra in her barge from Act II, scene 2, of *Antony and Cleopatra* :

> The barge she sat in, like a burnish'd throne,
> Burn'd on the water. The poop was beaten gold ;
> Purple the sails, and so perfumed that
> The winds were love-sick with them; the oars were silver,
> Which to the tune of flutes kept stroke, and made
> The water which they beat to follow faster,
> As amorous of their strokes. For her own person,
> It beggar'd all description. She did lie
> In her pavilion, cloth-of-gold, of tissue,
> O'erpicturing that Venus where we see
> The fancy out-work nature. On each side her
> Stood pretty dimpled boys, like smiling Cupids,
> With divers-colour'd fans, whose wind did seem
> To glow the delicate cheeks which they did cool,
> And what they undid did.
>
> *Agr.*   O rare for Antony !
>
> *Eno.* Her gentlewomen, like the Nereides,
> So many mermaids, tended her i' th' eyes,
> And made their bends adornings. At the helm
> A seeming mermaid steers. The silken tackle
> Swell with the touches of those flower-soft hands,
> That yarely frame the office. From the barge
> A strange invisible perfume hits the sense
> Of the adjacent wharfs. The city cast

Her people out upon her; and Antony,
Enthrone'd i' th' market-place, did sit alone,
Whistling to th' air; which, but for vacancy,
Had gone to gaze on Cleopatra too,
And made a gap in nature.

Agr.   Rare Egyptian !

This passage, opening with the promise: "I will tell you", has the firm intention to describe; Enobarbus sets out to convey the rare and irresistible impression Cleopatra made on Antony seeing her for the first time and his words do strike the imagination with the vivid sense of Cleopatra's presence, of the power and splendour of what, as queen and woman, she was. I think the passage conjures up a picture, in the visual sense, but its sensuousness is not confined to that. We observe again, as in the Keats, that it is built up from fragments of evocation, from quite generalized hints, which create finally a single sensuous impression of great force. This is an "image" not only because of a certain amount of *visual* content but because a central idea, the commanding "effect' of exotic and erotic splendour, radiates through complex sensuous evocation; for not only is each of the senses, sight, smell, hearing, and touch, in turn assailed, but through the whole there runs the appeal to strong sensual feelings of various kinds.

The passage illustrates well the complicated nature of the image of verbal description, ambiguously positioned between a constructed idea and the illusion of sensuous realities. Neither as the creation of Enobarbus in the play, nor of Shakespeare, does it represent a visual reality, Cleopatra in her barge, in time and space. Those who ever saw this scene saw something different or partially so, for each would have his own variant picture. Cleopatra, we may assume, was always there, but views and reports of her would vary. This particular image is Enobarbus's, and beyond that it is Shakespeare's, put into the mouth of Enobarbus at a particular moment of the play and with a precise relevance to the whole purpose of the action.   In short, it is integral to a tragic interpretation of life in which this appearance of Cleopatra's, and its description by one character to others, is one factor.

This example demonstrates both in itself and in its dramatic context, how the representational image is always an image constructed so as to perform a function in a particular context.

vi. REPRESENTATION IN HISTORICAL WRITING

We may usefully conclude this section with a brief reference to the relation between history and the kind of representation found in art. History as the *record* of events consists of collated evidence or testimony, which gives it a basis of fact. History as the *description* of events tends to move away from factual objectivity and approach art. What is involved are the different kinds of truth contained on the one hand in records and on the other in description. Much historical evidence derives from statements, spoken and written, of the type: A prince was born an hour ago, or: Parliament has just passed new taxation laws. Such statements are simplifications of very elaborate situations; they summarize in broad general terms events of great complexity. Their truth lies in their generality and the testimony of several or possibly numerous witnesses, and they are the bare bones of history.

Any attempt to present events and situations in all their complexity leads, first, to a much greater detail of the actual happenings the sum total of which would constitute the 'birth of a prince an hour ago' or the 'passing of taxation laws by Parliament', and, secondly, to adequate description of scenes and persons. The latter derives also from evidence, written or spoken, provided by participants or eye-witnesses. This brings us to the distinction crucial for our principle. This latter kind of evidence, that is, descriptions of complex situations in their sensuous aspects, is both fragmentary and partial; it is the limited direct experience of separate persons, conditioned by character, temperament, and the particular nature of the personal link with the events described. As such it constitutes an "interpretation" in the sense of this chapter. We are familiar with this kind of evidence from autobiography and political memoirs or from a historian like Clarendon who himself witnessed so much of what he recorded. Theoretically, such historical contributions could amount simply to a cataloguing of objective "facts". In practice some attempt is usually made, and often with notable success, to present the record in an animated and pictorial style. In this form historical testimony, though tied to a framework of objective chronology and geography, subjects itself also to the laws of representational art.

Historians are not always participants. In that case two ways of dealing with such descriptive evidence are open to them. They can incorporate in their narrative as many separate pieces of descriptive evidence as they have collected, thus giving a composite, multi-faceted record of events; or they can by selection and interpretation construct a new descriptive record. The first method, besides being clumsy, could never be complete. The second discharges the primary debt to chronological and factual truth without neglecting to do justice at least in some degree to that elaborate constitution of all events and situations which requires sensuous description if its different kind of truth is to be conveyed at all. History comprises representational art in proportion to its vivid presentation of the sensuous complexity of situations, contributed either as the view of a participant, or by the historian through skilful collation and re-constitution of evidence.

vii. REPRESENTATION IN DRAMATIC ART

Drama is allied to visual art by its stage settings and scenery and by its use of actors, and to literary art by its use of words. As to the latter one point should be made at once. Dialogue is itself, as an extension of persons, as part of their behaviour, representational in a direct way, and so differs from the verbal representation by evocation that we discussed in the previous section. In this it comes nearer to the method of the visual arts in the sense that it is an imagery in the same mode as its original in nature, in this case the speech of persons, just as painting is an imagery in the visual mode. Literary art, by contrast, mingles evocation with the propositional meanings of third-person report.

The visual and auditory presence of scene and actors makes drama a highly representational form, the detailed problems of which will be discussed in a later chapter. For the moment we need only apply to drama the principles already observed in the arts to which it is allied and note one or two consequences. And at this juncture we are speaking not of characteristic styles of dramatic writing (which will be discussed later) but of the stage-scene and actors as elements of representational art.

In the first place the scene and persons, however "realistic", are an imagery in which is embodied not reality but a vision or inter-pretation of it. And the law of functional relationship of all the images to a predominant purpose (whether idea, or impression, or emotion) holds here as everywhere. The stage-setting and appearance of the actors are integral to the dramatic conception. But only their appearance, the appearance they have from the auditorium. For the aesthetic purpose the actual properties of the stage, together with the private bodies of the actors, are non-existent. They only exist for dramatic art as a carefully constructed pattern of imagery. For a symbolical corroboration of this we need only look to make-up which at close range is meaningless but at audience range creates the desired illusion, and to stage lighting which gives the appropriate illusionary lustre to properties and costumes, making rags look like regal garments. It is of course possible to construct a stage set which is physically the equivalent of reality. The furnishings of a contemporary drawing-room can be set on a stage, or a period room can be faithfully copied, with genuine pieces of furniture, as is usually done, for example, with Ibsen's plays. But they still belong, as such, to the author's presiding aim with his play as a whole.

The actor's, as distinct from the spectator's, conscious sense of the image breaks through frequently in two ways; first, in the irony of comedy, which often requires exaggeration and a very deliberate aiming at the effect on the audience; and secondly, when the actor simulates his own art within the role he is playing.

In connexion with literary description we noted that Keats used general undefined images (the owl, the limping hare, etc.) to define a precise total impression. I think there is something analogous to this in the relation between actor and role in drama, although it may seem at first paradoxical. Different actors play the same role, say Lear, presenting us with quite different physical appearances, though no doubt certain traditional conventions offer a stabilizing framework; two Lears must always be more like each other than a Lear and a Hamlet. But we are not disturbed by these physical differences between one Lear or one Hamlet and another; we accept them as possible variants and do not feel that they cancel each other out. And this is because any given impersonation of Lear functions as a *general*, or "variant" image, like the owl and the hare in Keats's passage, within a *precise* context. The actual detail of the appearance is of little account, except within the limits set by the general features of the character, such as age, rank, time and place, cultural milieu, and so on, because the whole context of the play is what finally establishes itself and its meaning in our minds. The point applies equally to stage-setting and production generally. What we require from a producer is not a copy of an "authoritative" or "original" or "particular" version of a play, even if such ever existed, but a version consistent in itself and faithful to the spirit and meaning of the play. *Hamlet* in modern dress may be possible. But *Hamlet* played as though it were *The Tempest* is not, nor is a *Hamlet* in which Hamlet appears in modern dress whilst every one else is in costume.

A further point concerns dialogue. Here again the particular problems, especially those of style, will be raised later, but in connexion with the topic of this chapter, representational images, we observe that dialogue is ambivalent. On the one hand it is highly representational, being one aspect of persons, and persons in a play talk after the manner of people in real life. And on the other hand it is highly fictive, since no dialogue of drama is a representation of an actual dialogue in life. In this respect it differs from the graphic arts, where representation almost invariably implies an original scene or model, of which the work of art is, as we have maintained in this chapter, an "interpretation". Representation with dramatic characters and speech is always oblique. It is not true to actual particulars of life and people but it is modelled on them in such a way that it borrows their truth for its own images.

viii. CONCLUSION

We may sum up this chapter as follows; first, in simple language. A representation in art refers to something represented—a landscape, an object, a person—but it is always a certain selected aspect, never a repetition of the "object" itself; yet the object is important as the source of interest. The main interest may be visual, or it may be emotional reaction to the visual, but representation includes a clear reference to the object as the source of stimulation.

A more elaborate statement can be made in terms of images and the contexts in which they function. Art-images are like impression-images (from direct perception) in the sense that similar processes of observing are involved; we "look at " a natural scene, and at the picture of it, at the model for a piece of sculpture and at the sculpture, or at a social setting for a play and the play, and " see " external objects. But they are like purely mental images in another sense because they—the painted landscape, the sculpture, the stage scene

—are not natural objects, but constructions of a deliberate kind, both less than and more than originals; they are a fabricated, a newly constituted imagery, differently patterned from, though still related to, the models in nature. Thus they form a particular kind of context; not a context of ordinary perception, nor simply of remembering or day-dreaming, but an aesthetic context. Such a context may be established in face of objects; when this happens the observer, who has then become in principle an artist, shuts off the flux of impressions, and fixes his "vision"; and the technical artist embodies "vision" in a medium.[11] This vision does not hold the total possible visuality of objects. It develops some aspect of them and so becomes independent and "creative". It is a process of mental faculties elaborating a certain kind of context of thought, which has a focus and a unity, so that we can speak of its "predominant" idea or tone or feeling.

To help to clarify such a context we used a contrast. Representations which seek the highest possible degree of faithful reproduction we called "scientific copy-imagery". They are based on a normative selection, are essentially analytic in intention, and made to serve conceptual thinking, for which reason we ascribe them to contexts of scientific theory.

Expressing the differences in terms of "symbolism" we could say (1) that the perceptual world is a 'symbolic representation of the physical world' (as quoted above); (2) that scientific copy-imagery is a symbolic representation of the perceptual world, made as precise as possible but by necessity remaining approximate; and (3) that representational art-imagery is a symbolism simultaneously of appearances together with an emotional reaction to them.

The representational aesthetic context is thus a field of imagery with a focus of unified meaning and emotional tone. The simple way of indicating its difference from the original object is to say that the images of perception are selected, or modified, or even "distorted", as they are incorporated in the aesthetic vision; but it might be more accurate to say that some of the perceptual images are discarded and others, newly imagined, substituted. What is important is that in this process, which is partly receptive and partly constructive, the changes or substitutions all contribute to composition, and to a unity of meaning, and because of this we see that the imagery, no longer a matter of simple reference, is important by its *function* in relation to the meaning of the new construction. All the images are influenced by this process; they are all "modified" or "reconstructed", as a colour varies in tone when juxtaposed with others. A simple example is the function that the image of a tree might have in a landscape painting. It may itself be the focus of interest, in which case the images of other objects fall into functional relation to it with a correspondent diminution of their own identity and importance. But the main aim of the picture might be to portray a tempest. In that case the image of the tree, and all other objects, would be assimilated to the central meaning and made to function as signs of atmospheric agitation and the dramatic sense it occasions.

This process is of the greatest significance because it emphasizes even in representational art the impulsion towards metaphor. The images mean something that is not only themselves. Such obliquity is the infallible sign of the transposing imagination and the secret of all expressiveness in art. We now turn to the elaboration of other aspects of this principle.

CHAPTER THREE

IMAGES AND FEELING

i. ART AND FEELING

ART HAS OFTEN, indeed usually, been associated with the expression of feeling and, as with many generalizations about the subject, the idea contains something essentially true but at the same time simplifies too much. We find its clearest exemplification in love-lyrics or lyrics of mood, in expressionistic art where the distortions of normal form and colour in objects symbolize a dynamic world of emotion, and of course in music, conventionally accepted outright as the purest language of the heart. Other forms of art do not depend quite so clearly on feeling or at least are not focused on it. Didactic and epigrammatic poetry, geometric art as well as architecture and its associated decorative and useful arts, and even the severer musical forms like fugue, dubbed "intellectual", owe much of their character to other motives than feeling in a narrow sense. But it is none the less one of the best directive words for approaching the particular nature and function of art in contradistinction to other kinds of thought. What, we may ask, is there in works of art that we do not find in other productions of the mind? The simple answer to this question is undoubtedly that they do not only interest our intellect, our reason, our desire for knowledge or science or religion, our practical desires, and so on, but *move* us, as we say, making a direct and striking appeal to our human emotions; and we assume that every artist is "moved" to make his work, and that unless he has been moved his work will probably leave us cold.

The events characteristic of human life and its fortunes, the behaviour of other people, furthermore natural scenery, are amongst the things that arouse strong emotional responses in us, for which reason they provide an inexhaustible source of subjects and themes for artists. Hence most art that from one point of view is representational, because it depicts or evokes the world of objects, is at the same time expressive of feeling. And as we said above, pure and absolute representation *in art* can only be theoretical, if for no other reason than that some irrational or affective influence at least determines the interest of an artist for any given subject. But these emotional reactions to what we see in the world around us spring from a life of feeling that is part of ourselves and our existence, and is something autonomous. It is active and dynamic; its responses to external stimuli are only one of the forms it takes. Life and experience always include in their meaning this foundation of the life of passion, feeling, and emotion, which are sometimes a responding factor to events but always a shaping factor as well.

This autonomous life of feeling, as distinct from emotional excitation by external objects, seeks its own expression in art and we observe in particular two tendencies. Either the objects of nature are used arbitrarily as signs of emotion, or signs without any representational or literal significance are specially constructed for the purpose. In the one case the normal meaning of objects is displaced and their visual form modified, perhaps distorted, as we often rather loosely say, in favour of a substituted affective meaning, whilst in the other case forms that are abstract, or non-representational, are filled with an emotional significance. This process we now wish to examine more closely. In doing so we shall repeat our method of the previous chapter, trying to isolate the "purest" examples of the image as feeling, or formula for emotion, just as we tried to distinguish the purest examples of representational imagery. In this way we shall establish two poles, one being representational imagery with a minimum of affective "distortion" (e.g. a Dutch still-life or sea-scape) and the other being non-representational images that are highly expressive of feeling.

ii. THE IMAGERY OF MUSIC

In spite of the great amount of "abstract art" in painting and sculpture of recent decades the obvious and without doubt still the most frequently invoked example of non-representational art is music. Certain reservations have to be made about this, which we shall examine later. For the moment we will agree with the general notion, because when music is thus singled out it is "pure" music that is meant, music in its most uncompromising form, as we find it for example in the art of the classical symphony and string quartet and before romanticism introduced its literary interest into musical style.

Thinking of music then in this pure sense we can describe it as a system of auditory and rhythmic images appealing to the imagination through the auditory and motor senses, to the exclusion of other kinds of sensational experience, above all the visual, for music is on the whole blind to the world of objects. This imagery consists of melodies, harmonies, and rhythms built up into elaborate patterns, in which also such phenomena as dynamic contrast, which is extra-musical, since it does not pertain only to music, play a considerable part. A further point to notice is that, although we distinguish melody, harmony, and rhythm, we can only do so by analysis, since they are largely contained in each other. A harmonic system is usually implicit in the form of a melody, and a sequence of notes without rhythm would be felt as chaotic, or at least as unmelodic.

We have no choice but to use such generalized and abstract terms for the quintessential modes of an esoteric art. But we can take comfort in a certain dual character of music, for though on the one hand its grammatical organization is complicated and abstruse, its appeal, on the other, whether by melody or harmony or rhythm, is extraordinarily direct; direct in the sense that one is subdued at once by melodies, tunes, or motifs and becomes a contented participant in a state of self-sufficient meaningfulness. The elaborate imagery expresses, as we say, "feelings", by which we mean that it is not simply an ingenious game but has intimate connexions with experience. It is the product of imagination linked, in ways both direct and devious, with the life of feeling, sensation, and sensibility, the impelling force. It is a formula in sensuous terms externalizing something inward and making it repeatable. This dual aspect is seen both in the simplest tunes and the most elaborate compositions. In the former we observe often quite clearly a nameable quality or mood of joy, gaiety, sorrow, melancholy, aspiration, and so on; in the latter, in the grander forms of symphonic, choral, and instrumental music, we find evidence that the musical imagination can work on a scale equal to all the complexity of experience and the greater spiritual conceptions of humanity.

Certain forms of music give support to this more tangible aspect of its character, especially song, in which we find both its earliest manifestation and a long tradition of vocal composition. The voice provides the organic link between feeling and its expression in music; we use our voice to project sound, and the uttering of exclamatory cries is one aspect of natural expressive behaviour. But also the striking effectiveness of musical sound is conditioned by vaso-motor reactions and the nature of sound itself in relation to our auditory sensibility.[1] The early uses of music are explained by these physical and psycho-physical conditions, as for instance its connexion in early ritual with dance, which is also an imaginative extension of expressive behaviour; and they explain too its legendary apotheosis in the myth of Orpheus who tamed the wild passions of men and beasts with his art and even moved inanimate rocks and stones. We know that music as an art is a form of imagination transcending the organic and physical, but these conditions and associations help to account for the fact that its non-verbal meanings are so impressively persuasive.

We can also add in this connexion that rhythm is often a clear bridge from musical phrases to something nearer the representational, or to a definable expressive meaning, especially when we think of dance forms, choreographic music, and the elaborate musico-rhythmical expressiveness of ballet, associated as it is with story and miming. But the same may apply to melodic shape and harmony. A congruence can be traced between the structure of the music of, for instance, Chopin's Funeral March, and the gestures of sorrow and grief, especially in the heavy, wearied repetitions and downward movement of the motifs of the opening section, which are a counterpart to bodily gestures of mourning. Overlaps and analogies of this kind reduce the esoteric mystery of music. The *S. Matthew Passion* of Bach offers a wealth of examples of the most frankly eloquent expressiveness in musical forms.[2]

The unbroken tradition of vocal music makes a powerful contribution, both directly and indirectly, to this view, because it shows music explicitly attached, as an interpretative organ, to particular verbal meanings. The music of a song, it is true, takes its structure—the shape of melody, the colouring of harmony, the compositional form—from the poem set, so that its form deviates from the forms of instrumental music; but we do not feel that as music it is different in kind. On the contrary we observe constantly, above the differences, a similarity of style in vocal and non-vocal music by the same composer, for instance in Bach or Mozart. Composers may have found many ways of imitating in musical figures the sense of words and also, in the seventeenth and early eighteenth century, of the devices of traditional rhetoric; Bach is particularly fertile in this kind of invention.[3] If vocal music had only done this it would have decidedly constituted a special kind. But we look upon such figures not as the central focus of expression but contributory. Our real test for the music of a song or an aria is whether the musical form altogether is *congruent* with the import and "feeling" of the words. This involves in one sense a certain generality in the relationship; for which reason several, or even numerous, musical settings of the same words are possible. But it involves particularity also, since the congruence is necessarily with the same words. I think that instrumental or "absolute" music has the same quality of generality, for instance in the predominant mood of symphonic or sonata movements, and that it also conveys by implication a sense of particularity similar to that of song in relation to words. However that may be, a vast amount of music being vocal and choral it is clear that its definite links with verbally explicit meanings are numerous and continually being affirmed and renewed. The question of programme music and literary motifs is related, and there are a large number of instrumental works specifically based by their composers themselves on a programme, as for instance Berlioz' *Symphonie Fantastique*, or Mendelssohn's symphonies, or Liszt's *Tone Poems*. We recall also the well-known habit of Haydn, after all a master of the symphony and string quartet, of composing with a romantic story or a scene from nature before his mind's eye. Finally, support for this view may be derived from the results of the comparative study of style which shows a period sensibility asserting itself simultaneously in literature and other arts.

I have stressed this feature because it is essential to understand that music is not simply a transcendent creation but, like other arts, stands in relation to experience. Only with this firmly in mind can we grasp its most remarkable characteristic, which lies in the combination of the greatest abstraction and the intensest evocation of feeling, of the most independent imaginative constructiveness and the profoundest sense of emotional reality. The simplest tune shows this, for however clear its mood, however near the brink of verbal explicitness it may hover, it is still a formula of imagery; not an object, not a real feeling, but a constructed formula of sound-images, a creation of the auditory imagination. But the point is clear above all from the compositional features of the predominant musical forms in which a few "subjects" or "subject groups" are developed, elaborated, transposed, placed in sequence and contrast, all in an intricate system of tonal and rhythmic relations, and in one sense a sublimely untrammelled play of creation. Here lies the abstraction of music, the free rein it gives to the inventiveness of the imagination, and the chastened ideality of the result. Yet it is, in the constitution of music, counterpointed against the most striking affective power. No other art is at one and the same time so ideally rarefied and so passionate in the very nature of its means.

This feature we can elucidate in still another way. The art of musical composition is loaded with "theory", precisely because of its abstract nature. Harmony, counterpoint, "form", orchestration, all require an intensive kind of study that is far removed from the visual "observation" of the painter or the novelist and more like the preoccupations of mathematicians. Yet all this theory is wasted unless the motifs and phrases from which a composition develops are initially vital. Those short phrases the working out of which make a composition, the "subjects", as they are technically called, of fugues, sonata movements, and so on, contain the central emotional meanings; and the large-scale "formal" relations are the systematic unfolding of formal relations already implicit in the shape of the subjects themselves and their relation to one another. In this way the emotional power of the subjects radiates throughout a whole movement or composition; and this applies as much to a Bach fugue as to a Beethoven symphony.[4] "Formal elements" or "relations" are unfortunate and misleading terms since they suggest something imposed upon musical themes or subjects, whereas they are of course inherent in the sound-imagery and only analytically separable. As a pure theoretical concept "formal relations" can be exemplified in the exercises, fugal and other, that music examinations require from candidates, and that fall short of expressive meaning. On the other hand we can most of us make snatches of melody for ourselves which in a small way have momentary meaning for us. Musical genius conceives these two things infolded in each other.

Music offers us the perfect example of how a formula of imagery without representational significance, or object-references, or verbal associations, can be accepted as meaningful because it corresponds to "feelings". I propose to call this feature the *expressive formula-image*, which is the least ambiguous term for it of many that have a claim to relevance. "Symbol" has too many meanings; "formal images" is too simplified and carries a legacy in the epithet; whilst "constructed" and "abstract" are not precise enough.

We have isolated, as we purposed at the beginning of this chapter, the non-representational image in as clear and pure a form as possible, as the counterpart of the representational image. These are the two broad classes of imagery found both separately and also in constant interplay in the arts. And it seems to me useful to conceive both as *imagery* since the facility of their interaction in certain arts is more easily accepted as un-mysterious and also because it helps to establish rationally the kinship of music with the other arts, which represents a step forward over theories that emphasize the separateness and peculiarity of music. The firm relation of the two lies in the fact that they are both imagery functioning in interpretative or expressive constructions of the imagination. We were at pains to show how for various reasons representational images are always an *interpretation* of the visible world and function as images and not as reality within that framework. The same applies to the auditory images of music. They relate to feelings but they are, being images and not reality, ideas or interpretations of feelings and function in unified relationship to that. Just as the image of the Madonna varies from painter to painter, so the image of the Agnus Dei or the Te Deum varies from composer to composer. Yet, as we have observed, these non-representational, or non-pictorial, images are in the last resort interconnected in an infinite variety of ways with the images of nature and human face and gesture, providing many channels of intuitive understanding by analogy.

iii. OTHER KINDS OF FORMULA-IMAGE

Music offers the most independent, but not the only, examples of the *expressive formula-image*. To them belong also the acoustic and rhythmic values in poetry, phenomena such as alliteration, rhyme, general euphony, and metrical form. Some hesitate to accept the notion of rhythmic imagery, no doubt because they see a difference between visual and auditory senses on the one hand and the motor sense on the other, and cannot accord to the latter the same sort of relationship to the imagination. Rhythm, however, is a complex sensation. Even if one can isolate a purely motor sensation there remain the many manifestations of rhythm in combination with either visual or auditory experience, as when we *see* the breaking of waves, the movement of wind over corn, a greyhound running, or when we *hear* waves breaking, the familiar rhythmic noises of a train, the rocking of a chair, and so on. So that against internally "felt" rhythm we have to set externally perceived rhythm, in which different kinds of sensation are correlated. This is always the case in art. Rhythm in poetry is both motory and auditory. But it is in itself an "abstracted" or non-representational imagery in the same sense in which linear design is.

In painting, too, there is formula-imagery. The lines are not merely a mode of spatial division or compositional ordering but have emotional implications, while the same is true of colour and its distribution. Even perspective can in itself become an emotional symbol.[5] Artists speak of "expansive" colours and forms, of warm and cold colours, or warm and cold forms. Line is a prolific source of expressive formula-images. As outline, of course, it belongs partly to representation, though it is an "abstraction". But artists have a strong sense for freely handled line as an analogue of feeling. Handbooks of drawings tell us that vertical lines express dignity, horizontals strength, stability, and repose, obliques movement, whilst curves add liveliness or joyousness. Line portraits and caricature show expressive lines abstracted from face, body, and limbs and, like the stylized gesture-images of ballet, provide a bridge between the representational and the abstract-expressive.[6] Nor should we forget that the great prototype in nature of the expressive image is the human face, for here we have the primary and intuitive experience of non-sensuous qualities appearing in sensuous forms. The noble features, the melancholy wrinkles, the gentle eyes, the strong chin, the majestic brow,—these are commonplaces of the moral interpretation of physical features, upon which the imagination of poets and novelists builds the greatest refinements. For this reason portraiture, whilst highly representational, is naturally expressive. The design, outlines, and spatial effects of architecture, too, affect us in such a way that we can say they express certain emotional and even philosophical attitudes to life, which we sum up in stylistic terms like gothic or baroque. In fact period style arises from the discovery of the system of formula-images that corresponds to the vital consciousness of the time. Michelangelo offers vivid examples of cognate expressiveness in representational and non-representational images, for his sculptures (Moses, David, the Medici tomb) share with his architectural forms (e.g. the Campidoglio, the Palazzo Farnese, the Medici chapel) qualities of grandeur, courage, dignity, power, affirmation, nobility, triumph, and splendour, showing the intricate interchanges in art between the pictorial and the expressive formula-image. Even the simplest schemes of interior decoration carry the sense of certain qualities which are thus evoked because they are desired and give pleasure to the feelings. In poetry and painting the expressive formula-imagery is subtly interwoven with other kinds, a feature of complexity which will be considered closely at a later stage. Architecture is nearer to music, in the sense that its forms are non-representational, which gave rise to its being called "frozen music"; but on the other hand its utilitarian aspect introduces a practical influence absent in music. I would also include here the larger rhythms of design implicit in the development of plays and novels. They mirror, of course, the "rhythm of events" in ordinary life and one could argue that they are to that extent representational. But they are also subtle constructions of calculated expressive effect, and of great importance for the sense of "re-enactment" (to be examined later) and its accompanying emotional responses.

The construction of non-representational imagery derives from the faculty of imaginative abstraction, observed perhaps in its most obvious form in the "abstractive seeing" which enables us to see one aspect of an object, as for example its outline, divorced from others. Abstracted forms and images are a step away from the organic complexity of nature, and the free invention of forms shows the imagination pushing still further the process thus begun. Experience of nature offers many signs of this process, for there is a multifarious commerce between natural phenomena and abstracted shapes. At twilight colours are slowly subdued until landscape, with its hills, meadows, ploughed fields and trees, is a composition of opaque shapes. From the top of a mountain outlines, mass and configuration predominate at the expense of crowded and multi-coloured detail. The stones and pebbles on the sea-shore are washed and ground until the latent contours of their uneven density appear as shapes of strange beauty and expressiveness. Similarly there is a natural world of sound, evident in wind, waves and tempest, or in the cries, utterances and songs of animals and birds in which at least there are relations of pitch and rhythm. Through these connexions we are reminded that the art-images conveniently called "abstract forms" (or "formal elements") are closely bound up with organic nature and sharply to be distinguished from the particular abstraction characteristic of scientific theory and illustration. We observe, moreover, that if we are to be aware of these "abstract" forms at all they must, though abstracted from one context of nature, be reset in the sensuous, however rarefied. That is another way of saying that they can only exist as images. For that reason these images, however freely invented or elaborated and apparently divorced from the pictorial, retain their link with the natural world, as the imagery of music does with the psycho-physical, and thus they preserve in their transformation, by the ingenuity of mind rooted in nature, the passionate quality of the living universe. The whole process is implied, I think, in a comment of Picasso :

> "There is no abstract art. We must always begin with something. Afterwards we can remove all appearance of reality; there is no danger because the idea of the object has left its indelible imprint. It was the object which provoked the artist, excited his ideas, stirred his emotions. Ideas and emotions will be securely imprisoned in his work; whatever they do, they can't escape from the picture; they form an integral part of it, even when their presence is no longer discernible. Whether he likes it or not, man is an instrument of nature; she imposes her character and appearance on him. . . . We cannot contradict nature. She is stronger than the strongest of men! It pays us to be on good terms with her. We can allow ourselves some liberties; but only in details". (Quoted in H. Read, *Art Now*, pp. 146–7).

This devious connexion is not to be confused with aesthetic theories based on "natural forms". Organic form is without doubt important for art forms, whether in obvious or intricate ways, but if based too simply on outline or linear pattern it gives little help towards clarifying the expressive power of art.[7] The essential feature of art is not good design in an external sense but the use of forms which, though derived from nature, have been transformed, reconstructed, or re-structured, into analogues of sense and feeling. Art begins where organic forms are functionally applied—by human sensibility—and therefore modified, in a context involving thought, feeling, and experience.

The essential point to grasp in this question is that the formal aspects of a work of art are not exclusively "intellectual" or "structural" as they have so often been called. Such terms are appropriate in connexion with the design of non-aesthetic work; for every effort of mind has to have a shape of some sort. A book of philosophy, a memorandum, a leading article, a prospectus, and so on ad infinitum, all these things show a certain order in their presentation, as do all the manifold kinds of pictorial illustration, but this does not make them into works of art. In the aesthetic context what we often call form or composition or design does not make an analytical or ratiocinative order under which a material world is subsumed; it is an aspect of imagery which interprets the material world and expresses feeling. Once we are willing to see this, and to understand how in the first place apparently "abstract" forms derive ultimately from natural and cosmic phenomena, and in the second how our own psycho-physical forces continually erupt into the objects and forms of nature and their imaginative elaboration, then the artificial barrier in theory between representational and non-representational forms disappears. Helpful in this respect has been the extension by psychology of the idea of images from the visual, which for long held a prerogative over the word, to other kinds of sensational experience.

To illustrate this problem further some points made by Paul Valéry about rhythm and poetic composition are instructive. He has called attention to the process by which a rhythmic pattern declares itself in the initial stages of writing a poem, before the ideas and subject are yet grasped :

'Je me suis trouvé un jour obsédé par un rythme, qui se fit tout à coup sensible à mon esprit, après un temps pendant lequel je n'avais qu'une demi-conscience de cette activité latérale. Ce rythme s'imposait à moi, avec une sorte d'exigence. Il me semblait qu'il voulût prendre un corps, arriver à la perfection de l'être. Même il ne pouvait devenir plus net à ma conscience qu'en empruntant ou assimilant en quelque sorte des éléments *dicibles*, des syllabes, des mots, et ces syllabes et ces mots étaient sans doute, à ce point de la formation, déterminés par leur valeur et leurs attractions musicales. . . .' ('La Création Artistique', in *Vues*, La Table Ronde (1948), p. 300.)

42

Or again:—

> 'Something quite unexpected wakes the poet in the man,
> some incident within or outside himself: a tree, a face, a
> " subject ", an emotion, a word. Now it will be the desire to
> express that will start the ball rolling, the need to translate
> something felt: now it will be some formal element, the first
> rough draft of an expression seeking its cause, its meaning,
> in the spaces of his spirit. Note well this possible duality of
> stimulus which can set the poetic invention moving: sometimes
> it is a feeling that desires to express itself, sometimes the
> medium of expression seeking employment.' ('Poetry and
> Abstract Thought,' in *Essays on Language and Literature*,
> Ed. J. L. Hevesi, London, 1947, p. 109.)

When Valèry writes 'the medium of expression seeking employment' he is really suggesting that the imagination is aware of certain
non-representational forms, say rhythms, which are potentially
correlates of some emotion and therefore expressive. His previous
words 'the first rough draft of an expression seeking its cause' strike
still nearer the mark. If it were possible to write a poem completely
in a rhythmic scheme alone the poem would already be written.
Something approximately comparable in the graphic arts would be
an *abstract* composition in pencilled *line* only. From this point of
view the study of "technique" in art is nothing less than an exploration of different kinds of imagery in order to discover their peculiar expressiveness and the ways in which they may best interfuse in
the total complexity of finished work. One of the marks of finished
art is that it is an organic interstructure of differing kinds of imagery.

Having considered both representational and non-representational images, having observed that they are closely related by being
images, and having hinted that their distinction lies in their function
within a certain kind of interpretative and expressive context, we
can now proceed to a more particular statement about such contexts
and the functions of imagery, leading on to the question of words
and images and then to a definition of art and poetry. But much will
be gained if at this point we introduce a brief consideration of
metaphor. For metaphor is the most patent instance in poetic
method where images are not valid in themselves but by their
function, a feature towards the elucidation of which our argument
is now tending.

iv. METAPHOR

Metaphors belong to effects of style for which the common language of literary criticism reserves the term "imagery" and they are of an importance for poetry that we can scarcely overestimate. This is particularly so in the English tradition, for which through their abundance they have become one might almost believe the principal feature of the poetic in general. My purpose in this chapter is to treat of metaphor in the light of the broader theory of imagery here being put forward. I want to indicate one or two salient aspects of metaphorical expression; above all, the question of how images assume various functions and how they are changed in the process. My treatment will be brief compared with the scope the subject offers but my aim is to place metaphor in relation to the general argument.[8]

Metaphor in its simpler uses is illustrative, consisting often of a visual image which gives vivid support to meaning. For instance in the sentence 'His speech aroused a storm of disapproval' the metaphor contained in the word storm produces a combination of lucidity and brevity better than anything that abstract definition could achieve. Metaphors of this kind contribute much to vivacious prose and show imagination at work even though it is harnessed to the relatively sober purpose of illustrating thought. This use of metaphor, so customary that we overlook the degree to which it is present, at least in the form of " faded metaphors", even in the most ordinary speech, and its extraordinary efficiency in the achieving of vigorous statement, is in itself evidence of the extent to which our thinking is dependent on images.   At the same time we can still speak of content and form in metaphors used in this way. A meaning is presented in the form of metaphor. In illustrative metaphor the thought is directed towards a rational meaning which, being achieved, can discard the instrument. In poetry this duality disappears.

The more subtle effectiveness of metaphor lies in its mode of appealing to the feelings. If we say a man has a "fiery nature" the metaphor of fire uses one object, fire, to suggest certain properties of another, a man. It can do this because there are properties in common to fire and a passionate nature: heat, movement, tempestuousness, danger, consuming power. The metaphor short-circuits the statement of these qualities, relying simply on the way we react to the idea of " fire ". Thus the man is described by way of our emotional reaction to the properties of fire. A complex meaning is implicit in a psychological response to a single word. Numerous instances suggest themselves easily. In phrases like 'he was a lion in the battle' or 'the voting produced a landslide' we get the sense because we get the "feeling". This is to use extra-intellectual psychological factors in communication, so that the hearer is appropriately "moved" and thereby understands. To move in this way is to tell.

Metaphor thus has a composite appeal. Through its use the imagination exploits the excitements of sensational experience and at the same time clarifies some idea. This is a very remarkable process because it runs counter to two pronounced tendencies in human nature. On the one hand physical and emotional excitement alone, even when only imagined, obscures the clearer faculties, as one sees in the effects of anger or passion, or even in simple self-abandonment in happiness; whilst on the other hand the rational faculty stakes its honour on the elimination of irrational factors in its attempts to state truth. In metaphor the excitements of experience are conjoined with clarity of statement. Moreover, the image used being oblique, that is, remote from the reality under view (as with "landslide" and "voting" in the above example) it is obvious that it is a mechanism of thought. It declares the imagination.

But obviously an instrument that can perform such a function is perfectly suited to make statements about the life of sensation and experience itself. That is, by drawing on multifold analogies it can evoke the appropriate responses in such a way as to secure a certain kind of enhancement and clarification. And this gives us the reason for its prominence in poetry, which mostly puts some aspect of experience before us. Take, for instance, the following :—

> Tomorrow and tomorrow and tomorrow
> Creeps in this petty pace from day to day
> To the last syllable of recorded time . . .

Here the metaphor 'creeps in this petty pace' is as much illustration as the simple examples above; it tells us how slowly these tomorrows pass. But its great power lies in its giving us so vividly the "feeling" of the slow passage of time, reinforced as it is by the second metaphor of 'last syllable' and "recorded". This feeling is the point to be grasped, or rather the experience to be repeated in imagination; and therefore the meaning is not simply in a thought towards which an illustration tends, but it resides in the image, drawing the mind back to it again and again. It remains unalterably fixed in the pattern, insisting on its presence in the "idea" presented in the passage. Discard it and the experience disintegrates. In an argumentation the metaphors are discarded along with the whole verbal apparatus when the demonstration is completed. In a poem the words and images circle upon themselves because, though ideas (i.e. product of mind), they follow the structure of living experience. Or consider the opening lines of *Richard III* :—

> Now is the winter of our discontent
> Made glorious summer by this sun of York.

The image is a brilliant evocation of contrasting seasons of nature. It carries with it the sense of experiencing them, calling forth our habitual responses; and so the passionate sense of life is preserved amidst the intellectual function of clarifying another situation from life (viz., the one with which the play begins). Modern linguistic theory speaks of metaphor as the natural language of excitement. Voltaire said that metaphor, when natural, was a thing of passion. However functional images are, they retain the power of the physical universe and are therefore sympathetic to what in ourselves is linked with the physical and organic. The power of an image, as deriving from nature, corresponds to nature in ourselves. Beyond the immediate fitness that attaches to metaphors supporting thought there is an all-embracing propriety that nature outside ourselves should be the most adequate medium for clarifying what nature in its psycho-physical complexity effects inside us.

A further characteristic of the metaphorical process is that though a metaphor is functional, in the sense that it implies 'x is like y', its terms in the moment of conception become reciprocal and the contents of the image used to illumine some other thing are themselves forced into a heightened clarity :

> Thou still unravish'd bride of quietness !
>   Thou foster-child of Silence and slow Time,
> Sylvan historian, who canst thus express
>   A flowery tale more sweetly than our rhyme . . .

Full many a glorious morning have I seen
Flatter the mountain-top with sovereign eye,
Kissing with golden face the meadows green,
Gilding pale streams with heavenly alchemy . . .

    The wedded light and heat,
    Winnowing the witless space,
    Without a let,
    What are they till they beat
    Against the sleepy sod, and there beget
    Perchance the violet!

    Es schlug mein Herz, geschwind zu Pferde!
    Es war getan fast eh gedacht;
    Der Abend wiegte schon die Erde
    Und an den Bergen hing die Nacht:
    Schon stand im Nebelkleid die Eiche,
    Ein aufgetürmter Riese, da,
    Wo Finsternis aus dem Gesträuche
    Mit hundert schwarzen Augen sah.

Full of desire I lay, the sky wounding me,
each cloud a ship without me sailing, each tree
possessing what my soul lacked, tranquillity.[9]

The use of metaphor leads to an elaborate evocation of the sensuous
world in general, together with our responsive feelings, so that we
may say nature is present in poetry twice over, in the sense that it
provides the subjects, the story, the emotions, and then further
images of itself to make the picture true, vivid, and striking. The
imagination thus achieves the intensity and incandescence which
mark the sense of "heightened nature" or enhanced life emanating
from poetry. And it is in this total effect, this final achievement of
complex relations, that duality of form and content disappears.

Metaphors thus always have three significant references. They
involve an image from the sensational world, which may be simple
as in 'thus the curtain fell on his life', or intricate as in:—

When to the sessions of sweet silent thought
I summon up remembrance of things past . . .

but which always springs from the world of concrete experience. In the second place they refer to feelings which are stimulated by the image used. And in the third place they point to a propositional meaning. The total meaning, however, lies in none of these separately but in the relations, which are idea, created between the three references. All this derives from the *functioning* of the image. The image is necessary, the particular image of each case ; the image from the world of the law evoked by "summon" and "sessions" in the above passage cannot be replaced by another. But the image is not the thing meant, though it suggests something similar. It often belongs therefore to a representational context without itself being the thing represented. But it is also expressive because it works, as we have seen, by appealing to appropriate feelings and emotional reactions. And so it appears related to the expressive formula-images considered above, without itself being one. It is thus intermediate in its structure between the representational and the non-representational image.

We now return to our argument.

V. MUSIC, METAPHOR, AND SYMBOL

The above analysis enables us to see metaphor as a focus for the understanding of aesthetic imagery, since it is intimately related to both the principal kinds of imagery and in addition illustrates so clearly how the importance of an image lies as much in its function as in itself. In considering representational images we insisted that they are never without some degree of affective influence; they are never objects, but images of objects viewed under emotional stress of some kind, or in relation to some idea or emotional purpose. They contain, in other words, an element of expressiveness, which is observable in the degree to which the image of the object is " distorted ", or in the manner in which selection and emphasis of naturalistic imagery, or the mutual adjustment of images in a unified context, are carried out. The imagery is thus partly symbolic of objects in nature and partly a formula for feeling ; for the artist it is equivalent to 'the object and myself'. Its significance lies in this ambivalence of its functional position; and insofar as it is functional, that is, stands both for itself and for something that is not itself, it *tends towards* metaphor. We need not say that it *is* metaphor, since the latter is a well-defined phenomenon in literary art; but it *tends* to participate in the nature of the metaphorical. Clearly a symbolic process is involved here, but to say simply that we are dealing with "symbols" is perhaps too general and does insufficient justice to the subtlety of the process.[10]

Common to metaphor and non-representational images, on the other hand, is their property of evoking feelings directly. There is almost always implicit in metaphor both a simile and a symbol; indeed a metaphor is often a contraction of a simile by intensified symbolism. Instead of: 'Our discontent is turned into contentment by this son of York, as the sun turns winter into summer", the poet writes:

> Now is the winter of our discontent
> Made glorious summer by this sun of York.

"Discontent" remains here as a general clue and the meaning is concentrated in the "winter", "summer" and "sun", which function as symbols of the feelings to which the speaker refers. The presence of the direct clue establishes the metaphor and keeps the method on this side of complete symbolism. But it is the element of direct symbolism that gives metaphor an impulsion towards the non-representational, or expressive formula-image. The latter is more overtly a "symbol", without the intermediate clue always found in metaphor. And yet the closeness or kinship of the two processes is clear, and perhaps we may see it still more clearly if we think of song again. We said above that our test for the music of a song was its congruence with the "feeling" of the words; that is to say, whether it expresses in its own way the meanings of the text. This relationship involves something very close indeed to metaphor. For the music of a song may be described as standing by its *function* in metaphorical relation to the words. It fortifies their meanings by evoking directly strong emotional responses; which is precisely the function of metaphors in a poem. Metaphors are to the propositional meanings of a poem as the music of a song is to the propositional meanings of the text. If propositional meanings are omitted entirely from a poem only symbols are left, exercising evocative influence on the feelings ; if the words of the song are deleted, again only "symbols" are left —the expressive formula-images of music.[11]

Metaphor rests on the possibility of finding innumerable different analogues for the same or closely similar feelings. If this were not so poets would long ago have despaired of new expressions for re-current human sentiments and experiences. The most vivid example of this phenomenon is to be found in the love sonnets of the Renaissance; in Spenser, for instance, the universe is pillaged for images to illustrate the one passion of love and the one beloved. Metaphor shares this feature with music, and with all expressive formula-imagery. There is an enormous range of sensuous symbols for the same emotions; how many instrumental movements express the common "moods" with equal clarity! Or one may observe the process within a single movement. Bach shows this repeatedly. The first movement, for instance, of his two harpsichord concerto in C major is an elaborate association of musical motifs with the same expressive purpose, a complex of sense-analogues within the same general tone, all contributing to a radiant, joyful, and triumphant march of feeling. The individual particularity of musical pieces has been used often to emphasize the absoluteness of music, its aural detachment and chasteness, and to reject its programmatic and directly expressive quality. But this is to misconceive individuality. There is no unique musical phrase for the expression, say, of serene joy. There are many; nevertheless they are all *instances* of serene joy.[12]

In order to complete the argument and cover the main possibilities a brief reference must be made to one other kind of image function. It belongs to common experience that emotional significance can accumulate about an object with such force that the object itself is finally less important than the feelings it releases. Any object, a tree, a particular street or building, an animal, a chair, or a group of objects such as a room and its furnishings, can assume significance in this way. When that happens it has become an emotional symbol. What occurs thus in life is repeated in art; extensive use is made of symbolic objects for the purpose of expressing emotional meanings. In such images a non-representational expressive significance is substituted for a representational one. Or in other words a representational image is converted into an expressive formula-image by virtue of its function.

CHAPTER FOUR

IMAGERY AND THE INTERPRETATION
OF EXPERIENCE IN ART

i. IMAGERY AND THE WORLD OF EXPERIENCE

BEFORE PROCEEDING TO some problems of language
and imagery, and thence to a definition of poetry and art, it
would be well to sum up the position we have now reached.
We have spoken of images and of something to which they relate.
We know that the meaning of aesthetic imagery is in itself since it
is "idea" and not object, and since it is not simply a language of
report communicating knowledge of events. Nevertheless it is the
world of experience that provides the materials of thought, including those of aesthetic images. So that two things are involved;
on the one hand a world of experience and on the other one of
imagery related to it.

We may divide the former into the world of objects and of
feelings, but they are not necessarily separate spheres; there is constant interplay between them. Hence we envisage three divisions;
(1) the multifold objects and events of the external world; (2) these
objects and events associated with emotional reactions or other
affective influences of varying force; (3) the subjective world of
autonomous feeling.

The imagery of art corresponds to these divisions in the following way. (1) A perfect naturalistic representational image of an
object (say, an apple) would be a perfect symbol of that object.
As we have seen, it is extremely doubtful whether such images
exist at all or are not simply hypothetical; or they are perfect scientific
copy-images. In art-imagery nothing pertains quite simply to the
world of external objects and events. The latter is the uninterpreted
world, or the world that in a different mode of thought may be the

object of scientific analysis. (2) Images corresponding to the second division are symbols of "objects (and events) modified by feelings "; that is, a double symbolism, embracing both an object and the feelings it releases in the observer, inheres in a single image (an *ideal* landscape, a *pastoral* scene, a *tragic* portrait, a *dramatic* situation). Such images are always a selection from the possible images offered by objects and events in nature, and are carefully attuned to the feelings involved. This implies some degree of "distortion" as against naive or scientific reality. (3) Under the third group, where the subjective world of feelings is projected into sensuous terms, we have expressive formula-images, as in music, architecture, and "abstract" art; or pictorial images functioning not as symbols of objects but as expressive formula-images, as in "musical" styles of painting and, at its extreme, in "expressionism".

The above groupings apply to all the arts and also to the primary imagery of literary art, by which I mean the appearances of life and nature found in the plot and persons of narrative and drama or evoked by the lyric poet, together with the auditory imagery of spoken language. Metaphor, which is a secondary imagery, takes up a special position; it belongs to no group separately but is linked with all three. It springs of course from the nature of language in the sense that the latter has constantly sought to increase its powers of connotation and evocation by refining analogical processes ; metaphors are instruments of great economy and efficiency. The point about metaphor as secondary imagery is that it is a frank mechanism of the imagination. It reveals with a certain histrionic flourish the imaginative process itself, at least in one of its aspects. From this point of view it exposes unmistakably the ambivalence of the world of imagination. The more representational an image is the more it obscures the ideality of art. The more non-representational it is the more it obscures the experience of which all art is an interpretation. Metaphor, in which images are instrumental in illuminating something not themselves, functions between sense and abstraction, phenomenon and idea. It shows plainly the peculiar role of the imagination, as it establishes a world of idea and identity out of a world of sensation and experience. This all art does, though the process is veiled. For this reason metaphor has always enjoyed a peculiar prestige in literary art. For this reason, too, we have assigned it its special place in relation to the other kinds of imagery.

ii. THE RELATIONSHIP BETWEEN DIFFERENT KINDS OF IMAGERY IN ART

In discussing images we have, for the sake of analytic clarity, drawn a difference between a representational and an expressive emphasis. But it is useful to insist once again that all images in art are new constructions isolated from the instinctive world of continuous sensation and fixed as a mental imagery. They are not, even when pictorial, transcripts of perception, but elements of a newly-constituted context of aesthetic idea. This means that the important thing about the art-image is not whether it is, in any exclusive sense, representational or expressive, but what it is, and how it *functions*, in its characteristic context. We have said that the representational image in art is always expressive as well; it symbolizes both an object and a feeling about it. We have also said that an image of an object, like objects themselves, can become a pure emotional symbol, and is then by its function an expressive formula-image. The reverse kind of transfer, though more rare, also occurs. The metre of poems and the rhythm of songs frequently help to evoke visual descriptive images (the rhythm is 'suited to the sense'), as in Schubert's *Erlkönig* and *Die Forelle*. Certain types of music, like Debussy's ('Impressions de Mer', 'La Cathédrale Engloutie'), or the programme music of Wagner, Berlioz, Liszt and their successors, have a pictorial effect sometimes startlingly vivid.

The prominent feature common to all art-images is thus their constructive adaptability to a context. They may sometimes, especially in the plastic arts, be akin to the images of perception, but they nevertheless differ by being re-structured to support an interpretative-expressive idea. The different kinds of imagery, which we separate by analysis, are assimilated to each other and to something else—a presiding "idea" or feeling—in the synthesis of the aesthetic context. This sets art-imagery apart from other kinds; from perceptual images, from ordinary mental images or memory-images, and from scientific copy-images, all of which belong to other contexts of thought or sensation. It also means that the symbolism, or symbolic functioning, of art-images has to be distinguished from common kinds of symbol like language or mathematics, where given signs have given meanings, or the rational symbolisations of fable, allegory, or heraldry, or even the unconscious symbolism of dreams.

Thus what any art-image is depends finally on its function; on its contribution, by sensuous character and evocative effect, to the "total image", the context of imagery which every poem, painting, play, symphony, etc., is. We may be expecting an image, perhaps of a tree in a landscape, to be representational, but we find that it is a symbol of mood. We may be expecting the rhythm of a poem to be a support of some "musical" effect, whilst in fact we get an imitation of a galloping horse, or a swooping windhover, or a limping man. The image, although always a sensuous form, is indeterminate in itself and receives its true character from its contributory function. This feature is central in art-imagery; we might describe it as metaphorical functionalism, borrowing the term from the nature of metaphor and its mode of operation as analysed above.

iii. BEAUTY, DESIGN, AND ART

This metaphorical functionalism in all art-imagery throws light on one of the most vexed questions of aesthetic, the relation between qualities of design, which inhere in all art and give it "beauty", and qualities of expressiveness. For here again we have an opposition which is more theoretical than real; or at least it arises not from fundamental difference but from relative emphasis.

It is a commonplace that harmony and proportion are elements of "beauty". Design, the relation of parts to the whole, unity in variety, clarity, sequence, all contribute to the beauty of formal perfection. The first thing we note is that this kind of "beauty" appertains to contexts of thought outside art, and also to cosmic and organic patterns. I would maintain that it is not a purely "intellectual" phenomenon, even in its most abstract and abstruse manifestations, as in mathematics, or logic, or philosophical system, but that some affective element is always present in it. There are basic factors of psychological and physiological pleasure and well-being in the response to harmony and proportion. This being so it is easy to see how sensuous forms embodying these qualities, though not art-imagery, have a *tendency* to become something very close to expressive formula-imagery. And thus the beauty of design, order, and clarity insinuates itself naturally into the expressive imagery of art. This beauty, which as we said may pertain to things outside art, is not in and by itself art; but applied to expression, fused with expressive imagery, it reinforces art. It is like organic form in nature, which also is not art, but exploited and transposed in conjunction with feelings and ideas reinforces the power of other expressive imagery.[1]

Three orders constantly interfuse in art, though in an immense variety of ways : design or "formal beauty"; the picture of life or nature and the emotions it evokes; and expressive formula-imagery, the sensuous analogues of the life of feeling and sensibility. The balance between them differs from work to work, from art to art, from style to style. Sometimes they are wonderfully reciprocal, as in the Parthenon sculptures and Michelangelo, in Titian, in Shakespeare, in Racine, in Cézanne, in Bach's great choral works, in one or two of Mozart's operas. In such cases there is no problem of beauty against expression, or art against life, or classical formality against warmth of feeling, to mention a few common spectres of art discussions. The greatest complexity and ingenuity of imagery and formal relations contains in such cases the greatest complexity and intensity of reference to the world and the feelings. In this intricate equivalence resides the ultimate secret of art. Art never originates simply in strong feelings; it arises from the faculty of "making", the gift of rhyming, singing, painting, and so on. But these can be trivial and are only interesting in a sustained and major way when applied to "life" with all its richness and all the qualities of human character and mind. The mere play of forms, even beautiful ones, quickly tires the mind. The great human discovery implicit in art, and renewed with every successful work, is that the play of forms and imagery can be made to embody feelings and aspects of experience that are self-evidently profound and not otherwise available to expression.

CHAPTER FIVE

IMAGES AND WORDS

U P TO THIS POINT we have with one exception avoided the problems of verbal meaning in literary art. We have done so in order to emphasize the importance of images, which are of various kinds and fulfil differing functions, but belong to the very nature of art, including poetry. Before coming to the question of verbal meanings we have been insisting on the fact that meanings can be adequately expressed in imagery that is independent of words, as in music, plastic art and mime, and, by implication, in images that go with words.

In poetry words offer in themselves, as spoken sounds, a series of auditory images; and many words, according to the poet's purpose, evoke visual and other images in the imagination so that as we read a poem we "see" with varying vividness places, persons, scenes, objects, and so on, or we are at least aware of a world of sensation which is important as such. Poetry and literary art rely to an enormous extent on these systems of imagery, and on metaphorical figures which imply image-thinking replacing abstract definition. It would be wrong to call these images non-verbal, because words are used to produce them; but clearly, though poetry uses words, its relations with them are problematic, in the sense that its mode of using them has a character of its own.

The predominant feature is that poetry, in using language, exploits the image-value of words, their sensuous structure, associations, and evocativeness. I do not think that the poetic use of language can be distinguished as a selection of certain *kinds* of language. Words are used by everybody for numerous non-aesthetic purposes, for instruction and command, for information and explanation, for philosophical argument and homiletic exhortation, and many activities have their own peculiar technical language.

Poetry can incorporate all these uses to which words are put. When the mind interprets in poetry, that is, in a medium of words, what it observes, it may quite naturally use any of its own contents of ideas and knowledge which are often indissolubly linked with words and therefore pertain to the medium used. Poetic language is not a question of different areas of language but of the manner of using it. Poetic language means a certain way of thinking, and we recognize it when we observe that linguistic statement, which is not in itself poetic, is assimilated to a complex system of imagery which includes rhythm, sound, metaphor, sensuous evocation, and design.

The ambiguities of language make this easier than might at first be thought. For words move between the poles of the "concrete" and the "abstract", between proximity to the sensuous impression and remoteness from it in conceptual thinking. Even much abstract language preserves a link with sensuous perception. If, for instance, I say : virtue is its own reward, which is an abstract generalization, it is well to remember that I am likely to make such a statement, sententiously, in face of a given example; in which case the preliminary observation is really: such and such a person has performed a perceptible act of virtue and he will be put into a contented state of mind which is a reward requiring no supplementary material reward. There is still in the mind a fresh impression of the conditions out of which the generalized statement might be produced. Or if, on the other hand, you suggest to me, starting a line of argument: virtue is its own reward, isn't it ?—I shall start to think, and in apprehending the sense of your statement, or question, I shall probably refer "virtue", as an abstract, to a " virtuous person " or a " virtuous action", and through my mind will run, concurrently with the abstract statement, a modification of it: virtuous persons doing virtuous acts tend to feel sufficiently rewarded by the act itself, a modification which preserves a certain generality of statement but is much nearer to the concrete, to an image.

This is a very brief and from the philosopher's point of view possibly crude analysis, but it will serve our present purpose if it illustrates one of the ambiguities of language as a sign of mental processes establishing independence amidst dependence on concrete reference or sensuous imagery. At one end of the scale is a particular perception, at the other the most abstract generalization; at one end an "image", at the other a generalized statement in which echoes remain of particular images. And perhaps even the most abstract statements rely for their being understood on constantly revived references to sensuous perception.

The importance of this for poetry is that since images are implicit in so many words, or at least are drawn upon for the process of thinking and vivifying meanings, there is no significant area of language as such that on principle need be excluded from poetry. What determines the poetic quality of language as against the abstract is how it is used; that is, how the stock of words which is available to any writer and is the same for all is manipulated, to what purpose and with what intention. Moreover, the distinction operative hère is not between prose and poetry, nor between a baldly contrasted "emotive" and "abstract", but between the use of language as part of a system of complex imagery and its use to achieve the theoretical accuracy that we sometimes call "scientific", or an extreme degree of conceptual statement. A similar distinction may be perceived between design in art and geometrical figures. It is perfectly true that painters often compose on a foundation that may be called for practical purposes "geometrical". But it is never more than reminiscent of geometry. The figures, used for non-mathematical purposes, are converted into images of nature or formula-images for emotion. Geometrical figures as geometry have no sensuous appeal, being valid alone as an approximation to concepts the whole point of which is their non-sensuous, theoretical, or logical accuracy.[1] In certain uses of language, as for example the scientific or the legal, a similar attempt is made to eliminate ambiguity and reach theoretical exactness of definition. This effort would not be necessary if opposing forces were not released by language itself, and they derive from the ambiguity noted, the fact that words point at one and the same time towards images, and evocations with numerous affective tones, and abstract concepts. The tendency of scientific language is to proceed by a series of class words. For instance the word flower indicates a class of objects, of which rose is a sub-division, tea-rose a further sub-division, each step in this process securing a more particular reference but still remaining essentially generalization. A scientific conception of a particular flower will finally be made up of many references, going beyond the above kind of general names to exact classifications of the stem, leaves, petals, stamens, all the several parts of the plant, thus accumulating a sum of exact references which constitute the scientific formula for the flower. A theoretical formula, however, not an image, since the method is conceptual, achieving a kind of accuracy which is only consonant with generalization at every stage. The words denoting and describing each part of the flower refer not to particular images but to classes. When the botanist has sorted out the relevant classifications, only his eye can show him the rose again, and only the word "rose" says what he sees. It is not accident that science tends more and more to mathematical forms. The ambiguity, the essential inaccuracy of isolated words, impels scientists to use symbols that are more adequate to theoretical exactness than language.

The scientist's attitude to the imagination confirms this process. Every scientist uses imagination; he conjectures, guesses, experiments, makes working hypotheses, "imagines" possible relations between the various facts of the physical universe as he knows them and may still know them. Scientific discovery is to a large extent the confirmation of an imaginative hypothesis by effective evidence or experiment. But the aim of science is to state laws; once these are conceived the imagination is abandoned, as belonging to the means but not the end. It is valid as an instrument but not as science.

Poetry, by contrast, draws language back from concepts and abstract theory. It does not dispense with concepts or conceptual words; but it uses language in such a way as to bring out to the full its implicit imagery and its potential use as metaphor. As we said above it is not a question of selecting suitable words and rejecting others, but of placing words in a context of expressive imagery. The scientist escapes from the ambiguity of language by seeking extreme theoretical formulations and shedding the pictorial or auditory evocativeness of words; the poet by seeking precisely the latter qualities and playing down the conceptual. Poetry secures its own kind of definition and precision in the cross-relations of words and images both visual and auditory in a context. Or, putting it another way, poetic language is the opposite of literal language; it defines images by escaping the conceptual definitions of separate words. Hence arises its whole apparatus of "figures of speech" and all the devices by which abstract thoughts borrow the vividness of sensuous or concrete detail. Abstractions may for example be personified, as often in eighteenth century verse :

Slow rises worth by poverty depressed.

But the personification and the concrete verbs subdue the abstract generality of the two nouns and hitch them to an image.

When poetry makes language as far as possible the vehicle of images it brings it into harmony with non-linguistic or pre-linguistic modes of consciousness and meaning. Here no doubt lies the reason why it is sometimes called more "primitive" than prose and why theories have been put forward that it is the "original" language of men, natural to a stage anterior to rational analysis and differentiation. Such language is the sign of naive immersion in the organic world, the immediate world of nature in which man is plunged and labours, not yet knowing a challenging vehicle of distance from it such as the language of the independent reason. It may be true that poetry is more primitive in this sense. Yet man is still in bond to nature both outside and inside himself, and scientific statement is only one mode of knowledge. But, as we said before, poetry, using words, can use all words; it can enter and leave at will any part of the verbal world, which contains all the knowledge of human memory and science consolidated through centuries. If in one sense it is more primitive, it is in another more intricate and complete; for, whilst preserving the power of the vivid image from nature, it can incorporate all the power of thought which man has developed and established as continuing knowledge. Poetry is thus a subtle interplay between non-linguistic meanings and those of verbal consciousness; between the sense of order and coherence realized in the imagery of words and the order pertaining to verbal propositions; between verbal contexts of apprehension and contexts of meaning that exceed purely verbal connotation.

From this arises a paradox of poetry, observable in the tantalizing way in which the word itself is both present and absent.

> Where, like a pillow on a bed,
>   A Pregnant banke swel'd up to rest
> The violets reclining head
>   Sat we two, one anothers best.
> Our hands were firmly cimented
>   With a fast balme, which thence did spring,
> Our eye-beams twisted, and did thred
>   Our eyes, upon one double string;
> So t'entergraft our hands, as yet
>   Was all the meanes to make us one,

And pictures in our eyes to get
  Was all our propagation.
As 'twixt two equal Armies, Fate
  Suspends uncertaine victorie,
Our soules (which to advance their state,
  Were gone out), hung 'twixt her, and mee.
And whil'st our soules negotiate there,
  Wee like sepulchrall statues lay;
All day, the same our postures were,
  And wee said nothing, all the day.

Words are here everything, and nothing. Nothing, because, as we
read, the situation of the lovers and their state of mind is presented
so completely as image that the medium collapses silently and leaves
us simply enveloped by the sense of a present scene, an illusion or
idea of reality. Words are everything, however, because to change
the context, or the metaphors, or the rhythms, would disturb the
interplay of imagery and deface the image as a whole. So that
although we forget the words we come back to them. In completing
the reading the words glide into absence, yet their presence in this
unique arrangement is essential in order that they may thus efface
themselves in the image. Perhaps this is one meaning of Keats's
well-known passage : 'Poetry should be great and unobtrusive; a
thing which enters into one's soul, and does not startle or amaze
with itself but with its subject'.

Poetry, by existing as an "intertexture" (a word of Coleridge's)[2] of
differing kinds of awareness, expressed in different kinds of imagery
associated with words, provides a self-awareness of mind more
intense, delicate, and complete than any other we know. Its range
of meanings, verbal and non-verbal, visual and rhythmic, sensuous
and logical, is as extensive as their organization is intricate. And so
it comes about that its statements transcend the specializations of
one faculty or one activity of the psyche, and indicate a condition of
'spiritual sensation', as Blake said, or, as Coleridge has it, one in
which 'the whole soul is brought into activity.'

CHAPTER SIX

MEDIUM

W E HAVE REACHED a point where we can make a decisive statement about complexity or intertexture, which is crucial for our understanding of different kinds of poetry, literary art, and drama. But it is convenient to intercalate here a word about the artistic medium. Our inquiry into the functioning of images enables us to re-define the problem of medium.

Medium is a word used often in a loose way to refer both to the material of an art, like stone, or paint, or words, and to forms like lyric or novel. It is better to regard the latter, however, as different ways of handling the same medium. Although we shall recognize a connexion between medium and kinds it makes for lucidity to distinguish them in the way suggested. The medium is a physical factor, the kinds or "forms" the result of its varied handling. For example, words exist outside poetry, and are therefore a medium; but the form of lyric poetry is intrinsic to literary art, being one mode of the poetic use of language. If this is the difference, the connexion lies in the fact that they are both aspects of the image-making process.

Every artist has a relation to his medium which expresses itself in two ways. On the one hand he submits to it, and on the other exercises a command over it. He yields to it, explores it, caresses it as an object in nature which he has not made and cannot alter except in a limited way; and having done this he asserts his own power in making it subservient to his mind. Hence emerges that peculiar intimacy between the creative mind and its medium to which the onlooker responds when he gains the impression from a work of art that the medium is part of the experience; for example, when even simple people will say that the whole of Shakespeare is in the splendour of the *words*, or when critics find in some archaic Greek sculptures more of the quality of the stone itself than in later work of the fifth and fourth centuries.

This sense of the medium is highly important. But there can be no doubt that where it obtrudes, deflecting attention from the artistic idea to the display of the material itself, decadence has set in. If the material itself must not obtrude, or in other words, if the artist's idea (or vision) is all-important, why does the medium count at all? Why is the artist so fond of it? Why do we recognize a merit in the work that shows intimacy with the medium?

We have taken the image as the foundation of art; in accordance with that we can say that the medium is nothing more nor less than a constituent part of the imagery. As we observe the appearance and character of paint, or of musical sounds, or of stone, or wood, or the sound and evocations of language, we make images; and the artist assimilates the images of the medium to the visionary images which he desires the medium to portray. Turner, and the impressionists, very "painterly" painters, as we are told, explore in the images of pigment an imagery of light. This assimilation is most apparent when a subject is peculiarly suited to a medium. For instance, a sculptor who wishes to express monumentality has an advantage over a poet or musician, because it is a quality of the very material in which he works. Stone itself projects an image of the monumental which is congruent with a "monumental" design shaping itself in ·the sculptor's mind. Art, it is true, always expresses far more in any medium than just what suits the medium best; to make this tractable is one of its triumphs. Yet it will never deviate too far from the characteristic imagery of the medium. Impressionist paintings could hardly be reproduced in wood-cut; and the attempts sometimes made to write poems by verbal sound alone have always been failures.[1]

What this argument affirms is that from the point of view of art the medium ceases to have importance as a "thing", as "material". In this respect it is a conditioning factor only, and even fortuitous; we remember how certain forms are dependent on the materials and tools available in any particular culture or period, as for example engraving, which developed in the fifteenth century with the progress of paper-making. It is essential to be clear on this point because it arises continually in aesthetic speculation. Many writers raise the problem in connexion with "craftsmanship", or the "sense of craft"; they stress the role that the handling of the material plays apart from the "forms" it is made to take. The plastic arts contribute heavily to this notion since they consist so obviously of physical objects which can be touched, moved, defaced, destroyed, like any other objects, and since the artists have clearly made them out of blocks of stone or wood or bits of pigment, which argues some interest in their physical character. And yet when we contemplate a sculpture we yield to something totally ideal. Even a comment on its "texture" will be related to the idea or the visionary quality of the work. And I would say that the much quoted love of the artist for his material is a love not of a physical object but of its appearance, or in other words of the imagery it occasions. For, as we said in the first chapter, as soon as we go beyond perception, by which we recognize that objects are *there* and are such and such (a table, stone, chair, etc.), we begin to construct images and see relations between them. So it is with the artist contemplating his medium. The possibilities of expressiveness in a medium lie in its imagery.

And so we may say that here too we discover the metaphorical process at work, beginning with the medium itself. The stone, the paint, the melody, the words, themselves initiate the process by which a vision is stated in a pattern of imagery.

The common statement about poets, especially since Mallarmé, that they "love words", means doubtless that they affect especially the imagery of words, their audibility, their sound and rhythm, as well as their meaning or the visual images of things they evoke. They would not otherwise be alone in their love. Presumably everyone who uses language at all for precise purposes develops an interest in its possibilities. But love of words covers a number of different things. It may be a delight in lucid thought and vivid expression, which may appear in all kinds of prose. It may be a philosopher's love of meanings entrenched in felicitous definition. A poet most likely includes these enthusiasms in his own love of words, for they are occasioned by features of language that, strictly speaking, are only analytically separable and in reality interact all the time. But his specific affection is for words as he himself uses them, the material whose sensuous content and surface he exploits for his own trade in image and metaphor.

The corollary to the notion that the poet as artist loves "words" as the material of his art, is the idea, frequently expressed, that 'the poetry is in the words'. The latter idea must be corrected in accordance with our clarification of the former. It is an extremely fashionable notion nowadays, intended laudably enough to insist that the meaning of a poem is in the poem and nowhere else, not in ideas, or society, or history, or whatever. But it is a rough-and-ready phrase. We never say: the art is in the paint, or in the sounds. Art lies in the organization of images; poetry in the organization of imagery-in-language.

The theory here put forward accommodates under our major aesthetic principle the element of craft which has often been a stumbling-block to aesthetic. The medium as real object loses significance to the medium as imagery. But the medium has of course from one point of view an unassailable significance as real object. It assures the statement of vision. Medium does not make art, but it does enshrine it. Art is a mode of thought and knowledge, but its general effectiveness is only guaranteed by its appearance in a medium. Otherwise it remains isolated and private. As between artist and onlooker the medium makes possible the formula which enables our mind to re-imagine the image-idea intended and achieved by the imagination of genius.

CHAPTER SEVEN

ART AND EXPERIENCE

i. A DEFINITION OF ART

W E MAY NOW DRAW the various threads of this inquiry together and attempt a definition of art. Since we are especially concerned with several arts and with the complex art of drama, the sort of definition we require must contain a principle which not only indicates a unity in artistic creation and aesthetic experience but also covers the numerous overlaps between the various arts, those features which show them using common elements or encroaching upon each other. The real difficulty in finding such a definition is that unifying principles tend to minimize or deny the importance of the medium, sacrificing what every artist or sensitive person feels to be an essential element—the medium, the sensuousness, the particularity, the craftsmanship—to an abstract and over-philosophical idea; whilst on the other hand principles that do justice to these elements tend to lose in the particularity of a given sensuousness both the unity of art and the core of spirituality. I hope that our theory of the image and its functional use will help us to overcome the difficulties. We have held that art and poetry refer to something variously called nature, or the commonsense world, or external reality, from which images are derived, and also to the inner world of human thought, feeling, and spiritual insight. We have considered images of representational and non-representational kinds but we stressed both their common origin and the fact that their exact import depends very much on their function in relation to each other. We discussed metaphor and then the relations between words and images in literary art and established, as a result of these trains of inquiry, the idea of poetry as an "intertexture" of various systems of imagery and the conceptual meanings of words.

66

Using terms to be defined more fully in the sequence we may say that experience of the external and the subjective worlds goes to the making of art, which is, however, an independent, circumscribed creation or construction.

The definition proposed is this: *art is experience re-enacted as idea, a formula of imagery, or imagery-within-language, being the instrument of re-enactment.*

In putting it forward I am doing more than at the outset of this essay I set myself to do, since I said that I did not necessarily aim to produce an aesthetic but only to find a theory that would help to illumine the relationship between some of the arts, especially poetry and drama. Even now, with a definition proposed, the intention is not, in the strict sense, philosophical; I do not wish to masquerade as a philosopher, but to remain a literary critic trying to make a framework of theory for the understanding of poetic forms. But a tentative definition of art may well be the most convenient way of focusing the relationships. As we elucidate now the terms of the one put forward I hope it will be seen to satisfy the requirements stated above. It emphasizes the ideal or constructed nature of art, it does justice to varied media under a general and therefore unifying principle, it refers art to life or lived experience, and it is inclusive without being too general or vaporous. It can be applied to each of the arts, without exception, and in consequence also to their relations in complex or mixed forms.

ii. EXPERIENCE AND ART

In earlier chapters we said that even a pure pictorial image is not an equivalent of reality but a representation of a partial aspect of it. It is a selective image; and a representation of any object or scene is a selective image or pattern of images and may be called an " interpretation" of that object or scene. We also said that representational images were usually not pure, but had an admixture of subjective expressiveness, a charge of feeling. And we spoke also of expressive formula-images as sensuous symbols of feeling. When we use the term "experience" in our definition we mean the events that precede and lead to the formation of all such images, either the impact of the external world on the artist, or the feelings that he has and wishes to express. It is from these things that images issue and the reference to them constitutes part of their meaning. In other words, art is intricately linked with a process of living, and a definition must embrace this link, for which reason we use the term experience. It means what happens in *us* amidst the world that is *not* us, the world of nature, society, and supra-individual life. It arises from the impact of external things, and of the life that surrounds and transcends individual limitation, on our bodies and minds, and ranges of course from the minutest physical sensations to the most complex mental and spiritual disturbances. One cannot single out any particular class of experience as the material of art. The world of light and colour found in landscape painting, and built up from fine sensuous responses, involves experience just as the poems of John Donne, with their moral and religious issues, do.

But we must keep the meaning of experience in our definition quite general, distinguishing it sharply from the notion of single experiences as particular historical events. It often happens that works of art follow on single experiences, being jilted, seeing an operation, being in an air-raid, viewing a landscape, grief for a dead person, and so on; but art is not the record of autobiographical events in the artist's life; it is not simple recollection or memory. From what has been said above about imagery and interpretation of nature we know that works of art can never be history in a strict sense; they can, even at their most realistic, only present a selection of the happenings of life and such a selection is already something different from life.[1]

But if we reject the idea that art is equivalent to real situations in which the artist was involved, we do explicitly insist that the origins of art lie in experience understood as the vast reservoir of sensations, impressions, actions, and events suffered that each life provides as it is lived and on which the artist's thought and imagination do their work, combining and re-combining images and memories. Positivist critics fifty years ago never tired of looking for the real life models on whom authors based the characters of plays and novels; but authors themselves have for the most part deprecated the search as being of little significance, not because they never used models, but because the meaning of their art was other than the meaning of the real persons who may have helped to set their imagination in motion. For something from *all* experience enters into a work of art. But experience there must be; there must exist the contact between the imagination and the life of man and nature. The precise relations between an artist's work as a spiritual sequence and his personal life as a biographical sequence are always complicated and differ from one artist to another. But certain it is that artists, like others, have characteristic dispositions of the feelings, obsessions, unconscious desires, a temperament and compulsive interests, which are all real, existing before the work of art, flowing into it, and continuing to exist after it. They alone give genuine character and consistency of style to a series of works, being the life from which these emerge, and endowing them with sincerity. Works of art are not made by the imagination turning on itself, reflecting itself and its procedures in mirrors; they are made from interpretations, from thought and judgements about life and the feelings and ideas it evokes. And for this reason novelty, which goes with personal vitality and sincerity, is a legitimate criterion of art. Where novelty is present, in its genuine form, there is also the "contemporary spirit". And since this creative process is natural and organic an artist is likely to be more genuine and contemporary when absorbed in what seems to be his own personal problem than when trying hyperconsciously to generalize about his time and "represent" it. An artist has only to be true to his own feelings to be exact about his age.

The 'return to nature', the slogan of many revolutions in poetry and art, and productive of very different sorts of "nature", is one of the general ideas under which artists free themselves from the sentiments, beliefs, and consciousness of previous generations and seek to define their own, which entails always new "forms" and a new "diction". Thus it was with Dryden and Pope, with Herder and Goethe in the early 1770's, with Rousseau, with Wordsworth, with the pre-Raphaelites, with the realism of the mid nineteenth century, and also with the search for emotional honesty in the twentieth century after Victorianism. The reproach of the succeeding generation against each movement of 'return to nature' is usually that it was artificial; not unnaturally. The process of education in childhood, bound up with language and existing art forms, cannot but transmit ideas and beliefs not strictly relevant to the new life developing in the child, for the sum of language and art at any given moment represents the degree of illumination achieved by those who use that language and art and have extended its expressiveness. The child, though assimilating knowledge and ideas which it will need, is still faced with the task of clarifying its own life which is ahead of the verbal system and art forms of its parents and teachers.

The deliberate effort of revolt is required by every generation in order to counteract successfully the very process of education by which it is put in possession of knowledge and art at all, and achieve its own identity. The imagination is the most potent of the instruments disclosing the secret of new feelings and beliefs.

Hence the jealous sense of vocation and mission in young artists and poets, their sense of being heralds of new truths, and a notable predilection for shock tactics. These do not in themselves guarantee the finding of the new vein of ore. On balance they proclaim the spurious as often as the genuine. But they proceed from the deep instinct of the imaginative temperament, in league with strong impulses, to seek words and images for its ego, its own sacrosanct spirit.

Experience in our sense embraces both object and subject, but the exact relationship takes innumerable forms. It obviously includes strong elements of individuality and of the artist's own emotional character, since these things always determine his reactions, as they do everybody's. It includes the original interest we spoke of in an earlier chapter, the compulsion, pre-rational and pre-conscious, that directs in artists as in everyone their interests and tastes. This we understand when we hear for instance of Proust's delight in noting and analysing what happened to him; this is an individual trait distinguishing him from people who do not experience this form of delight, and it has consequences for his art. Eliot has written that "experience" is what happens to us as we do the things we want to do. So the basis of experience always implies a particular person, acting and re-acting in a particular way, being moved or excited by things and events. But in the sensitive person it always implies also thought and imagination operating in conjunction with action and reaction and influencing them. Experience thus comes to mean more than what just happens to us; it is that together with our knowledge and understanding of it and the way we relate it to all our knowledge and understanding and to the continual process of living. So we supplement our acknowledgement of the factual and personal element in experience with the notion of the imaginative elaboration of it. As Henry James observed, artists do not necessarily need to live through all the violent or great experiences portrayed in their works; they need the imagination that unfolds significance from trifling hints. One need look no further than Shakespeare, or indeed any of the great tragic poets, for examples of this truth, for after all they are not themselves the murderers they portray with such convincing psychology. And this is, of course, an aspect of the perpetually invoked "intuition" of genius.

The communion between living and having intuitions about living is, of course, the matrix from which art arises, and the reason why the voice of genius is always both personal and impersonal. A personal disposition is always sublimated in the style of art; but the life that speaks through the individual is supra-personal. It is a life that flows through all the differentiated phenomena of nature and man, and in which the artist as a man participates as others do; but as an imagination, a medium of intuition, he achieves a vaster knowledge and sense of it and becomes an instrument of something far transcending his personal self and its actions. Through the imagination he is in touch with the spirituality surrounding and permeating human life, and his voice in consequence is larger than himself. The lyric poet's first person is for example generally a convention or a deception, since it conceals a general voice.

All art is thus at one and the same time a metaphor of the artist's self and a metaphor of humanity in general, since it feeds inescapably on both these sources. It shows a search for self in congruent sensuous analogues, a symbolic delineation of the deep, secretive self in the materials of not-self. It is the imagery in which self and the world co-habit. Self is submerged in the world, but the world speaks out of this self. It is this process that is consummated in the metaphorical structures of art, which are not "object" and not "subject" but both together in an ideal transformation and construction; and it accounts for their resonance and reverberation, the sense of infinite significance residing in finite forms. Life and intuition, process and imagination, historical particular and supra-historical effectiveness, merge in art and in this way experience is re-enacted as idea.

Great thoughts, or "spiritual insights", do not alone make poetry, because, although arising within the framework of life, they do not incorporate the world of sensuous process but are formulated as detached abstractions. But they can form part of poetry when allowed to appear in a larger context embracing the imagery of experience, as they do, to take a striking and very pertinent example, in Wordsworth's *The Prelude*.

The case is similar with mysticism, a brief mention of which is appropriate, since a poet and a mystic have often dwelt in the same person. Here the essential point is not to confuse the true mystic experience with the record of it; nor with poetry, when the record happens to have poetic qualities. Mystics have described their visions, it is true; but the genuine mystic experience lies beyond any description or report, inaccessible to mere readers. The mystic, however vividly he may record, experiences something that his readers cannot. But mystical writing—and this is its ambivalence— partakes of the poetic when an attempt is made to construct an imagery of the experience. Formulated in a medium the experience declines from the truly mystical and becomes something different; it is then a re-enactment in sensuous terms. It is a poem, and accessible to others.

iii. RE-ENACTMENT AND IDEA

The images of art, deriving from acquaintance with the external world and the self, are idea-images embodying interpretation and expression of experience in the generalized sense just expounded.

Because it is idea, art exists outside the flux of experience; but because it is always imagery it is a re-enactment in sensuous appearances. In this curious nature of the idea-images of art, and the functional relation between them in a unified system, lies its ambiguity. It is lit from two worlds simultaneously, the world of time-space appearances and the world of the interpreting mind. The two things, idea and re-enactment, go together without any possibility of being separated.

Poetry and art use the appearances of the real world, but with a subtle re-adjustment which removes them from it. They are a creation of mind; they are *idea*, products not of external nature, but of human thought. Even if we call them 'expressions of feeling', or 'pictures of life'—common, useful, but very general and therefore mildly misleading terms—they are still the products of thought. The stone of a statue is a real object, but the statue itself, its shape and expression, is, from the point of view of natural objects, unreal. Nor can we say that a hand has produced it, the sculptor's hand "instinctively" shaping it. A hand cannot do very much until it is moved by a will or a passionate idea. Again it is not "feeling" that has produced it, though this idea, as well as the former, is widespread. In one sense art includes an activity that starts as behaviour, as the spontaneous expression of feeling, but then it goes far beyond that. It is the result of events that take place inside the mind and in which conscious as well as unconscious, ratiocinative as well as emotive and affective, processes all play their part. A painter, for example, is attracted to a given subject, say a landscape, by unconscious impulses, by all the compelling forces in his nature which determine his outlook, feeling, tastes and pleasure; it is this conjunction of something external and something internal that constitutes a vital sensation and excitement which is spontaneous, real feelings following a real stimulus. But the choosing of images of paint with which to fix his vision and feelings in a formula involves a complementary conscious process, attested by "sketches", by trial, selection, and rejection, until he has found the images that he knows to be the right formula, the images that his judgement confirms; the purpose of this whole process being to clarify in the imagery of the medium an *idea* of what he sees and feels. In short, the excitement out of which the art creation issues is emotional, affective, extravolitional, and real; it "comes upon" the artist. But the creation of the imagery that enshrines his idea of and feeling about his subject depends upon his imagination and conscious judgement and is a process of ideation.

The idea of inspiration, linked with that of the sensuous imagination, and doubtless extremely pertinent, cannot be said to contradict the above analysis, though it sometimes is used for that end; just as some would like to credit everything to genius as a wholly irrational power. This involves an over-simplification. In the first place it fails to allow for the education and development of their powers that great artists undertake and achieve with deliberate study, converting a natural activity or spontaneous form of behaviour into a form of thought embracing various powers of their mind. And secondly it confuses an extremely efficient though unconscious *mechanism* of thought with something that is outside human thought altogether; or, to use the terms often invoked, it calls the processes of genius "irrational" and implies thereby something vitalistic and akin to organic life from which rationality and ideality are absent. This error appears in its crudest form in the view, vague but widely held, that works of art are conceived instantaneously and executed without hesitation, sprouting and unfolding into bloom by that dispensation of nature that produces the silent unconscious world and its beauty. From the sense of unity gained from works of art this view seems to argue retrospectively to an initial fabulous act of creation in which all was seen and done in a flash. There is much evidence that the main features of some great works of art were conceived simultaneously, and evidence, too, that poems can be sometimes conceived with dream-like immediacy. Even so we must not confuse a mechanism of thought with the absence of it. How ideas occur to us, whether upon deliberate thinking, whether spontaneously, belongs to this mechanism, and the sudden irruption of ideas into consciousness, or the sudden success in ordering related ideas, does not alter their character of being ideas, nor does it exclude the possibility of long unconscious gestation and slow conscious working out, as may be seen with the most persuasive force, for example, from Beethoven's notebooks.[2]

Again the fact that a work of art is the result of processes of thought, which means that it grows in time, and the fact that it uses the illusion of sensuous life, i.e. of life in time, does not put it back again into some category other than thought. It takes time to compose a poem, and time to read it, and time may be in its subject, but the poem itself is placed outside human biographical time because it is *idea*. And we know it is idea because it is fixed in a formula and is repeatable in thought and only thus. A poem cannot "take place", nor can it be "an experience", until someone reconstructs it as thought by reading it, which is an act of will or of particularized and conscious desire. The same applies to music, or mime, or ballet, the only difference being that an intermediary is needed, the performer, who realizes the images of the formula for us, so that we may reconstruct the work of art in our thought.[3]

But the character of art as idea emerges strikingly from another feature of our preoccupation with it. The notion of "unity" or unity-in-diversity is a commonplace of aesthetic and criticism and here again the suggestion is constantly made that we "perceive" the unity—of a painting, or of a poem—in a flash, by way of some "intuition" or instantaneous recognition that seems to exclude the slower, familiar mode of thinking and reasoning step by step. Again, I think, a mechanism of thought obscures the fact of thought. "Unity" is not a sensuous experience, but an idea about it; it is an interpretation. And similarly with a work of art; the unity is the result of the artist's imaginative thought; he has constructed it. Our perception of it, although it may be rapid, especially if we are experienced, is a construction commensurate with the artist's. The case is clear with forms that require performance. The "unity" of a symphonic movement is not an accidental instantaneous illumination but results from the knowledge of its parts, and this establishes itself in the mind in the course of performance and repeated performance by following the musical images and remembering their sequence and thus gradually seeing their relations. The understanding of unity cannot be other than a product of thought working with the materials of memory. Ease and fluency of understanding, which are sometimes confused with "intuition", result from practice. Events, including action and behaviour, are in time and unrepeatable; art, though necessarily experienced in time, is intrinsically a construct of thought, of extra-temporal ideas.[4]

From this insistence on the ideality of art we turn back to the notion of re-enactment, since only the two things together, idea and re-enactment, can do justice to its ambivalence. Any definition has to include within its scope the sensuous terms of art, the feature of repetition, or reflection, or imitation, or mimesis, or representation, or presentation, or simulation, or illusion, of life. All the terms just recalled arise because art uses the time-space appearances that also characterize life and nature. A drama is not real life, and the time required by its subject, or story, is not the same as the real time involved in a performance, but it has to create the illusion of time in order to represent its subject at all and to let it evoke the right feelings. A sculptured figure imitates in the imagery of stone or wood the spatial, tactile and dynamic conditions pertaining to a real figure in life. Even in architecture and abstract art the apprehension of the meaning involves the illusion of "feelings", for example the sense of a resolution of conflict or of the balancing of contending forces, or the expression of some definable mood like joy, peace, gaiety, or of experience of a quality desired, as we expounded in connexion with expressive formula-images; Gothic style expresses the Christian sense of the numinous, baroque the dramatic sense of the duality in life, modern "functional" architecture provides in general an ingratiating image of a cool, honest and rational economy joined to a simple sensuous pleasure in textures and the clean play of light on surfaces. Viewing such art renews the sense of the qualities it embodies, and gives pleasure. Hence "re-enactment" is an appropriate notion even here. It is more adequate than traditional terms like representation, or illusion, or any of those just mentioned, because it applies equally to the representational and expressive aspects of imagery. The re-enactment of feelings as idea in music or architecture, for instance, is a more lucid and comprehensible notion than that of "representation" of feelings, and retains within the general idea of art symbolism a useful analytical clarity.

Thus the proposed definition: art is experience re-enacted as idea, a formula of imagery (or imagery-within-language) being the instrument of re-enactment, attempts to reconcile the difficult and contradictory features of art within a single principle.

iv. INTEGRITY IN ART RECONSIDERED IN RELATION TO EXPERIENCE AND IDEALITY

Our theory of imagery and definition of art enables us to put the problem of the integrity of works of art in a new light. By integrity we mean their characteristic of being a self-contained world, a world with an order and perfection of its own and framed off, exquisitely, from the common everyday world. Most people agree about this quality, though it has been explained in different ways. But there has always been much disagreement about its implications for the question of what art has to do with life. The conflict finds for instance a convenient focus in two extreme views, the one holding the value of art to consist in some social relevance of a direct and obvious kind, and the other maintaining that its value lies in a transcendent idealism inhering in it and effectively separating it from "life", which in such a view is deprecated as vulgar. The one opinion minimizes, the other maximizes, the idea of integrity so far that they end by denying a great deal of art—all the art, in fact, approved by the opposite view. A historical example of this is the opposition between the naturalist social novels and dramas of the late nineteenth century and the contemporary symbolist style in poetry. Such partisan solutions cancel each other out and we are bound to conclude that they misconceive both art and integrity.

We began this chapter by emphasizing that art arises from experience and that it is not a creation out of the void. We have said it is a mode of thought, but thought implicit in sensuous forms, representing nature and expressing feelings. Let us also recall here a point from our first chapters to the effect that its meanings are only available to us if we can compare and contrast them with other kinds of experience and knowledge; by setting for instance a landscape-painting against the landscapes of naive realism or of scientific truth.

And in fact, putting it bluntly, art is only interesting and enjoyable because it does illumine life for us, the life in ourselves, the life of objects, and the life of men and nature, society and history. We could not live by "geometric" art alone, or the arts of pure pattern; these are expressive in their degree, but we need more frequently still the direct effect of the great poems and paintings on our feeling for the nature of life and destiny. The power of all "abstract" art depends precariously on whether it convinces us that "feelings", or "felt ideas", or "intuitions", and sincerity, are relevant, however difficult to analyse.[5]

The problem is thus to admit that art, as created by an artist, has clearly some close connexion with "life" or "experience", that its significance in some way depends on the connexion, but at the same time to acknowledge that it is after all different, framed off in its final perfection of statement, and raised above and beyond the chains of the physical and organic.

The answer to this enigma is that the work of art is *an issue*. It is a result, the special result of experience, that experience which is compounded of the external world and an artist's response. As an issue from these antecedents it is still linked with them as a child with its parents. But, being an issue, it is a new thing. Both these positions belong to the work of art, and the reader or spectator is aware of both; he sees both the life and the transfiguration in art, what aspects of life have moved the artist and how he has given them an ideal form in images, whether modelled closely on originals or freely combined and elaborated.

Such observations show that the integrity of art is a condition of perfection that in no way prejudices the question of origins. In technical analysis it is useful to say that art is not "about" anything, in the sense in which a book on furniture is "about" that subject; art is itself. But in simple language it is equally useful to say that art is always "about" experience. This clear point should prevent also a misinterpretation of our view of "ideality" as an intellectualist one. Emotions of some kind, whatever their force or degree, are invariably involved in the processes of art, and we shall examine their incidence more closely in a moment; but in the finished work of art we have not emotions but *ideas* of emotions fixed in the formulas of imagery. This is the point of Wordsworth's "emotion recollected in tranquillity", or, as we say, re-enacted as idea.

77

v. (a) ART IN RELATION TO THE EXPERIENCE OF ARTIST AND RECIPIENT
(b) THE PROBLEM OF "REAL" FEELINGS IN ART CONTEMPLATION

Two problems about art and its relation to experience call for special comment, the one concerning both artist and recipient, and involving the question of understanding and judgement, whilst the second concerns the recipient and the sort of feelings he has in the process of contemplating art.

In the preceding section we said that although art contains its meaning in itself, which we call its integrity, it issues from experience. Similarly, we now add, it can only be understood by observers who have sufficient experience of their own to bring its meanings to life. Nothing is more absurd than the notion that we need no equipment for understanding art, in spreading which idea some enthusiasts have unwittingly joined forces with the barbarous and the Philistine. We all know how gradual is the growth of our understanding of poems and other art works from late childhood or early adolescence onward and how frequently we experience in later years the feeling of suddenly "understanding" a poem or line of verse for the first time. Why should this be if not because it is only as we increase our knowledge and gather experience that we provide the field of reverberation for the poems we read? Wordsworth's ode *Intimations of Immortality* contains an encomium of childhood, for instance, but one quite beyond the understanding not only of children but of all young people. In other words the work of art cannot entirely of itself create or induce in any given person at any given moment the conditions of understanding. On the contrary it has to find a context of knowledge and emotional preparedness. Fortunately, in this as in most features of art creation and reception, we are not always faced by a cruel alternative of total understanding or total lack of it; works of art give us much enjoyment even when we only partially grasp their sense and beauty. But the pursuit of art does imply the search for those felicitous moments when a work and ourselves meet in perfect or nearly perfect coincidence. For having once occurred such moments impose a standard and force us to seek them again. This is a natural process in those interested in art.

Examining the problem more closely (and to avoid a laboured phraseology I will refer simply to poets and poems, taking them as typical for artists and art in general), we observe the crucial feature to be a continuous interaction between real experience and imagination; and this applies, though there is a point of view of the poet which differs from that of the reader, both to the making and to the contemplation of poems. A poem occupies a certain historical place in the life of the poet, and of course we mean his spiritual life, not merely his biography. It is related to his previous life and experience; it is the product of a particular stage in his total development as a sentient, thinking, and creative being. It could not have been produced before that stage, and if it were postponed it would not be the same poem but another, the product of a later stage of development. On the other hand you have the reader who, reading a poem, is doing so, no less than its maker, at a particular stage of his life. He is at a certain age; he has a given equipment of experience and knowledge; he is a given person at a specific moment of his total development. All this bears on his reading of the poem.

From this we see that any "understanding" or "response" to the poem is necessarily related to the two worlds of experience involved; it is the product of a point of intersection between them, and they are both relevant to the reading. By that I mean that some forces, and some meanings, overflow from both into the poem; I do not mean that there is a capricious or chaotic commerce between them.

Any reading of a poem thus falls somewhere on a scale between the near-naive and the fully initiated response. A naive reading in the strictest sense is an impossibility in view of the premises from which we are arguing, since any reader must be assumed to have some degree of equipment. One might be tempted to call a reading naive where there is a simple intersection between a poem and a response which has not been preceded by any special preparation; this is the case generally when we read a poem for the first time and, allowing it to make a clean, fresh impact, seek its particular note of beauty or interest. And indeed the art of putting prejudice or irrelevant matter out of one's mind in order to let the poem make its own chaste effect in this way belongs to reading and is very properly emphasized nowadays in the teaching of criticism. But it should not be misunderstood; dismissing irrelevant matters is not the same thing as making one's mind an innocent blank, and one cannot in fact do anything at any given moment in one's life but use the mind one has, formed, developed, stocked, furnished and intricately functioning as it is.

The idea of the perfectly innocent reading can thus, once the simplification involved is exposed, be dismissed as a myth. What we really have with a poem and its readings is a series of variants conditioned by two things: (a) the general experience and preparedness of the reader both as regards life and poetry, and not forgetting his character and temperament; and (b) the reader's knowledge and understanding of the context of the poem in its *author's* experience, by which is meant, as we said, not simply its place in a chronological or biographical sequence, but in a spiritual life. In this complicated relationship lies the justification of literary scholarship and commentary.

But the analysis is not complete without a special reference to the role of the imagination, which is nothing if not a compensating faculty. We have sufficiently emphasized that a poem is not the documentation of particular events. To write his poem the poet needs a certain quantity of experiences and a certain degree of imagination (that is, command of imagery, and perception of relationships and meaning); the elaboration of the one by the other, or in other words, their mutual fructification, produces the intensity of intuitive statement that astounds us in poetry and art. The exact relation between the two varies enormously, but clearly, given *some* experience, the imagination when powerful tends to render the historical details of experience irrelevant and to a large extent even superfluous. They are important genetically, as being the occasion of the growth of the poem; but ultimately the latter is valid by nonhistorical meanings.

Now this gives us a second relationship between poet and reader, which, parallel to the first one discussed above, we will describe as occurring at the point of intersection between the *imaginative powers* of the poet and those of the reader, between the poet's visionary process and the reader's capacity to respond to it. And again, this relationship varies very greatly.

These two sets of relationships—experience and imagination—influence each other all the time, and in general it may be said that the second set provides compensation for the lack of correlation under the first, a generalized imaginative constitution of experience —which is idea—replacing a simple conceptual understanding of similar factual experiences in two persons. A paradoxical result follows. On the one hand the intricacy of these relationships, always different, has the consequence that readings of a poem, either by different persons or the same person on different occasions, are varied. But on the other hand the effect of the imagination, in its relation to experience, is to cross-refer and generalize; every poem, as a formula of imagery, is precise and particular, but as a system of meaning it involves a high degree of generalization and cross-reference. This generalization is not conceptual, but its effects are in some ways similar. The most important is that it helps powerfully to give a poem a consistent identity, to which every reading is an approximation. I mean it reinforces the quality of objective ideality in a poem; which means that when a hundred or a thousand or a million persons read Donnes *Twickenham Garden* they are not simply creating *x* independent "personal" poems but are in fact at the same time being attracted away from their personal orbit into that of an impersonal idea, the poem *Twickenham Garden*.

Our view is based consistently on the idea that a work of art exists potentially in a formula of imagery and is realized by the recipient as a reconstitution of its imaginative pattern, with supporting feelings. There is no doubt that readings vary; we know it from our own experience and from discussion with others as to theirs. But the variation is slight, and in no way a replacement of an original by some entirely new thing. It is erroneous, though very fashionable in recent years, to exaggerate the idea of individual or "personal" variation into a provocative dogma. The worship of personal deviation can merge in a cult of eccentricity equivalent finally to intellectual isolation and suicide. The views of Valéry and Eliot, to the effect that poems once made leave the orbit of their author's control, becoming different things for different readers, have contributed to the fashion perhaps more mischievously than either poet intended. For however difficult it is to say what exactly a work of art "is", apart from its material instrument—the piece of stone, the pigment on canvas, the signs on paper or the noise in the air—it is certainly not simply the sum of *x* "individual" realizations if each is at liberty to deviate as it likes. The formula of imagery is not the work of art, since this is the reconstitution of the imaginative pattern; but it *is* most assuredly the key, the guide, the directive.   It is the link with the starting-point. I mean that varied realizations must be "of" something; something must be realized and something varied. We can willingly admit that the artist, having completed his work, may reconstitute it even for himself subsequently in different ways, but even he must accept an implied starting-point, which we may take to be the moment in which he successfully achieved his formula. The arts of interpretation offer notable examples of varied rendering and we derive pleasure from having different versions of, for example, a musical work. But however liberal we may be in our attitude towards interpretation we still have a desire to recognize the work being interpreted; the Pastoral Symphony has to be the Pastoral and not the Fifth, and it has to be played in the style of Beethoven and not of Bach or Wagner. Nor have I ever heard even the most idiosyncratic of musical amateurs maintain, as they listened to the Jupiter Symphony, that they were hearing the G minor. Such symptoms, which belong to experience, are just as potent as those that give us knowledge of deviation in interpreting, and they point to the over-riding common factors which make all the readings of a work of art at least into a *class*. In short we must not underrate the ideality of art, its high degree of generalized and supra-personal statement, even though its reception must always be sensuous and particular, in favour of a too facile emphasis on the individual's "experience" of it. Art intends the ideal; and the "personal experience" of it is worthless except as an initiation into its ideality and generality.

Two further effects of these intricate cross forces may be mentioned. One is that the validity of first readings is reduced. In these the context for comprehension is too restricted, but obviously age and experience are a corrective; and by age I do not mean old age, but rather the *appropriate* age. There are many poems and works of art which are realized most fully in a context of youth or at least early adulthood, and the question of their rank or value cannot be settled without taking this into account.

The second effect is that by virtue of the imagination—i.e. of poetry and art—one can, to a certain important extent, transcend one's own real experience; which has as a further, reciprocal consequence that one's capacity for, and understanding of, real experience is increased. We need some experience in order to respond to the meanings of works of art; but they always add to it, enlarging, supplementing, transmuting, completing. Only with some previous experience can *King Lear* make sense, but it then changes all subsequent experience.

The second problem to be considered about art in its relation to experience is the question as to whether the observer of art has "real" feelings during the process, and if so, what they have to do with the feelings expressed in the work of art, and why they are commensurate with ideality and integrity in art.

In the first place we shall leave out of account as irrelevant all purely private emotional uses to which a work of art may be put. It is psychologically true that poems and pictures may have quite different emotional significance for different people. I can for example cherish an aria of Handel because I heard it sung on an early summer's evening in Florence by a particular friend, and every time I hear it I have real feelings arising from these circumstances. You, on the other hand, associate it with a second-rate choral concert once heard in the fog-bound Midlands, and the memory always obtrudes very really on any performance you hear. We each can link works of art in innumerable such ways to our own lives. But psychological facts like these, however true, do not belong to the analysis of art except to be noted as impurities. They are arbitrary private behaviour, not contemplation of the creations of imagination. Any object in nature, say a flower, in a particular garden or vase, may be appropriated to emotional uses in the same way, but though it can thus come to "mean" different things to different people, there is still a sense in which it is *a flower* and not a mere stimulus.

If we speak of real feelings being present in aesthetic contemplation we mean at least feelings that are in some way relevant to the work of art. Simple examples are those called into play when following a story or drama. We pity Lear and Cordelia, we "hate" Goneril and Regan, our "indignation" rises at their behaviour, our "sorrow" and "grief" fetch tears from us at the end. In short we follow stories always with our feelings keyed up to a certain tenseness as we "sympathize" humanly with the characters and follow their fortunes and misfortunes with correspondent emotions. Or, to take another example, with lyric poems that evoke moods of joy, or sorrow, or grief, or hope, or melancholy, and so on, we may experience something very like these real feelings.

I think we have to remember that all conditions or acts of thought are part of a continuous physico-mental existence. A man lives and his thinking is a part of his being alive; he doesn't stop living, in order to think, and then, ceasing thought, take up life again. What does happen is that many of his activities cease when he wants to do some thinking or are carried on automatically without his being conscious of them. Thus philosophers and others are able to walk to their daily office completely sunk in a train of thought and oblivious of passing their friends in the street. But those unseen friends in their turn might observe the man's lips move and, hearing a murmured O dear! infer a grave turn of thought, or see a smile and infer a satisfactory one. Hence we admit that certain forms of behaviour accompany thought. We also know that reading books, of no matter what kind, and including the austerest works of science and philosophical argument, may induce real feelings of depression or well-being, surprise, excitement, suspense, indignation, and so on. Pure thought, or pure thinking, is an abstract conception, whilst real situations, i.e. real-men-thinking, are thought in a complete psycho-physiological context. But the crucial point is that we can admit all this and yet believe that the behavioural aspects of the real situation are entirely subordinate. They are not of the essence of the matter but accidental; the essence of the matter being that the thought—the science, or philosophical argument, or whatever— is precisely an *abstraction*, and that to conceive it as a physical situation, even in part, is to offend its aspiration. It intends the abstract.

Art, being through its ideality a form of thought, follows a pattern similar in some respects. The real feelings felt during various kinds of reading noted above—surprise, excitement, etc.— are experienced also in observing art. But in addition, since art employs the appearances of life, we are aware of feelings very like the real feelings stirred up by the various aspects of the subject of an art-work. We have to admit that a beautiful religious picture puts us into a religious frame of mind. Hard-boiled aesthetes deny this, but they probably with some faint dishonesty suppress their religious response, or, if they do not feel it, they can be convicted of missing at least half the point. A painting of the Nativity, if it loses its religious meaning, is devoid of sense. Similarly poems, or pictures, or music, induce "moods" of various kinds which have emotional reality, whether of joy, triumph, sadness, romance, happiness, aspiration, edification, merriment, nostalgia, or whatever. But the emotional intensity of a mood may vary a great deal and it seems to me that what we have to do is differentiate between the emotion, say *joy*, that is a constituent of an *actual* experience (the joy of meeting one's lover or friend) and the *mood of joy* that a work of art might induce, whilst admitting equal *reality* of feeling in both.

We may put the matter perhaps in the following fairly simple form. Reading a poem, for example, calls into play various emotional factors that are present in other kinds of experience but with

a different, balance. In an aesthetic situation the final goal is comprehension and enjoyment of a total work of art in its completeness
and unity. Part of the process of reaching this goal involves having
real feelings varying from stage to stage. They are not as strong as
they would be in situations of action, but they are real in the sense
of being psychologically of the same kind.

There is a further important aspect of this problem. Apart from
real emotional behaviour aroused in the course of aesthetic observation, and apart from the sympathetic evocation of particular
emotions, there exists also the phenomenon of what may be called a
certain tuning of the emotional sensibility that accompanies contemplation of art. It may be observed at its most vivid, perhaps, not
in ordinary reading and listening and viewing, but in the arts of performance. Every lively performance of a musician or actor or dancer
rests on some real and central vibration of feeling which diffuses its
influence throughout the whole and makes it "live". Otherwise
the performance, and the art, do not "come off". All musicians and
actors know that sometimes their performance is "dead", because
for some reason or another they cannot bring about in themselves
the right emotional tuning. What applies to performance pertains no
less to reading and observing. Not being "in the mood" for reading poetry, or going to a concert, and so on, are common enough
phenomena, as are periods of merely mechanical attention during
reading and listening (I do not mean distracted attention, which is
something else). I think there can be no doubt about the *reality* of
this emotional tuning—it is not imagined or thought—and it helps
to account for the fact that performers and others are sometimes
actually moved to tears by works of art and by great performances.

Summing up the matter, we observe that in art-reception the
imagination and the feelings are in close contact. We distinguish
especially a generalized tuning of the emotional sensibility, the
presence of real affective reactions at various stages of the experience, and a sympathetic response of particular emotions. But
if we are thus willing to admit the play of real feelings in the aesthetic
situation, we also most decidedly circumscribe it as a situation *sui
generis* in which the relationship and interaction of imagination and
feeling is of a special kind. We distinguish it sharply from other
situations characterized by a prominent relationship between
imagination and feeling. Of these the pathological cases are obviously in a class to themselves, from hysteria to the various

symptoms of mental disturbance or derangement, in which real feelings may lead to illusions or, vice versa, imagined causes induce real emotional conditions. There is also another notable class of cases, namely, actors, or people of histrionic temperament, who over-dramatize themselves. Such people are carried away by their gift or temperament and end by having the real feelings they begin by simulating. They then often effect a deft exit from the consequent situation and are able to behave as though nothing remarkable had happened, which is bewildering for others.

In other words there may be, as we admit, real feelings involved in the aesthetic situation, but they are under a certain kind of control which distinguishes them from the pathological cases where the feelings themselves sweep their victim along. The musician or actor has to be in the right mood and simulate the feelings called for by his piece; and to simulate means here to induce the appropriate sympathetic supporting emotions. This is a matter of his own control; not in the sense that he can always and invariably do it at will (we said that he sometimes feels "dead") but in the sense that it is a consciously initiated and terminated process. A singer must, after all, change his mood for each successive song or aria on his programme. This, like all the features mentioned, helps to show that the aesthetic situation admits of real feelings and yet they are in the final count tributary to the imagination. They are part of the apparatus deliberately used by the performer or reader (listener, viewer, etc.) to reconstitute in his own imagination the work of art from the formula of imagery before him. The formula itself is not the work of art but only its key. The feelings one has are not the work of art but only its necessary resonance or sounding-board. The work of art is the reconstitution of the imaginative pattern. In this sense a work of art shows the abstract, or idea, constituted within a framework of living emotion. And perhaps this is why in fine art we always have the simultaneous impression of serenity and of great events or feelings. The latter are involved, real feeling is present as well, but the imagination has all under its control.

vi. ART AND PRESENT-DAY CULTURE

The definition here put forward falls into line with the changed position of art in contemporary culture. Formerly, when religious belief was still firm, art took its place in a scheme dominated by religion. Men lived by religion, not by art or science, and in consequence they assigned to art a particular role and were clear about the purpose it could fulfil within the scheme. Briefly we can sum this up by saying that its business was to create something "beautiful" and thus make a specific contribution to human life which would be added to the achievements of religion, morality, and philosophy, which were concerned with God and with the "good" and the "true". Within the framework of orthodox belief art was an additional witness to God and his Creation. Medieval poetry and art show best, perhaps, how prestige was achieved by functional subordination, whilst as late as the earlier eighteenth century we can note how, though they no longer directly serve orthodox belief, the arts still imply the primacy of religion and a function for themselves of a specialized kind.

In the last two centuries we observe the progressive autonomy of art, as also of science and philosophy. We have, in the result, lost any simple, clear, or dogmatic sense of what art does or what it exists for. We can no longer assign it a function within a framework of belief accepted by everybody and moreover we avoid saying that artists "create beauty". We accept it as a phenomenon of natural genius, but of uncertain incidence and wide variety, and we accept our interest and pleasure in it as natural too. We do not, however, believe that the "pleasure" art gives is of an ordinary kind. For gradually the notion has become widely established that art provides a certain *kind* of experience, differing from the ordinary experience of living and with an integrity of its own.

For this reason art, though giving pleasure, is "serious", the impression of seriousness arising no doubt from the sense of its ministering to some needs, not easily defined, of those who enjoy it. My own view is that there is nowadays in this prevalent attitude a belief, whether acknowledged or not, that art fulfils a complex function in the individual's life, the main features being as follows. In the first place it always has a documentary value, by which is meant that it always illumines life by putting into articulate form something that essentially is observed in life, either as a record of relatively simple experience, or one compounded from various experiences or from experience amplified by imaginative intuition and cross-reference. In consequence all art is part of a vast illumination of experience, in the knowledge and understanding of which we desire to participate, either by sympathy, when it resembles our own, or out of curiosity, when it differs. We are interested in art because of our interest in life itself. And I think the essentially modern feeling that art has to be taken cognisance of derives from this feature. Nowadays people, in quite large numbers, feel that they must know about modern art developments because they would otherwise be "missing" something, the meaning of life, or whatever. This is sometimes described as being 'at the growing point of conscious-ness' of the time, a phrase most symptomatic of the condition to which I am referring. The feeling is not restricted to a small group of self-appointed prophets and their disciples; it is shared by writers, artists, scholars, the educated, and also the partially educated. It results, insofar as it is a peculiarly modern phenomenon, from secular philosophy and an extended educational system; but I believe that even orthodox religionists accept the idea, since their own beliefs have been affected by dynamic conceptions that mitigate the static nature of dogma.

In the second place art has a cathartic function, in the widest sense, for both artists and recipients. In its simplest terms this means they achieve through art a resolution of conflict or an expression of vital desire. There is of course an enormous range from minor to major needs, and perhaps it is best to think of art in this connexion as a function of living, which is sometimes a simple and sometimes a complicated matter. Take, for instance, the simple qualities of beauti-ful objects, their proportions, colour-harmonies, texture; these give us pleasure, and we call them beautiful, because they satisfy ele-mentary needs of a psycho-physiological kind. We avoid boredom and monotony, we seek interest and variety, we take pleasure in our natural activities and responses. Belonging to the organic order of nature we are constantly affected, physically and psychologically, by the symmetries and functional appropriateness of everything organic. From this point of view the sense of beauty in objects may be directly linked with the sense of being in tune with nature. At the other end of the scale we observe how art reflects the disturbances of the emotional life, clarifying and appeasing them, or affirming desire, and thus acquiring a ritualistic value, of which we shall say more in a later section.

I think these are now implicit assumptions in regard to art. It can no longer be viewed only as an aesthetic activity giving support to meanings accepted from religion or philosophy; it is itself an instrument in the search for and assertion of meanings and indeed in the assertion of life itself.[6] We can freely believe that it perhaps always performed this office ; but its operation was veiled by the primacy of the beliefs that in earlier epochs provided a clear frame to human life. Since the nineteenth century and the subsequent widespread philosophical indefiniteness and insecurity this function of art has not only shown itself in a more naked light; it has enormously increased its relative value as a spiritualizing agent and its prestige in the social collectivity. I would say that these beliefs were in fact implicit in the attitude of Roger Fry, R. G. Collingwood, and others, although they apparently endeavoured to refine the idea of art as something pure and separate, which altered into non-art at the slightest contact with other aspects of thinking and living. Their notion of a pure art, exemplified most challengingly by modern and abstract styles, differs strikingly from the *l'art pour l'art* beliefs of the nineties which, at their most chaste and sincere, depended on a genuine mystical aspiration. The view of these thinkers is, not only from the religious but also from the aesthetic point of view, secularized, and only its aesthetic exquisiteness, precision, and aristocracy make it superficially appear more nearly related to the nineties than to the view I am here putting forward and with which I think it actually concurs more closely.

Art represents life, or expresses feelings, that we recognize and confirm through comparison with our other experience. It has an authority of its own, the authority of being at least part of an intensely lived and created life, both as the product of an artist or as the acquisition of a recipient who recreates it for himself. It bears witness to an imagination, to a mind, to a person. If its method is representational it bears witness also to something recorded from the external world, whilst non-representational forms embody effective symbols of emotional circumstances and experience. And it is always a clarification, an assuagement, a catharsis. Sartre has said explicitly: 'The Theatre must speak in their (the audience's) most general preoccupations, dispelling their anxieties in the form of myths which anyone can understand and feel deeply'. ('Forgers of Myths', in *Theatre Arts*, June, 1946).

A symptom of this situation appearing in the recent past in, for example, literary criticism was that a literary work was judged neither as a message from some transcendental spiritual realm nor as an artefact made according to certain well-established conventions or patterns and assignable to a clear *genre*; instead the critic sought to discover, in the evidence of ideas, images, and language, the *quality* of the thinking and the imagination. The sign looked for was the complex and sensitive mind, the mind and sensibility that respond in an adequately intricate way to experience and succeed in expressing this response in a language. This criterion has emerged in organic relation to the development of literary art itself in the last hundred years or so, and has received support from T. S. Eliot's idea of a poetic idiom that should match the complexity of modern life. Its extreme has perhaps by now been reached, first, in the tolerance of personal forms in literature, especially in the novel, which, always perhaps an "elastic" form (as Henry James said), has become the repository of much besides 'a story'; and, secondly, in the elaborate exegesis of chosen "difficult" poems familiar from the so-called New Criticism. The first of these features emphasizes originality, particularity, individual thought and research brought to bear upon experience in the forms of imagination, private deviation taking precedence over communal conformity. The second feature, by placing an enormous apparatus of seriousness and complex learning at the service of poetry, acknowledges implicitly its newly felt function of being a central focus of the meanings of life and culture.[7]

vii. RE-ENACTMENT AND THE RITUALISTIC FACTOR IN ART

The conception of art as a "re-enactment" covers also its ritualistic element. By that I do not refer simply to kinds of art in which ritual is the predominant feature and art an accessory; I mean a natural ritualism of the broadest kind inhering profoundly in the activity of art. Perhaps the simplest example is architectural style, which shows, transformed into images, what values and feelings predominate in a period. The achievement of such a style is at once a clarification of the feelings and values involved and plainly an affirmation of them in all the insistent presence of buildings which in the sequel propagate what they symbolize. In this respect art is always a rite by means of which we solemnize the acceptance, affirmation, and re-affirmation of our own way of existence.[8] The ritualistic art of religions is a public form of this phenomenon, whilst most art that would not apparently come under this heading belongs to private ritual. Not being a psychologist, I do not want to fall into pseudo-psychological explanations of this aspect of art; but we do have to acknowledge the phenomenon of compulsive repetition, in obedience to profoundly rooted impulses; the fact that we read and re-read poetry and the same poem, seek out paintings again and again, go repeatedly to hear music and the same music. The old idea that the "beauty" of a work of art was constant and universal, for which reason one continually returned to it, presupposes too easily a moral decision and takes too little account of purely psycho-physiological need and pressure. It seemed to imply that because beauty was a "universal value" it should be cultivated with an up-lifted sense of ideal spirituality and achievement. Such a view completely underestimates the simple potency of the spell art casts over its amateurs. It is spiritual, without doubt; but it is also drenched in primitive and elemental vital impulses. It is always either a desirable world willed into creation by unconscious compulsion, from Greek gods and Indian temple sculptures to the drawings of Toulouse-Lautrec or the landscapes of Monet and Cézanne; or it is an image of human fear, from totem masks, cathedral gargoyles and the gro-tesque scenes of Hieronymus Bosch to the indictments of Goya and Picasso. On the one hand we see the worship of life, its ecstasies and triumphs, on the other the exorcizing of devils, the sacrifices to hostile powers. And some forms of art, like tragedy, which consti-tutes what is loved within the framework of what is feared, partake of both these ritualistic characters. From this point of view "beauty" is the flattery of desire, "ugliness" the flattery of fear. The studying of art as part of the history of ideas and culture tends to obliterate this psychological significance, which is none the less one of the profound meanings of art as a function of life. The teaching of "criticism", too, if it suggests that the end of reading or art-study is merely judgement, implies a degradation of art enjoyment into Pharisaïsm.

viii. RE-ENACTMENT AND THE ELEMENT OF
PERSONAL TASTE

The idea of psychological function comprehended under that of re-enactment allows also for the personal element in taste, which has always been one of the most difficult problems for aesthetic and a stumbling-block in criticism, but which is best linked with the feature of ritual. We may differentiate between taste for one of the several arts, or for a genre, taste for particular artists, and taste for particular subjects or kinds of subject. One man is fond of poetry, drama and music, whilst another prefers the novel and painting. This means that temperament and the needs of sensibility, darkly felt and unexplained, take us to works in our preferred arts, which, whether we judge them good or bad or indifferent, always have some interest for us merely because they *are* those particular art forms. This proclivity is an infallible sign of sincerity because of its origin in our very nature; it can in no way be attributed, as could a taste "for the best" in "all the arts" to extra-aesthetic motives, moral or educational ones for instance, or to a less respectable culture snobbishness. Persons who have educated their sensibility to an appreciation of several arts can still distinguish between the art that moved them from the first by its elemental nature and those that interested them later as secondary extensions of their taste. This factor plays a part in the emergence of the separate arts and kinds, which appear from this point of view as varieties of natural ritual promoted by different psychological types. For all the arts, in their origin, are given in natural endowment; the impulse and ability to sing, dance, draw, mimic, etc., are a gift, and all art as we prize it is the complex and extensive superstructure produced by applying such primary impulses to all the possibilities of experience.

A taste for particular artists or subjects forms itself just as naturally within the framework of one's preferred art. We have said above that an artist treats his subjects because they interest him and hold his attention in a special way. Obsessing him, they become part of his life; they agitate and disturb; they are the things he has to reckon with emotionally, this man with nature and landscapes, this with portraits and human psychology, this with religion, and so on. After Racine had turned from classical subjects to the Bible he found Athalie, an old compulsion asserting itself amidst his new-won piety. The same applies to the recipient; few affectations have been so foolish as the recently fashionable one that the "content" of art didn't matter. The preference for one artist as against another may rest on like-mindedness as to subjects, or on temperamental affinities, the romantic, the sceptical, the ironical, the sentimental, the elegiac, and so on, each attracting their like. We all construct for ourselves out of such selections according to our nature our own particular world of chosen art.

The process may be followed also in individual differences in apprehending works of art, for at the moment of impact each one of us sees first the feature to which his taste is most attracted; in a picture, for example, one person sees the colour first, another the draughtsmanship, another the "story" or other non-pictorial meaning. In short we each abstract the images that are most important to ourselves. Such images are not distortions; they are partial aspects having special meaning for our particular sensibility; they are not the whole picture, and they do not necessarily prevent the progressive widening of understanding by further contemplation. A person of trained taste will of course discern at once, in spite of his own preferences, the characteristic feature or strength of a work. His preference will not say draughtsmanship when his trained judgement says colour. But his preferences exist all the same.

Such is the strength of the ritualistic aspect of re-enactment. Our definition speaks of the 're-enactment of experience *as idea*', linking the two together precisely because the quality of ideality is real but always related to a psychological function, to a state of preparedness or predisposition in artist and recipient without which the work of art does not come alive. Idea or ideality in itself is essentially of the nature of art but it has no power of its own to generate a response unless other conditions are fulfilled. This explains why works of art have their seasons in individual lives and artists theirs in history. We commonly try authors and discard them, to take them up again, perhaps years later, and discover a greatness quite veiled from us at our first attempts. Or we read an author and "exhaust" him, feeling that we shall never again find life or beauty in his work. This does not mean that we have found his work at last to be inferior, exposing its inability to remain of "permanent" significance; it is still potentially significant for others and even for ourselves at a later date. It simply indicates the absence of the proper conditions of psychological function. Similarly with artists and periods. El Greco lay for centuries virtually unrecognized, as Hölderlin did throughout the nineteenth century, until people were prepared by the particular circumstances of their own knowledge and experience to understand them.

The presence of genuine taste, as here described, makes a person's aesthetic experience authentic. It need not conflict with education from a narrow to a more catholic taste. A taste too exclusive shows poverty of imagination and human feelings, spoiling its sincerity with obstinacy and hard temper. At the other extreme we should suspect the too catholic taste of shallowness and docility. But the gradual extension of sympathy and curiosity naturally accompanies the process of living and learning, and a taste become more catholic by such assimilation is not a betrayal of character but an affirmation of a developing humanity. A true aesthetic culture is thus poised between the authenticity or sincerity of a personal taste and the effort to transcend self which is of the essence of all thinking and creating.

ix. PAST AND PRESENT IN THE WORK OF ART

I think we may also use the dynamic relationship between re-enactment and ideality to illumine another vexed question of aesthetic before bringing this section to a close. Because in one of its aspects art is experience re-enacted (a ' documentation of experience', as we said above) it always has a contemporary reference which later passes naturally into a historical one. The poetry of Spenser, Milton, and Wordsworth was in the first place poetry of and for their own age, which has as a consequence that some of its meaning can only be thrown into full relief by historical study and the sympathetic reconstruction of a past situation. But on the other hand, because art in its other aspect is always idea, it is liberated from historical into symbolic truth and remains available to the imagination of posterity. Every work of art is the field of a conflict between its present and its historical existence, the vital power it exercises over us, the present recipient, and that felt by former generations, including the one that gave it birth. The conflict is most obvious in comedy and in many novels on account of their ties with the social setting. Lyric poetry rides the centuries more easily though we may sometimes think the conflict non-existent when in fact it is merely hidden. This applies to all poetry governed, as for example courtly poetry or sonnet-writing were, by firm conventions, for they implied aesthetic assumptions widely different from those of the present day, and if we are perhaps still moved by such poetry it may not be in the same way as contemporaries were. The interaction of present impact and historical significance modifies constantly the pattern of appreciation.[9]

CHAPTER EIGHT

THE PRINCIPLE OF CHARACTERISTIC INTERTEXTURE OF IMAGERY

i INTERTEXTURE OF IMAGERY

THE DEFINITION put forward in the above paragraphs refers to all the arts; it reconciles them, in spite of their varied media and sensuousness, under a unifying idea. It acknowledges the central importance of imagery; art as re-enactment and idea exists only in and by its images, and this applies to language which only becomes art through its image-aspects. For the general definition of art the kind of imagery used by any one art is unimportant so long as it is imagery. But clearly we need now, to supplement and fortify our general idea, a further principle that accounts in terms of imagery for different arts, for composite arts, and, within literature, for various "kinds" or "forms".

A salient feature about the arts has already been adumbrated in the remarks on medium, of which we said, applying our theory of images and metaphor, that it becomes in the process of art-creation an aspect of imagery. Instead of differentiating the arts according to medium, which is a convenient but provisional word, we can substitute the idea of a *characteristic imagery*, amplified by that of certain *interfusions* of imagery in the case of more complex art forms. Music in its instrumental aspects, and the plastic arts of painting, sculpture, and architecture, come under the first head as relatively simple examples, since in the one case auditory, in the others visual imagery are predominant.

Other arts with a more intricate composition have to be conceived as textures made of the interplay and harmonious co-ordination of different kinds of imagery, sometimes together with language. Under this head come the collaborative forms of theatre: drama, opera, and ballet, which combine in varying ways spectacle, acting, poetry, dance, and music. Here, too, belong the forms in which music combines with poetic or other texts, as in cantatas, oratorios, or *Lieder*. Less obviously, but no less certainly, we include poetry itself in this class, contrary no doubt to the common view which sees it as a product of the simple "medium" of language. We do so because language in its poetic uses is, as we have seen, a very complexly sensuous phenomenon, inducing, apart from its propositional meanings, effects which include visual and auditory imagery; for which reason we are obliged to classify it as composite. The structure of such composite arts is governed by what we may call the principle of a *characteristic composite imagery*, or a characteristic *intertexture* of imagery, to use Coleridge's vivid and suggestive word.

Before commenting further on particular characteristic inter-textures we might observe in general that the composite image structures of art have a prototype in nature with which they are still linked, though their own elaboration carries them much further. Perception, sensation, and images deriving from objects, scenes, and events in nature are always complex; visual and aural, aural and kinetic, kinetic and visual, interweave constantly. One of the dictionary definitions of "image", as used in psychology, is 'a revival, reproduction by memory, in the mind, of some sensuous experience undergone in the past, including the visual, auditive, tactile, and other impressions associated with it.' If art were pure representation its composite imagery would simply mirror the compound perceptions and sensations which make up our apprehension of nature; the coloured sound-film is the nearest approach yet made to such a mechanical reflection. But, as we know, art is constructive, and works by abstracting, selecting, re-combining, modifying, inventing. Naturalistic images can assume the functions of expressive formula-images, whilst these can be constructed from any of the sensational contexts of nature. They can also, by the same process of abstraction and reconstruction, be re-combined in the most varied ways. The only essential is that this restructuring means giving functional unity to all the images used; they must all serve in their adapted form, in their distortion, their adjustment, or their invented shape, a central expressive idea.

For this reason certain natural phenomena offer a more precise model of the processes of art. A simple example is the image of waves breaking on the sea-shore. Here the sound is inevitably attendant on the sight of the wave, as its crest rises, rolls over, and breaks in a splash of foam. A similar organic co-ordination of the seen and the heard arises when the wind blows over a field of corn or sways tree-tops. By contrast, the physical appearance of a person singing, and the sound of the song, are disjunctive. There is a causal physical relation between the two, but there the link breaks off; the appearance of the singer is not relevant to the song.

Another example of organic relationship, of the greatest importance for drama, may be found in the ordinary gestures accompanying speech. Think of someone giving a warning cry: Look out! Here the word, the meaning, the tone of voice, the raised hand and the anxious turn of the head, form a composite impression characterized by organic unity. This is the quality imitated by art, and in a later chapter we shall analyse in detail the development of drama from this basic paradigm.

Arts like *Lied*, opera, and ballet achieve the composite structure which in the preceding example is natural by conjoining imageries otherwise separate. Thus dance, if conceived without music, remains close to a natural expressive behaviour of a simple type, with opportunities only of a limited kind for sophisticated stylization. But elaborated with music into ballet it shows the constructive reinforcement of one imagery by another, something only possible to the inventive imagination. The same holds of the various forms for words and music. In such complex forms we observe a sympathetic interfusion of images, a discovery of cognate expressiveness in different systems of imagery.

Turning to poetry, with which we are more concerned in this study, the question of intertexture has already been raised in chapter five, where, drawing on our analysis of images, we emphasized the part played by imagery in verbal art, though the conceptual nature of language makes the problem more complicated than in the non-linguistic arts. All our earlier argument, with its wider application of the idea of the image, was calculated to show the ubiquitous presence of images—in verbal sound, rhythmic pattern, in sensuous suggestion and evocation both in the subject and in figures of speech—or, to put it another way, of a mode of expressiveness not identical with language but intra-linguistic, working through language, and linking verbal art with other kinds.

The simplest formula for the characteristic intertexture of poetry, using the term in its current sense of verse, and leaving complications to be dealt with later, is the combination of metre, verbal sound, figurative language, and propositional statement. Whatever the subject, whatever the verse form, and however much or little figures of speech are used, the presence and interaction of these four elements signifies poetry as contrasted with other forms of language. The idea of "poetic" or "lyrical" prose does not, as some may think, invalidate this view; it confirms it. The qualities of such prose are always a more intensive use of figures, of rhythm, and of verbal sound, so that, as in many passages of Joyce's prose, the form moves towards the intertexture characteristic of lyric poetry, but stops short of the final transition into a metrical form which would establish the intertexture completely. It is close to "free" verse, which however belongs to metrical forms, since it is not as free as its name supposes.

The interfusion of the characteristic elements is inextricable, so that the "poetry" is not the sum of the parts but the product of mutual assimilation. This enables us to recognize poetry not only when a whole poem is before us but from fragments or brief quotations.

A slumber did my spirit seal . . . .

There is no mistaking this as a fragment of poetry that could hardly be used as prose although it includes a simple proposition. The beauty of the double metaphor, the quiet iambic rhythm, the well-knit pattern of verbal sound, establish at once a characteristic intertexture of imagery in language. Nor can a better example be found of the commanding principle of such an intertexture, that it has a unity conveniently called organic by analogy with the organic structures in nature, in which a whole is made up of perfectly functioning, mutually adapted parts, the whole being something that, exceeding the mere sum of the parts, has an identity of its own. Such unity means that a single alteration in any word changes not only that word but all the relations of sense and imagery in the context. It is not an addition or subtraction; the whole context becomes something different. Similarly in music the alteration of a single note changes all the melodic and harmonic relations, or a single change in the length of the notes affects the whole character of the context. Frequent obvious symptoms of failure in organic complexity in poetry are mechanical rhythms, inappropriate metaphors, and strained rhymes.

The ideas of *characteristic intertexture* and *organic unity* go together. They are not of course different terms for the same thing. The former refers to the kinds of imagery used by an art or art-form, words and rhythm, verse and gesture, music and dance, and so on. The latter refers to the condition in the relations between images that is the distinguishing feature of good art. But they belong together because organic unity, the effect of the mutual metaphorical assimilation of images in their function of clarifying a central idea or feeling, is all the more imperative where there is complexity. Poetic or artistic genius is the power to conceive interstructures of imagery having this kind of unity in complexity; whilst on the other hand all criticism of poetry and art is directed to confirming its presence or analysing a failure to achieve it. The quality of the intertexture is decisive for recognizing true art; it is the organic unity of the image-structure, seen in every part, that bears witness to the genuine creative imagination, and not, as is so often suggested, the architectonic "unity" of the whole work. Factitious art can easily have the latter kind of unified design, whilst fragments can be of genuine poetic texture though not elaborated into a whole. One or two poems and a number of fragments give evidence enough to convince modern readers that Sappho's great reputation in antiquity was deserved. In recent times the fragmentary and uncompleted late poems of Hölderlin bear witness in spite of their lack of unified design and meaning to a resplendent imagination. The immediate recognition of art, that is, of quality in an art-work, rests on this phenomenon; and this admits also of the fact that, quality being at once recognized, mature consideration may discover faults of one sort and another, including those concerning unity and design. The same applies to all the arts; we recognize the genuine imagination, the impress of style, in any part of a musical composition or in any fragment of a canvas without knowing the whole.

The force of the principle of characteristic intertexture is apparent in all composite forms, by which we mean not the mixing of different forms in a varied pattern, as when lyrics or dances are interpolated in a play, but song, or opera, or ballet, or drama, or, as we have seen, poetry itself. In opera, for instance, the music must be qualitatively dramatic. It may not be what one might call "ordinary" music adapted to a plot. The musical structure itself, in all its melodic, harmonic, and dynamic complexity, must be a unified image of the dramatic, as it is in the mature works of Verdi, the best single example to recall. In other words its nerve is a dramatic nerve and in consequence its shape, in all its details, is characteristic; not an adaptation of music in its other shapes, but the musical imagination giving the immediate image of "life as drama", as conflict, passion, agony, and so on. It provides an expressiveness cognate with that of the gestures, words, and meanings emanating from the libretto or text. Mrs. Langer has argued, in *Feeling and Form*, that in opera and song the words are "assimilated" totally to the music; these are not really "mixed" forms, but simply music. It is a tempting view, especially when we remember how powerful music is. But it solves the problem by evasion. The composer of a song, not having abandoned the words, expects us to hear them; that done, we cannot dissociate the music from them. We listen to such music in a different way from instrumental works. We listen to it as music for particular words; as we listen we seek a congruence; we hear, quite consciously, the corroboration that the words and music have for each other. The same applies to opera, with a still more complex pattern of corroboration. Wagner was extremely concerned about the myths he set to music, Verdi about the drama of his plots. And who could maintain that the third act of *Der Rosenkavalier* is a case of music "absorbing" everything else? We have all felt for ourselves how listening to a radio performance of an opera, without a text, and without memories of seen performances, is completely unsatisfying. We must have the plot, text, situations and themes, the stage and the people on it. They are sometimes cumbrous, and slightly comic; but the whole makes sense, whilst the purely "heard" performance is incomplete, its meanings unfocused. The music-words-gesture-plot complex is a characteristic intertexture, in which a congruent expressiveness of different kinds of images and meanings produces a total unified expression.

Experience shows that there is a limit to the degree of complexity admitting of the best effects. The several arts have often collaborated, and there are composite arts; but the mere adding together of different modes of imagery does not enhance artistic value. For the scope of each is limited by its relations with the others. Up to a certain point combination produces a richer intertexture, whilst beyond it the loss may outweigh the gain. For instance, drama, as we shall see later, uses verse to its advantage, in the sense that

Hamlet is better in verse than it would probably be in prose. It might conceivably be argued that drama, in its most poetic form, shows a more richly intricate texture than any lyric or meditative poetry, for which reason it might rank higher in a hierarchy of forms. But it certainly could not be argued, on the same grounds, that opera was a higher form than drama. Opera has another element of expression, music; but it pays for this with serious losses in acting and sometimes in the text. It is a characteristic intertexture, but it exists on the boundary of what is possible as regards a satisfactory organic structure.

Having established the general principle of characteristic imageries and intertextures, and reserving discussion of certain details for following chapters, we turn to the problem of literary kinds and forms. The theory here put forward, and the inclusion of poetry as a composite art, enable us to state this problem in a new way, and to indicate the position of the art of drama in relation to other arts and to poetry.

ii DRAMA AND LITERARY ART; THE LITERARY KINDS RECONSIDERED ACCORDING TO THE PRINCIPLES OF IMAGERY AND THE DEFINITION OF ART

It is desirable at this point to clarify the position of drama, which is to be examined in detail in later chapters, as an important form. Strictly speaking, it is a separate art; it has its own characteristic image-intertexture. Its medium is not simply language, but persons acting and speaking. Nevertheless it is profoundly linked with literature, for on the one hand it often incorporates poetic expression not less intense than that found in lyric and epic poetry, whilst on the other both epic and lyric were originally not " literary" but sung or declaimed; they too depended on a 'person speaking', which implies some degree of genuine dramatic amplification or at least resemblance to the speaking of drama. Poetry preserves still in itself, even if but little read aloud or recited, the impulsion towards utterance by voice and amplification by person. The classical divisions of genre into epic, lyric, and drama, deriving from Aristotle, depend on the fact that in antiquity they were all of them spoken, or sung, or declaimed, and therefore could properly be conceived as branches of one thing.

The position to-day is by no means so simple, for a number of reasons. Many poetic kinds have been created in the course of three thousand years; the printed book brought great changes; and in more recent times, since the romantic liberation, there has been a powerful tendency towards individualized expression. Increasingly differentiated forms have in the end given support to the view that classification by genre is not only more difficult, and likely to lead to absurd sub-division, but, more important still, irrelevant to aesthetic value.[1] No one would minimize the difficulty. The sharp differences between Greek and modern drama make one wonder whether pieces so different as *Agamemnon* and *Antony and Cleopatra* can usefully be considered under one head. Or again, in plays like *The Cherry Orchard*, *Pelléas et Mélisande*, *The Playboy of the Western World*, *La Folle de Chaillot*, *The Family Reunion*, to name a few at random, the voice of the dramatist is so individual that the association in a form known as drama seems fortuitous and of little consequence. Moreover, as soon as one tries to isolate an infallible characteristic feature of a literary kind the task appears impossible. Drama can at least be segregated because, being acted, it is not literary in the strict sense.

The history of the nomenclature within lyric poetry also shows constant changes and mutations, sometimes sudden or arbitrary, sometimes gradual or natural, in the use of forms. Horace called his " odes " *carmina*, or, as we should say, songs. Petrarch's sonnets to Laura were called *canzoni*; the term *sonnet* thus assimilates the Provencal term and indicates in effect a genre of love songs. Ode, in the Greek, meant a "song", and was used of lyrical pieces generally. In modern literature its meaning became restricted, mainly under the influence of Pindar and Horace, but when we recall Cowley, Collins, Goethe, Wordsworth, Hölderlin, Shelley, Keats and others, we realize that even the restricted meaning allows a tantalizing variety of compositions. "Elegy" illustrates no less pointedly the vagaries of classification. Originally it meant a poem of mourning without reference to a particular metre. Then the distich became the conventional form for such poems. This form, however, came to be used for other themes and denoted any poem written in the form whether "elegiac" or not. In more recent times the term has relinquished its formal sense and reverted to its original straight meaning. Goethe's *Roman Elegies*, in honour of love and the classical world, are a modern example of the intermediate, conventional meaning based on the metre and not the subject.

Yet, in spite of the difficulties, we have to admit that history shows a number of forms tenacious over long or short periods, allowing variation without losing their main character. No one would mistake a sonnet by Wordsworth for one by Spenser, but neither would they confuse a sonnet with a ballad or an ode. If a pedantic attitude to kinds and forms makes them into lifeless theoretical figments or false models of correctness, there is an equal pedantry in obstinately rejecting them, for a radical denial of the kind " ode ", merely because the pattern varies, is really the same kind of mistaken theoretical extremism as the attempt to frame a unique ideal formula; both views are stiff and dogmatic. We should not, moreover, out of a sense of the present-day diversity of individual expression, underestimate the importance of set forms in the past to those who used them, especially in connexion with classical traditions. All the evidence shows that idiosyncrasy of form as well as conformity to general types exist side by side. Clearly every poem is unique in the same sense in which every human being is so; its exact conformation of words, rhythms, and images has never been realized before and never will be again, and this applies whatever the metrical form, regular or irregular. But the uniqueness of a sonnet is limited by the conventional form in a way not applicable to a poem in free verse. It is related to other sonnets. And when we say related we do not refer simply to an external classification based on superficial formal features, but a relationship arising from similarity of expressive motive, of which the structure is the external sign.

I propose to relate the problem to our definition of art and principles of imagery and try to arrive at a more flexible view that does justice to the historical fact of *genres*, kinds, and "forms", but also to the vast range of individual or, as I shall call it, idiosyncratic expression.

Both aspects of the creative process have to be borne in mind. On the one hand there are various forces converging upon production: the impulse to and need for expression, the urgent vision and the disburdening of feeling, which have both individual and social aspects, and are influenced by historical and cultural conditions. On the other hand there is the literary result, the aesthetic phenomenon, the epic, the play, the song, the novel, etc. The one corresponds to what we have called experience, the other to re-enactment by means of imagery and language.

It is convenient in the first place to distinguish three persistent tendencies that have undoubtedly been present from the beginnings of poetry, once it was beyond the crudest magic, and about which we must be clear before we can be clear about specific kinds or forms. They are best called story, song, and meditation. They are not in themselves "forms", for the generalization involved is too large to admit of any precise connotation of form. They are the preliminary conditions of form; they indicate deep-seated expressive tendencies shaping poetry from its origins. At the most they suggest a general notion of either representation, or musical rhythm, or a language in which feeling and thought intermingle; for which reason they correspond roughly to the broad distinctions between representational images, expressive formula-images, and language, expounded in earlier chapters.

This suggestion sets aside the hallowed trinity of epic, dramatic, and lyric poetry, but the developments in literary art, especially of prose and narrative forms, make this necessary. A declaimed epic in verse, with long passages of dialogue, a feature common in all epic poetry, was still close enough to a stylized verse drama for the two to be felt as branches of the one art of poetry, as we see by placing Homer next to Aeschylus or Milton's *Paradise Lost* next to *Samson Agonistes*. The modern novel, however, as a linguistic construction for reading, is so different from a play seen on a stage, that one is moved to think not of two species of one art but of two different arts. It is this sort of feeling that helps to justify our theory of image-intertextures, according to which drama certainly goes into a clear category of its own, whatever elements of poetry and language it may still share with literary forms. We still have to admit, of course, the poetic kinship of epic and drama in classical antiquity and in the Renaissance period; but we can bring drama under our suggested major tendencies by regarding it as a special kind of story.

The advantages of the broad classification indicated appear especially in connexion with the intermingling of narrative, dramatic and lyric elements in many works. It is a common feature and in fact has been used often as a weapon against over-precise distinctions as to kind. There are lyrical plays, and dramatic novels, etc., in plenty. And yet it is not, strictly speaking, the forms of narrative and drama and lyric that intermingle, for a form is a whole. A lyrical novel is not a lyric poem hyphenated with a narrative. The sense of intermingling arises from analogous qualities suggested by certain features of the material, or subject, or composition; by features, if we wish to use our comprehensive term, of the total imagery.

This difficulty and imprecision vanish with the idea of story, song, and meditation as tendencies rather than formal divisions. For these three tendencies operate constantly in literary art and, most important of all, they often do so concurrently. They interfuse; they are co-present. It is not only a question of having a form, as final product, which is made up of alternating sections, some of which are narrative, some lyric, and some meditation, though this sometimes does happen, but of a single form which has different aspects. The Greek dithyramb was a hymn to Dionysus incorporating story elements, which themselves provided the motive for the hymnic inspiration, about his life and death. The Pindaric ode, a laudatory, hero-worshipping poem, contained a narrative from myth as an integral part of the passionate glorification of the victor in the games. Dante's epic is a narrative imbued everywhere with the expression of feeling and intimately linked with a religion and a philosophy. English metaphysical poetry, and indeed most reflective or philosophical poetry, shows lyric meditation inseparable from fragments of first-person story or dramatization. Moreover, by far the greater part of what we invariably call "lyric" poetry is not the simple expression of feeling, which the term in its strict sense connotes, but meditation coloured by feeling, thoughts conceived in an emotional context. Novels, too, show the interfusion. They incorporate beliefs, so that their "story" is also a symbolic pointer to a " philosophy of life" and an expression of feeling about it. And finally we recall various prose forms like essay, sermon, and pamphlet, which combine a content of ideas with literary presentation and art, bearing witness to powerful imagination. The interfusion of story, song, and meditation occurs everywhere and with infinite variation in the individual result. In the last resort a writer's style (i.e., his choice of all the available imagery and language), whether in prose or verse, in a novel or a lyric or an essay, embodies inescapably elements of his feeling, reflecting his felt ideals and values, and this is neither story nor meditation but the "song", his own individual note, that rings through both.

Because of this dominating expressive principle the narratives in poetic forms are never on the one hand denuded of feeling and reduced to the status of factual record, or history; nor on the other hand is the song in poetic forms deprived of linguistic thought and reduced to a completely esoteric symbol, even though, as we shall see, lyric poetry has sometimes seemed to come very near to that. What we are bound to admit, however, is that as poetic and literary forms, shaped by the forces we have been speaking of, emerge, they do tend to show an emphasis in one direction or the other, influenced by the kind of vision and of feelings each poet has. The decisive factor here is that for many writers the motive for expression comes from an excited and emotionally tinged interest in the nature of human situations and destinies, to which everything else is subordinate, and these are narrators or dramatists. They express feelings, and we read their narratives not naively as a simple "story" but as a language for these feelings, but they are feelings of certain kinds, feelings generated by the story aspects of life, feelings about human character, action and fortune. To express them their source has to be shown in images simulating life and people.

With lyric and reflective writers, the motive for expression comes directly from feelings and thoughts, which determines a different pattern of imagery and language.

Certain evidence tends to confirm these general divisions as justified and deep-rooted. It is remarkable how creative writers themselves show on the whole a decided gift for one of these forms and a paramount desire to create in it. The number of predominantly dramatic, lyrical-meditative, or narrative writers in the class of genius far outweighs that of mixed talents. And the most frequent cases of the latter tend when analysed to confirm the evidence. Shakespeare's non-dramatic poems are sufficiently remarkable to give him high rank as a poet, but he does remain predominantly a dramatic poet. In a similar way Milton, with a small production of lyrics and one play in verse, is mainly an epic poet. Cases like Hardy, where the balance is very even, are rare. These features are matched by like tendencies in readers, who, as we noticed above, mostly have some decided preference. Hence it would seem that these broad divisions of expression owe their origin to psychological factors, being parallel to the accidents of constitution that make a man one particular kind of artist.

Whilst therefore story, song, and meditation interfuse constantly, the evidence is that they appear as major tendencies or modes of emphasis; and such tendencies are not a matter of external classification but have an organic origin in the natural psychological complexity of art creation and reception.

We associate all narrative forms, and drama, with representational features, involving emphasis on the object; the impersonal picture of life, of men, of nature, strikes us first and it is only afterwards that we disengage the personal and symbolic quality of the picture. We know that all seeing is interpretative and affective, yielding images that are selective and only a partial reference to real objects. But such images of narrative, although symbols of a selective interpretation, are justly called representational, because they do intend to give a picture, an evocation of people and events. One of the effects of art is to register such interpretative seeing; and in such art the forms of nature reappear in those of art; not in the sense of an exact copy-imagery, but in the sense that the imagery of a narrative, or a drama, has to some extent the same kind of structure and coherence, and meaning, as the images we make from observing life directly. In other words there is an overlap between real people and events and those of story; or between dramatic situations in life and the dramas of literary art. The character of these forms is determined in part, aesthetically speaking, by the common forms of perception and interpretation. And this is one reason why they persist; they can always be taken, simply, at this level, and *mean* something.

We associate forms of song and meditation, on the other hand, with a subjective emphasis, in the sense of a " first person " voice, which is of course a convention, expressing thoughts and feelings. If in story forms the author's feelings arrange themselves around people and situations, here the external world arranges itself around the subjective feelings of the " first person ". The inner life of feeling and thought is the central focus, for which reason the exclamatory cry, as Valéry said, is the primitive prototype of lyric forms. Fragments of story and pictorial description occur but always in pronounced functional relation to emotion or idea. The growing tendency of the last eighty years or so towards an ever freer manipulation of images become quite unrepresentational is merely a confirmation, at the extreme limit, of the essential feature of specialized lyric song. In essence a lyric poem, or song, is an evocative imagery of feeling. Meditative pieces, poems or prose, are also centred on the subject, or first person voice, and have their own characteristic balance between imagery, language, and thought.

Up to this point we have discussed a number of factors important as conditions of poetic forms of any kind. We have noted three tendencies towards a predominant emphasis and indicated that they are intimately influenced by psychological forces, which endow poets and writers with different expressive needs and different interests in the material of experience; so that story, or song, or meditation, are not "forms" chosen arbitrarily *for* conveying feelings, but are themselves natural symptoms of an expressive purpose. And this we can link with what we said in chapter seven about ritual in its individual and social aspect. These are the most general tendencies discernible.

We turn now to more specific forces favouring the creation of clear types of composition. I mean the kinds of feeling and thought that find an outlet in tragedy, comedy, ode, hymn, elegy, idyll, satire, ballad, and other such groupings. They show a second stage of crystallization of literary types. One can speak here of types of expressive impulse because they can be traced always to recurrent experiences and psychological contexts that show consistent features amidst variation throughout long periods of human history. A hymn, pagan or christian, is associated with religious emotions and sentiments, both personal and communal, which show some similarity whatever the precise theology involved, the language, rhythm, and imagery showing correspondingly related features of fervour, aspiration, ecstasy, and rapture. Crashaw, Novalis, and Hölderlin addressed their hymns to very different Beings and Powers, but there is a general kinship in their motives and their forms. A related example is the ode, which arises with formal celebration, generally of public or social interest; to this it owes its rhetorically elaborate design, the original models for which were Pindar's odes and the choric passages of Greek tragedy. We feel doubtless that an ode by Keats is far removed by the subject and theme of its inspiration, and by its metrical form, from Pindar's work, yet the motive of celebration is the commanding impulse of both, bringing them under one and the same expressive law. Elegy, too, is a type of expressiveness, if taken in its straight meaning as a poem of mourning, its original sense, and leaving aside the vagaries of the use of the elegiac distich. Tragedy, comedy, and satire may be looked on in the same way, their character being traceable to moral judgements, philosophies of life, or psychological attitudes.

Such kinds being so closely linked with psychological processes, they belong to human history, and without necessarily being permanent show a marked longevity or, if they for a while falter, a strong disposition to revive. Hence vigorous traditions exist for them at least throughout European literary history. They represent kinds of literary creation in the common-sense meaning of " kind", but they find so many different formal shapes that they cannot be confidently classified as "forms" in any clear-cut technical theory. They are more than merely descriptive groupings, being based on expressive function, on different kinds of meaning, subject-matter, feeling, and experience; but they are not structures in the most accurate aesthetic sense, because they are not strictly confined to one medium. Some of these kinds, for instance, extend beyond literary art; critics of various arts imply, consciously or unconsciously, the existence of such an all-embracing kind whenever they speak of Rowlandson's comedy, or Delacroix's dramatic force, or use the term 'high comedy' of the dramatist Congreve and the novelist Henry James, or speak of an epic film or symphony, and so on. In the same sense parts of any literary composition can bear the character of any of the "kinds" mentioned. Novels are bestrewn with passages, even whole chapters, which are virtually elegies, odes, hymns, idylls, satires, love lyrics, threnodies, or whatever.

On the other hand there exist opposite these categories certain well-established species distinguished apparently by their formal character alone. Such are sonnet, rondeau, ballade, heroic couplet, blank verse, ballad metre, octosyllabics, etc. It is useful to call them metrical forms, or in some cases just "forms", since they do impart a characteristic shape. But they are not in fact purely metrical schemes applicable to any subject-matter. Rhythm-in-words being but one aspect of an image-intertexture, they form part of the aesthetic whole and are therefore elements in a process of expression. Their rhythmic character is incontrovertibly related to theme and subject; plays could not be written in sonnet-form, nor would segments of blank verse have the elegance, point, or the musical eloquence of sonnets. Blank verse was discovered to have admirable properties as a verse-mode of speech and dialogue because it is near to the natural speech-rhythm of English and at the same time modulates easily into intensified expression. The Alexandrine, as a dramatic verse line, has clearly evolved in relation to the character of the French language and also the psychological traits of the French themselves. The Petrarcan form of the sonnet, which was profoundly adapted to the Italian language and spirit, proved unsuitable to English and in consequence was modified. These instances demonstrate sufficiently that even with such apparently atomic units of form a relation with some characteristic expressive motive, psychologically and culturally influenced, still subsists. They emerge, of course, as innovations, the inspiration of some individual poet, to which in the sequel other poets respond. Such innovations may be looked upon as intuitions valid for others, and in more than one way. The innovator discovers and brings to light a form with expressive possibilities. It is developed by others, until gradually, as its varied application becomes manifest in a long succession of works, its true character is revealed : it is a generalized expressive formula susceptible of extensive application in particular contexts and persisting for a long period of time. Its notation in prosody is not an attempt to fix its character rigidly but only to systematize approximately for ear and eye a common denominator, a process which is useful and deceives no one but pedants. The history of art, music, and poetry, shows many examples of this kind of fertile conception, in which there is an interaction between a general experience of a "formal" idea and the single writer using it. And we know that great genius, as in Shakespeare, Bach, or Mozart, has often shown itself even more in elaboration than in innovation. One man cannot do everything, as Mozart said. Poets and artists often work with an abstract ideal in mind but also invariably with a sense of realizable shape, of the potential expressiveness to be achieved when the abstract ideal is realized in the individualized form, the new work.[2]

Thus we observe two important groupings, currently called "kinds" and "forms", and the question now to ask is: How do these two groupings stand to each other?

The answer is that each term denotes an important aspect of poetic works but falls short of precision in regard to them as wholes. Kind indicates more decisively the expressive motive, form the external aesthetic shape. Yet we must admit each implies also something of the other. Tragedy suggests a certain kind of story or situation with attendant feeling ; we know that, whether in drama or novel, verse or prose, it will have to use representational imagery, persons and actions, and so on. On the other side we know that a sonnet will have a certain movement of thought, and intensity of feeling, a certain counterpoint of argument and emotion. An ode, we know in advance, will be an invocation or a celebration, and will need a rather elaborate pattern of rhythm to support grandiose or sublime or grave emotions. This implication of each in the other pays tribute to the sense that a poem is a unity of content and form, of theme and expression, of feeling and imagery, and accounts for the loose interchange between the terms, as when odes and sonnets are called indiscriminately kinds and forms. But because they are only partial the two words, and the classification they denote, lack a sufficient aesthetic precision; they retain a particular emphasis, each remaining on its own side of the central territory where they should meet and interfuse.

Let us be clear that it is the terms, not works of poetry, that are inadequate. They each offer one mode of classification only, so that each is by itself unreal to the extent that it is partial. A tragedy must have a form, the definition of which is not properly carried in the term; a sonnet must have a substance of which the formal scheme conveys no precise idea. The aesthetic reality—the tragic drama, the Shakespearian sonnet, the picaresque novel—is both kind and form, and using a strict language that does not break analytically asunder what is felt and known to be a unity, we can only call them types of poetry and literary art; or, more exactly and at the price of clumsiness, structural types of imagery-within-language.

It seems almost too easy to say that the aesthetically genuine type is the *tragic drama*, the *idyllic novel*, the *verse satire*, the *pastoral poem*, and so on; yet this is precisely the case, for the simple reason that such terms rest on the conjunction of the two essential features of art, an *expressive motive* together with an *imagery*. Comedy, if applicable to any art or form, indicates only an expressive motive; verse, or distich, or blank verse etc., indicate only variously partial aspects of imagery. They are inadequate concepts for a total structure. But works that show both a similar expressive motive and a similar imagery, or, in other words, a related origin in general experience or feeling and a related form of re-enactment, demonstrate the crystallization of a true type. Here we are no longer deluded by pseudo-kinds which hover uncertainly amidst descriptive classification; they are genuine characteristic types of expressive structure.[3]

To these considerations we add historical and social influences which are always operative and contribute decisive features to the forms of art and literature. Poetry is always a product of experience and imagination, of present life amplified and generalized beyond the present; and by "present life" we mean the present consciousness and sensibility of a writer or group of writers, formed and active in a particular historical situation. Every writer, whilst saying something which transcends his time, has to use terms inseparable from it. His vision is part of his historical self and its experience of life and time, including the culture of his epoch; and his very medium, his language, cannot but be also in a particular historical phase. To speak the language and offer the visions of the past is imitation and sham, whilst the language of the future only arrives with the future itself. When writers are called prophets it means that the general public are still living in the past but slowly awaken to the new present felt already by the "prophet". His present is still their future, their present already his past.

Hence poetic types are seen at their least ambiguous in their historical limitation and modulation. We observe over a period of time a need for a certain kind of expressiveness, as for example in the Pindaric ode, the Elizabethan drama, the Italian sonnet in Petrarch's day, the ballad, various European novel forms in the eighteenth or nineteenth centuries; and such a need discovers a type of structure, of imagery-in-language, which, suited to its purpose, becomes the vehicle for the expression. The type recurs because the need is felt in an approximately similar way by many people, first one poet, then others, and a responsive and even cooperative audience; and the typical formula, serving the need, maintains a certain identity amidst inevitable variations in its individual application. And of course the florescence and decay, the renaissance or total disappearance, of poetic types follow on changes in social life and culture, of which they are the symptomatic expression.

The allegorical epics of medieval times have vanished with the communal experiences and conditions that constituted their milieu. The sonnet flourished most splendidly during the Renaissance in certain conditions of polite education and aristocratic culture, and sonnets of later periods do not, however good, wear so natural an air or show the same superlative ease and poise in composition and rhythm. These are only two examples, simple and obvious, of processes that have sometimes very intricate results. The study of such patterns of social agreement as benevolent influences on literary forms is the business of a true sociology of literature. By true I mean broadly based on all the processes of thought and social culture, and not simply tied to a narrow doctrine of the Marxist type. Both large and small, national and international, social groups contribute to the shaping of literary types. To begin with there is the kind of near-universal response seen in drama, a form known to a wide diversity of human cultures throughout history; or in the profoundly romantic need, always breaking out afresh, for a hymnic or dithyrambic poetry. Influences operate then within the racial or national societies, as we observe in forms clearly the product of national genius and its language. Simple illustrations are the metres —already referred to—peculiarly adapted to different languages, the classical distich, Dante's *terza rima*, English blank verse, the French Alexandrine, and so on, none of which transplants easily ; or the Elizabethan dramatic form as contrasted with the French classical drama. And finally forms are sometimes linked with quite restricted social groups, as was the case with the audience of the Restoration theatre in England.

One has to make a distinction, of course, between the life-period of a type from the creative point of view, and the much longer life it has for appreciation. But the structure of such appreciation is extremely intricate and many factors obscure the actual degree of datedness. The sympathetic imagination, both in itself and when supported by thorough knowledge, enables us to extend our understanding of literary forms as of history and widely separate cultures. But certain it is that all historical specimens of a form slowly die, as the psychological and social links with its original circumstances become more and more tenuous. We do not now hear Homer's epic as the Greeks, or Shakespeare's Histories as the Elizabethans did, nor Goethe's *Faust* with the ears of Humboldt and the Schlegels. This conforms to what happens with all works of art, irrespective of the kinds or typical forms. They suffer rarefaction, each generation being left with an abstraction of the original, its beauty still possibly moving, yet partial and attenuated. When works or authors suddenly become alive again, usually because of the recurrence of similar problems or taste, they do not recover their former character uncontaminated; they are in a sense translated from an original context into the new one, as may be seen in the case of Donne and Hölderlin in recent decades, though these are only particularly vivid examples of a ubiquitous process.

Our theory of art and principles of imagery thus enable us to replace a static theory of kinds and conventional forms by a dynamic theory of typical poetic structures or, more simply, literary types. We abandon the idea of permanent, universal, "ideal" forms, conceiving instead temporary stabilizations of aesthetic patterns corresponding to expressive forces, all works and forms being crystallizations in a constant dynamic process. A given type comes into existence, by the mediation of genius, in relation to certain human circumstances and social culture. It is developed and varied by a succession of writers, it finds a responsive audience, and then declines, suddenly or gradually, as historical change makes other forms necessary. Sometimes it is revived though never without being adapted to a new situation; the epic recurs, though not the Homeric form of it.

iii. TYPE, VARIANT, AND IDIOSYNCRASY

The point of view here adopted allows for an aesthetic significance in typical forms without suggesting that type and individual character are mutually exclusive. Part of the meaning—the expressive meaning—of a play is that it is a play and not a novel; of a sonnet, that it is a sonnet and not an ode. Types of form are adapted, by a combined interaction of nature, psychology, and artistic tradition, to given subjects and themes, so that the general and repeated experience behind a form contributes to the significance of every example of it. Nevertheless every work is an individual variant and the relation between single works and the " type" always subtle. The drama speaks to us from Shakespeare, Schiller, Grillparzer, and Ibsen, but severally with their particular accents.

Since our conception of "types", linked as it is with expressiveness and natural ritual, is not simply a matter of classification, we do not hold that all works must of necessity belong to one or the other type, apart from their coming under one of the very broad general heads of story, song, or meditation. Vast numbers of literary works are idiosyncratic; their individuality lies not in variation of a type but in exclusiveness; they are alien to type. Possibly even a majority of what we call "poems" are like this; the feature of verse is sufficient to classify them vaguely, and beyond that we are aware of a multitude of themes, styles, and metrical shapes, amidst which firm types tend on the whole to be rare. Modern everyday usage makes the term "lyric poetry" cover nearly all poetry not plainly narrative or dramatic, so that in fact we feel uncomfortable as to what "lyric" here signifies; for true lyrics are also relatively scarce. Most poems, especially nowadays, are a very variable mixture of thought and lyric, meditation and song, philosophy and music. They are statements about some phase of emotional consciousness, highly idiosyncratic in form.

The same is true of the novel in this century. It has often enough been said that this is the most representative form of the modern age, but this conviction, which presupposes after all some conception of the "form", has not prevented an increasing bewilderment as to what novels really are and do. Goethe still spoke of the novel as a hybrid in a sense that sounds strange to-day. He thought of it as only half inside the sphere of art, the element of prose "report" preventing the fully-developed imaginative representation achieved by epic poetry and drama. The twentieth century novel certainly withstands such criticism; but if it is more defensible from the formal point of view it no less certainly shows a great variety of forms. However, the predominance of such idiosyncrasy can scarcely surprise us. The present age being one remarkable for the absence of compelling faiths and philosophies of life, as distinct from ideologies, the tendency of most creative literature is not to judge or interpret life and man by a standard but to explore "experience". And the range of experience and vision that narrative can handle extends as far as life itself, and to show one bit or one aspect of it, with its effective colourings, is to determine a form, or isolate an image, for that one particular and no other. A sophisticated age like our own, when extreme satisfaction of individual ideals is sought and allowed and a consequent tolerance of taste carried to great lengths, encourages idiosyncrasy.

In connexion with idiosyncrasy we have to make a distinction between genuine originality and failure to use a form properly. Byron's playwriting is an example of the latter. He was haughty about the theatre and his plays reflect it; they have some elements of good drama in them, but it is quite clear that he was satisfied with a compromise, too proud to study the medium.

Miss Compton Burnett's strange novels, on the other hand, are too original to be described as a compromise with a conventional form. Nor are they a hybrid between novel and drama, as a superficial view of her dialogue has suggested to some. Her dialogue, far from being the characteristic speech of drama, is a genuine creation within the more elastic framework of narrative. Embodying in seeming continuous speech two things—what is actually spoken together with what is only thought—it bears analogy with the phenomenon of combined aspects in Picasso's paintings. As such it is a profoundly original invention, formal and expressive in one, a wonderfully economical and fertile technique for representing simultaneously a surface of conversation and an underlying pattern of secretive and ever vigilant passions.

At the side of idiosyncrasy we also observe a few hybrid or inter-mediate forms, by which I do not mean any vague mixing of kinds or tones, but a form drawing on two or more genuine types as defined above. Browning's monologues in *Men and Women* and *Dramatis Personae* are an example. Being monologues, and therefore short of drama proper, they nevertheless imply potentially dramatic situations and are in consequence more than lyric. In terms of their image structure we should say that the conventional first person voice of lyric is partially displaced, and we find an incipient dramatic imagery, with a "person" or "character" projected, speaking from a situation on the axis of a possible dramatic development. The form thus faces in two directions. Goethe's famous early poem *Prometheus* is of this kind. A piece found in every "lyrical" anthology, it was conceived as a monologue in a play never executed; in it elements of the Promethean drama are telescoped into a generalized expression of cosmic defiance.

We can also use our theory of imagery to illumine the problem of style in writing that is not in the strict sense "creative" but which imagination enriches with various qualities. No one needs reminding of the many works in philosophy, science, theology, politics, his-tory, and so on, to which literary excellence is ascribed over and above their specialized importance. And the possibility of "litera-ture" thus arising from an activity primarily non-literary has been used as one argument against classical or traditional theories of genre and form. From our point of view such writing, in its artistic aspect, represents modes of idiosyncrasy; for our argument has been that it is the embodiment of an imagery in language that creates an aesthetic form, and that this produces a multitude of diverse forms amidst which we observe from time to time certain persisting "typical" patterns. The first purpose of scholarly and philosophical writing is not expressive but learned, and the step from one to the other is crucial. But what gives such work a literary quality derives partly from brilliant imaginative conception and language, and partly from an admixture of passion and personal character, which makes it to that extent expressive as well as learned. As Buffon said, in a famous phrase quoted usually in a truncated form, the contents of knowledge are outside man, detachable, but *le style est l'homme même*.

Finally we note that idiosyncrasy also occurs in those eccentric authors whose imaginative powers get out of control, or are not happily balanced by other intellectual and disciplined qualities. Outrageous or feeble opinions are often found presented with imagination and style, sometimes by authors who seem to suffer altogether from aberration, sometimes in the inferior work of good writers. The problem may also occur where one simply disagrees with an author's views whilst admiring his style; indeed this is probably its commonest form, and it extends to the problem of beliefs and poetry. For in assessing any writer whom we admit to literary rank at all we have to acknowledge power and quality of some kind, since we should otherwise disregard him. We are often in this strange position of admiring a man's imagination whilst rejecting his opinions and beliefs.

The conflict here is between vital disposition, which expresses itself in style, and reason, which is generalized truth, all opinion being attempted generalized truth. Style adds passion to thought, giving an image of a person. In this sense all writing that achieves style is "true", because the truth that is inherent in a living person by virtue of life pertains also to the image. But the writing is not necessarily "true" as reason, or generalized truth. The person and the image are individual; reason is general.

A great amount of prose exhibits this conflict. Originality of mind shows itself sometimes in the capacity to state general truths, which may of course be vehemently opposed before finally achieving acceptance. But it shows itself also in simple energy, vigour, and self-confidence. Originality in this sense is a sort of character or assertion of will-power appearing in the form of literature; it is a frequent attribute of politicians, and far from displaying a steady sense of general human truth may more often than not be wilful and egoistic. But it produces orations.

The phenomenon appears also in criticism and aesthetic, particularly where creative writers pronounce their views. Everyone knows the bias characteristic of artists' utterances, which are usually justifications of their own practice. A poet's criticism or aesthetic is an aspect of his poetry; it is part of all his personal speech taken together. The character of his vision determines the character of his theory, which consequently shares the "truth" of the former, in the sense described above. For this reason a poet's pronouncement has a distinct authority and, like life, is incontrovertible. One senses behind his assertions the whole power of his mind and its vitality, thought intricately linked with passion, vision with life, infusing into his opinions a force which removes them from ordinary debate and aggrandizes them into something more than opinion. But with all their individual power they do not necessarily express universally applicable truth; for philosophy they remain one opinion amongst others.

The same conflict between expression and general truth is felt in criticism of the arts. Some critics are opinionated and write brilliantly or amusingly; on the other hand a certain dullness often goes with sound, sensible, conscientious criticism. Academic writing which puts "truth" first is laid on one side, respected but not necessarily read. The best critics treat literature and art as poets treat life. They respond with imagination and describe what they see, feel, and think. They are sensitive in the degree to which their imagination can work in this rather specialized way, and persuasive in proportion to their ability to define a response shared by others and to make their language reflect what their imagination reveals. The energy of their mind thus disburdens itself in a personal imagery but without prejudice to their subject or to generally acceptable judgements; hence criticism is sometimes called an "art" and sometimes a branch of philosophy.

iv. CONCLUSION

This chapter has provided us with the implications of the theory of imagery for the many varying arts and art-forms. We may now accept the idea of a type of structure, for instance drama, which has significance as a form in addition to what any dramatist chooses to say with it. We shall look upon it as a typical pattern of imagery and language, showing a characteristic intertexture which marks it off from other forms, and related to expressive needs. But we also observe that according to the same principle many variations are possible and inevitable within the kind, each showing some delicate balance between type and idiosyncrasy. Equally germane to the central problem is the relation between different kinds of imagery within any given type of intertexture, the issue in drama being interfusion of speech, gesture, and scene. It is this interfusion that we must in the sequel examine more closely, and we shall see what powerful support we derive from having established the principle of the image and its functions. For without the single underlying idea it is difficult to understand the subtle relations between such things as rhythm and logical meanings, verse and acting, dialogue and *mise-en-scène*, and all the other combinations characteristic of art and poetry. For all images relate to nature; and their interfusion, reflecting the organic complexity of nature, is itself natural, as we said above, giving the example of the warning cry and gesture. Images, which rest on sensuous apprehension, interfuse naturally, and are opposed to the analytical character of verbal meaning. And yet language, even propositional language, may be used, as we saw above, in such a way as to exploit the imagery it embodies, and thus may be assimilated to other systems of image-meaning. Examining in turn the image, metaphor, expressive formula-images, the functioning of images, images in relation to verbal meanings, the idea that images interfuse in characteristic patterns making types of literary expression, we have laid the foundations, by means of an adumbrated theory of art and poetry, for a theory of drama which will do justice to its variety and illumine the ways in which it achieves style and poetic effect.

But before looking directly at the problems of drama, I propose to analyse more closely the relations between poetry and music, elucidating at greater length some aspects of pre-verbal meaning already touched upon. The problem of music and poetry has an urgent importance since the symbolist movement, which was responsible for the evolution of a peculiarly rarefied idea of poetry, affecting general notions of the "poetic" in drama, as in other literary forms, in recent decades.

CHAPTER NINE

MUSIC AND POETRY

i. THE PROBLEM DEFINED

THERE ARE THREE REASONS for introducing this subject into the argument at this stage. The first is that it gives an opportunity to explore a prominent form of overlap between systems of imagery and so illumines still further the idea of intertextures. Secondly, it concerns aspects of poetry which are exceedingly relevant to drama, in which the voice and its expressiveness play so important a part. And thirdly, this relation of poetry to music has been of great consequence since the symbolist poets introduced new ideals and techniques, the art of music being viewed more and more as an ideal form and used as a criterion of art altogether.

In the course of history there have, of course, been many kinds of alliance between music and poetry. Epic poetry was originally declaimed with an instrumental accompaniment. The choric poetry of the Greek drama was closely linked with music and dance. Poets in widely differing ages and communities have written lyrics which were sung to the lute or other instrument. The modern centuries have produced more complex examples of artistic forms elaborating the interplay of words and music : the masses, motets, and madrigals of the age of Palestrina, the cantatas of the age of Bach, opera since the seventeenth century, as well as minor forms like the seventeenth century English masque or the later German Singspiel. All these examples show different relationships between music and language, each of which can only be established by modifying the elements in partnership. The music of an opera differs from that of a madrigal; the poetic language of a cantata differs from that of a song. A process of mutual assimilation alters them, sometimes very considerably, sometimes only slightly, leaving neither able to stand alone.

There is another relationship between poetry and music not indicated by any of the forms mentioned. It consists not in an alliance of the two arts but in the approach of poetry itself to musical expression. Sometimes, as in lyrics of sentiment, certain qualities can bring a poem to the very verge of music, to the point where we are aware of mood or "feelings" (as we briefly say, meaning in reality complex patterns of emotion, feeling, and sensibility) to the entire exclusion of thoughts. Yet a poem remains a thing of words, and the ideas and images evoked by them. It stops short of music proper, of instruments, of melody and harmony, and of collaboration with them. This is the relationship we now propose to analyse more closely. What do we mean when we say of poetry, which in modern times is simply read in privacy, or spoken without accompaniment, that it is "musical"?

Some of the means of poetry are very similar to those of music. They both use rhythm and acoustic features, which include the sounds produced by the inflexions of voice and the various vocal devices of verse such as assonance, rhyme, and the play of vowels. This gives a simple, elementary overlap with music. The borderline of poetry and music is seen where reading a lyric seems to be on the point of becoming a song; or in recitative, where the word-meaning predominates over the melody. *Lieder* style itself varies, of course. The emphasis is sometimes on a generalized mood, with the words themselves vague and half-musicalized, whilst in Hugo Wolf, for example, a dramatic element makes words and music equal partners. Thus, though normally a poem read and a song sung are two different phenomena, between them they have a common element.

In this connexion the role of the voice is important and calls for a brief comment.

ii. THE ROLE OF THE VOICE. VOCAL IMAGERY

Most discussions about the music of poetry seem to assume tacitly that the music lies in the language. This is an error. The music lies in the voice, with language—considered as a spoken phenomenon—providing certain conditions within which the voice operates. It is essential to emphasize the fact that the voice, being the natural organ of feeling, has its own purely auditory expressiveness. We observe it in simple emotional situations. We cry out with joy, or pleasure, or pain, giving to each a different tone. We murmur with contentment, we growl, snarl, wail, purr, as writers of thrillers know. Speech receives its intended meaning from appropriate inflexions of the voice; we deliberately co-ordinate our voice with what we want to say. The simple sentence 'You are going' may be a statement, or a question, or a command, according to the manner of speaking it. Moreover, special effects of meaning are achieved by the calculated disturbing of normal vocal co-ordination. For instance irony, sarcasm, and mockery depend on a tone of voice that cuts across the literal meaning of the words. They are kinds of meaning brought about by the subtle disjunction of two techniques of expression that normally go under the same yoke. They would be impossible without the independent expressiveness of the voice itself. For the same reason, whether a language is musical or not really depends on how it is spoken. German, which is often said to be "unmusical", sounds musical when spoken by a musical voice. Italian, on the other hand, always praised as a "musical" language, sounds harsh when harshly spoken. Any language as such offers in its phonetic structure a range of potential musical expressiveness. Poets study this in relation to an ideal musical voice.

The music of poetry thus depends, in its aural or phonic aspect, not on language but on the voice-in-language. It is the musical voice that creates both tone and range, quality and variety of sound, and all the types of expression indicated in music by conventional terms like *amabile*, *affettuoso*, *furioso*, *allegramente*, *con tenerezza*, *impetuoso*, *nobilmente*, etc., and equally applicable to poetry reading. The sound images of words are only realized when conjoined with the inflexions of such a voice. The voice thus provides a supporting sound imagery which fuses corroboratingly with the pattern of the words and their evocations. It is in fact parallel to mime and gesture, another supporting imagery for speech. To put it another way, the music of the voice is already expressive in its own right, and the good reading is one in which this quasi-independent music is adequately correlated with the words, rhythms and meanings of the poem. A reading is less than musical, less than poetic, if the words only receive the expressiveness suitable to prose. It is too musical if the voice floods the poem with its own musical pattern where it is inappropriate. It would, for example, be absurd to make an epigram "musical", however decisive its rhythm or smooth its sound.

The relation of voice music to feelings is the same in respect of poetry as of music itself. In both cases art is involved, not spontaneous behaviour, which means that the "feeling" affected by the voice belongs, like the melody or the poem, to an imagery which is idea and not reality. In chapter seven, discussing the place of real feelings in the aesthetic experience, we allowed for a real tuning of the sensibility and a simulation of sympathetic feelings, but recognized that they occurred within the control of the imagination. When we say the voice 'expresses feeling' in singing and poetry we mean that it realizes the imagery of the music or poem in which the expression of feeling is implicit. In so doing the singer or speaker achieves style. When superinduced real feeling engulfs the pattern of the music or poem the result is bad or sentimental singing and speaking. It is the indiscrete real invading the image, crude and misdirected sentiment displacing the imagination. When involved in a real feeling we are under the power of the physiological and psychical which suppresses aesthetic imagination and awareness. The greater this pressure, the less we are clear and aware; we become angry, uncontrolled, blind, and finally mad with fury. In art, on the other hand, images are evolved from the real. For the artist in creating is not involved in experience but in creating images of experience. Style depends on the singer's or speaker's ability to re-create such images.

Judgements about the reading of verse often suffer from a failure to understand the preliminary dispositions of the voice, and the fact that they depend on an operation of the imagination, of the image-making energy, parallel to rhythm, or metaphor, and functioning like them as part of a complex intertexture of imagery, the whole and unity of which we call a poem. When actors read lyrics, for instance, they use too frequently the sound imagery of dramatic verse, supported by a psychological tuning to the dramatic style, a miscalculation that distorts a lyric poem. On the other hand criticism is frequently directed against the way poets read verse, especially if they beat out the rhythm too forcibly, or if the modulations of their voice seem not to be varied enough. Particular cases call for particular comments but the general criticism is largely ill-informed. Those whose imagination produces poems are not unlikely to possess a delicate sense for the imagination in the voice and to exercise a finer judgement of the voice-music integral to their poems. They are like the composer, in whose playing of music, whether or not his own, we notice usually a touch more intimate and poetic than can be found even in the most sensitive performer who is not a composer. This quality of the composer is to be traced not simply to a vague notion of ' deeper feeling', but to the more potent imagination that transforms feeling into image. It is a greater capacity to realize the musical image in performance, deriving from the primary ability of the composer to create musical images.

iii. NON-ACOUSTIC MUSICAL QUALITIES IN POETRY

From this preliminary comment on the aural aspect of poetry and its vocal foundation we turn to an introductory observation on another side of the problem. The musical effect of poetry does not emanate only from the physical and acoustic elements shared with music. Other influences, not necessarily more subtle, but certainly more difficult of analysis, are at work. They emerge in three statements on the subject which have become focal points in the study of poetry and art. In a famous passage in the *Biographia Literaria* Coleridge, using Shakespeare's *Venus and Adonis* to illustrate the qualities of excellent poetry, writes:—

'In the Venus and Adonis, the first and most obvious excellence is the perfect sweetness of the versification; its adaptation to the subject; and the power displayed in varying the march of the words without passing into a loftier and more majestic rhythm than was demanded by the thoughts, or permitted by the propriety of preserving a sense of melody predominant. The delight in richness and sweetness of sound, even to a faulty excess, if it be evidently original, and not the result of an easily imitable mechanism, I regard as a highly favourable promise in the compositions of a young man. The man that hath not music in his soul can indeed never be a genuine poet. Imagery—(even taken from nature, much more when transplanted from books, as travels, voyages, and works of natural history),—affecting incidents, just thoughts, interesting personal or domestic feelings, and with these the art of their combination or intertexture in the form of a poem,—may all by incessant effort be acquired as a trade, by a man of talent and much reading, who, as I once before observed, has mistaken an intense desire of poetic reputation for a natural poetic genius; the love of the arbitrary end for a possession of the peculiar means. But the sense of musical delight, with the power of producing it, is a gift of imagination; and this together with the power of reducing multitude into unity of effect, and modifying a series of thoughts by some one predominant thought or feeling, may be cultivated and improved, but can never be learned. It is in these that "poeta nascitur non fit".'

The thought here hovers between a reference to musical effects of poetry that are in fact audible and the more general analogy between the effect of a poem, and of music, as a whole. The 'perfect sweetness of the versification', the 'delight in richness and sweetness of sound', the 'sense of melody predominant', are particular phenomena for the ear; 'the man that hath not music in his soul', and 'the sense of musical delight—together with the power of reducing multitude into unity of effect', suggest a broader comparison, less precise, but perhaps still more operative. The whole passage, set in the context of a great piece of criticism, shows Coleridge alert to all the possibilities. Yet it relies to an astonishing extent on the assumption that to perceive *the musical* is, without further explanation seeming relevant, to indicate an essential feature of poetry. Coleridge places it first in his enumeration of the characteristics of good poetry, he seeks no closer definition, and has not escaped tautology. 'The sense of musical delight, with the power of producing it, is a gift of imagination' . . . this, after all, only says that if the poet's work is musical it is also poetry. But what is music? And the musical *in* poetry? Does he mean the art of music? Probably not, in any strict sense. He is content to use a quite general sense of some relationship between the poetical and "music". We note that the terms of the comparison cannot be reversed with the same effect, or the same feeling that something illuminating is being said. No one judges music by its approach to poetry. No one says that a first quality of music should be a sense of poetic delight.

The two elements uncertainly yet naturally juxtaposed in Coleridge's passage are typical of the comparisons often drawn between poetry and music. There is always the reference to more particular aural and rhythmic characteristics which bestow a greater degree of lyricism, and make us say of certain styles, like that of Spenser, for instance, that they are "musical"; and there is always the vaguer, imponderable analogy resting not on specific symptoms but on an impression of the total effect which we find difficult to define but of which we are decisively sensible. The more we look into it the more we discover that the actual phonic overlap with music proper (with song, for example) is only a partial contribution to the musicality of poetry. Indeed it might be said to mark differences as much as similarities. It suggests an initial approach to music and in the same operation cannot but draw attention to the limits set to such an approach. Certain general features of art, on the other hand, suggest relationships less obvious on the surface, but with results more profoundly felt.

The force of the general analogy with music was stated most vividly by Pater in his famous dictum on the relation of the arts to music:—

' All art constantly aspires to the condition of music. For while in all other kinds of art it is possible to distinguish the matter from the form, and the understanding can always make this distinction, yet it is the constant effort of art to obliterate it. That the mere matter of a poem, for instance, its subject, namely, its given incidents or situation—that the mere matter of a picture, the actual circumstances of an event, the actual topography of a landscape—should be nothing without the form, the spirit, of the handling, that this form, this mode of handling, should become an end in itself, should penetrate every part of the matter: this is what all art constantly strives after, and achieves in different degrees'.

These words, in their context in the essay on the *School of Giorgione*, express a persistent conviction that music obliterates more effectively than other arts the distinction between subject-matter and form; and since our sensibility tells us that the specialized value of works of art lies in their presenting subject-matter so penetrated by expressive purpose that they are unique statements about the feelings and sensibility, impossible of translation into other terms, music clearly, on this view, takes the lead. Pater has here seized on the most mysterious feature of art, *when it is perfect*, and believes that music shows it in the purest form. It is an extremely important idea because it makes use of music as a symbolic criterion for the perfect obliquity of art, the *non-representational aspect* of its expressiveness.

Finally, a passage from Valéry provides evidence of the symbolist point of view :—

'Ce qui fut baptisé le *Symbolisme* se résume très simplement dans l'intention commune à plusieurs familles de poètes (d'ailleurs ennemies entre elles) de reprendre à la Musique, leur bien. Le secret de ce mouvement n'est pas autre. L'obscurité, les étrangetés, qui lui furent tant reprochées; l'apparence de relations trop intimes avec les littératures anglaise, slave, ou germanique; les désordres syntaxiques, les rythmes irréguliers, les curiosités du vocabulaire, les figures continuelles, . . . tout se déduit facilement sitôt que le principe est reconnu . . . Mais nous étions nourris de musique, et nos têtes littéraires ne rêvaient que de tirer du langage presque les mêmes effets que les causes purement sonores produisaient sur nos êtres nerveux.' (Avant-propos, *Variété*.)

For our argument it is interesting to observe that Valéry's observations, though clear and precise in regard to the general intention of symbolist style, show some of the same kind of unclarity as that noticed in Coleridge's passage. 'Et nos têtes littéraires ne rêvaient que de tirer du langage *presque les mêmes effets* que *les causes purement sonores* produisaient sur nos êtres nerveux'. This does not say simply that language should aim at musical effects. The thought is not so rigidly precise. The expression 'presque les mêmes effets' suggests something a little short of that, yet also something more. Valéry refers to the sound of the words but seems also to leave the door open for some effects that, without being phonic in the strict sense, would nevertheless be, in a way, "musical". The reference to very varied symbolist style supports this vagueness.

These three documents span the nineteenth century and whilst they contribute something to a general idea of poetry they also illustrate one of its historical phases. Distinguishing between them, Coleridge's may be said to define the presence of something musical in poetry generally, in its "normal" condition, using normal here inclusively for all its different types. It is not a real or orthodox music, in the sense of musical art proper, but a condition in the texture of poetry securing more intense emotional expressiveness. It is the musical undertone in all poetry.

Valéry's passage, on the other hand, shows the programmatic aim of symbolist style, which was to musicalize poetry. This was, however, not as simple a procedure as it sounds. A refinement of rhythm and auditory imagery belonged to the method, but also an exploration of the way symbols in general (objects, nature, images, words, etc.) can evoke sensations and feelings and thus become a pattern of signs corresponding to some state of emotion or sensibility. We shall analyse this process later in the chapter. Here we need only say that the immediacy of expression secured by such symbolic means is comparable to that of music. Thus to a genuine intensification of the aural and rhythmic music is added the subtle oblique music of the symbolistic process.

It must, however, be stressed that this musicalization of poetry took place in the interests not of music but of *pure* poetry. Here arises the remarkable ambiguity of the relationship between poetry and music in the symbolist practice, and both theory and criticism have often lacked clarity in consequence. The symbolists used music not so much as an aim for poetry, but as a criterion for a perfect art, this being essentially the creation of forms for a quite inward experience and an idealizing sensibility. Pater's famous passage, written in the climate of symbolist poetry, is related. It promulgates a theory of perfect art—the conversion of all "content" into signs for feeling and spirituality—with music as the obvious paradigm of the process.

Any clear discussion of music and poetry must try to keep the general question of musical or intensely lyrical quality distinct from the particular features of symbolist practice and belief, though obviously the two things are related and do overlap. In the following pages I shall bear in mind a threefold distinction. First we fix on the idea of a "music of poetry" which is *sui generis* and normally present in some degree or other in all poetry. Then, as against this norm, we observe in some passages of poetry an intensive musicalization, again at any period and in any style, the conditions of which may be observed and defined. And, thirdly, there is a special development in the nineteenth century, between the romantic and symbolist styles, in which quite particular assumptions about poetry, combined with general philosophical and metaphysical beliefs, lead to special views about "pure" poetry and art and to the cult of a special relationship between poetry and music.

I propose first to consider briefly two or three modes of musical quality or effect, including the customary one of auditory and rhythmic imagery, and the less obvious one of music by symbol and metaphor, and then pass to a more historical review of nineteenth century developments.

It is, however, not easy to trace musical effect to any one cause in isolation from the others, nor, in consequence, to give pure examples of the one or the other. Rhythm, verbal sound, the play of metaphor on the feelings, emotional saturation in theme and subject-matter, aspiration and nostalgia for the ideal, all interact and none induces of itself alone the musical quality. There is no exclusive prescription, no single formula, for bringing poetry near to music, and the most elusive process of all, the inter-action of phonic and non-phonic elements, may perhaps be the most important. We cannot do more than indicate certain directions of emphasis. To speak of "types" of musical poem would be already too dogmatic, quite apart from the fact that musical intensity occurs far more frequently in brief passages than in whole poems. At the most there are "typical possibilities" of musical intensity.

iv. MUSICAL EFFECT BASED ON AUDITORY IMAGERY

What does the sound of words contribute to musical quality within the total economy of a poem? This is a large subject, to which we cannot do justice in the present place. Our purpose is only to adduce a few examples sufficient to illumine this phase of our main argument.

Spenser's style offers a type of harmonious and mellifluous verse, most insistent in its organisation of verbal sound:—

> Lacking my loue I go from place to place,
>> lyke a young fawne that late hath lost the hynd:
>> and seeke each where, where last I sawe her face,
>> whose ymage yet I carry fresh in mynd.
> I seeke the fields with her late footing synd,
>> I seeke her bowre with her late presence deckt,
>> yet nor in field nor bowre I her can fynd:
>> yet field and bowre are full of her aspect.
> But when myne eyes I thereunto direct,
>> they ydly back returne to me agayne,
>> and when I hope to see theyr trew obiect
>> I fynd myselfe but fed with fancies vayne.
> Ceasse then myne eyes, to seek her selfe to see,
>> and let my thoughts behold her self in mee.
>
> Sonnet lxxviii.

The stanza Spenser used for the *Faerie Queene*, and the sonnet form, offer him great opportunities in respect of formal beauty. They are both strict patterns characterized by moderate complexity of design. They invite a certain elaboration of idea, involving diversity, but the mould is firm enough to curb the excited imagination before it transgresses to the ornate, or the diffuse. In short, they are forms particularly calculated to display delicate examples of art as a sensuous pattern of unity in diversity, from both the point of view of the thought and of the rhythms and rhymes. Spenser goes much beyond the minimum possibilities, however, more especially in his use of assonance and alliteration, and of repetitions applied in various ways; e.g. to the vowels, producing either internal rhymes, or more often a kind of persistent vowel-echoing; or to whole words, which double the sound repetition with a meaning repetition, knitting the ideas together. Such composition obviates a motley of sounds as well as sharp contrasts. These latter methods, moreover, which can be applied in any metrical scheme, maintain the sense of well-knit texture in those parts of his work not written in strict stanza forms.

To these features must be added the negative method of avoiding harsh sounds, or at least, by the use of a skilful neutralizing process, cushioning unavoidable harsh sounds with soft ones. A fine ear for smooth sound produces a generalized melodiousness. But all these qualities would be less effective were it not for a certain verbal fluency and abundance. There is a tendency to make more words than are necessary, producing, to some extent, a conflict between amplitude of sound and economy of sense. This lulls the attention to logical meaning and makes the continuing sound and the sustained rhythm and rhyme design still more important, for good or bad.

Nowhere, however, are pronounced and engaging musical effects obtained unless the ideas and emotions combine with sound in a general sweetness or tenderness. In the sonnet quoted this is achieved through the theme of absent love and the sentiment of tender desire. We notice also that the visual world is dissipated, the whole tendency of the poem being for the feeling to negate the external world and set up an inward "image" of which, however, it gives no details. The sentiment is all.

Tennyson is another poet well known for his pervading euphony. It is based on verbal sound and rhythm, on deliberate harmonies, recherché sweetness, and the musical effect of repetitions and sustained echoing, often in the service of tender or sad or nostalgic sentiments. One could quote single lines or short passages almost at random to illustrate his command of melody and sensitive, idea-reflecting rhythms:

> Faint as a climate-changing bird that flies
> All night across the darkness, and at dawn
> Falls on the threshold of her native land . . .

> There lies a vale in Ida, lovelier
> Than all the valleys of Ionian hills . . .

> Be near me when my light is low,
>   When the blood creeps, and the nerves prick
>   And tingle; and the heart is sick,
> And all the wheels of Being slow . . .

> Lo! in the middle of the wood
> The folded leaf is woo'd from out the bud
> With winds upon the branch, and there
> Grows green and broad, and takes no care,
> Sun-steep'd at noon, and in the moon
> Nightly dew-fed; and turning yellow
> Falls, and floats adown the air . . .

The last example illustrates beautifully the transference of a rhythm of nature to a rhythm of words. But, passing from brief passages to whole poems, the poem from which it is taken, *The Lotos-Eaters*, forms a single, elaborate unfolding of a vast lulling rhythm and bemusing sound sequence, imaging an eternal motion-in-rest or rest-in-motion like an infinite sea-music. As an example of a single short poem of intense musical effect we can take the following from *In Memoriam*:

> Sweet after showers, ambrosial air,
>   That rollest from the gorgeous gloom
>   Of evening over brake and bloom
> And meadow, slowly breathing bare

> The round of space, and rapt below
>   Thro' all the dewy tassell'd wood,
>   And shadowing down the horned flood
> In ripples, fan my brows and blow

The fever from my cheek, and sigh
  The full new life that feeds thy breath
  Throughout my frame, till Doubt and Death,
Ill brethren, let the fancy fly

From belt to belt of crimson seas
  On leagues of odour streaming far,
  To where in yonder orient star
A hundred spirits whisper 'Peace'.

Here the predominant long rich vowels create a rhythmical and musical equivalent of the progressive expansion of space to the physical and emotional infinity of the last line.

In the poetry of Stefan George, a great master of music in verse, we can distinguish many degrees of approach to the musical. He writes from the beginning under the influence of the contemporary French school. In opposition to materialism in society and the realism of prose forms in literature he studiously evaded every too obvious reality, or logic, or meaning, every plain subject or content or thought, and aimed at *Stimmung*, through metaphor, rhythm, and verbal sound. Throughout his work, even in his direct comments on culture, history, poets and artists, philosophy, religion, ethics, which all contribute to his beliefs, he maintains his ideals, so that almost any of his good poems could be adduced as an example of the musical in verse.

Briefly and in the most general terms, I think the reason is to be found in the conjunction of an imperiously emotional nature and a superlative command of unified rhythmic and tonal design. The one generates intensity, the other produces an adequate imagery adequately controlled. In these conditions is achieved the characteristic effect of music, keen feeling at once imprisoned and liberated in a strict order of images wholly or partly esoteric. Nearly all George's poems show the same pattern of formal resolution; gravity of sentiment, or emotional fullness, clarified in beautiful composition. Within the general ideal he set himself, however, he wrote poems called *Lieder*, recognizing thus a special type of lyric, to be distinguished from other forms; and he contributed many of the most beautiful in the German language. Here is one from *Der Siebente Ring*:—

| Im Windes-weben | Nur Träumerei. |
| War meine Frage | Nur Lächeln war |

Was du gegeben.	Nun muss ich gar
Aus nasser Nacht	Um dein Aug und Haar
Ein Glanz entfacht—	Alle Tage
Nun drängt der Mai	In Sehnen leben.

This is a good example of composition by musical principles. The poem is built rhythmically on a short, mainly iambic line with two stresses, and tonally on two predominant vowels, *a* and closed *e*, associated with closely related vowels and diphthongs, together with the predominating consonants w, l, m, and n. This establishes a decisively composed and unified sound-pattern, yielding a rich, warm, and urgent expressiveness. But this music of verbal sound would be meaningless without certain other marked characteristics. The poem works with hints only, with suggestions and fleeting evocations. Its sensuousness is delicate. As in the Spenser poem, the visual is avoided. " Ein Glanz" is not pictorial but a sign of feeling, just as "nun drängt der Mai", which could have insisted on a picture of spring, avoids the picture and indicates a state of passion. The last lines name explicitly the predominant emotion, longing. The conditions of lyric intensity are here a recession from visual images, a clear urgent emotion, and a care for verbal sound and rhythm in which the auditory pattern is important both in itself and for the expressiveness of particular sounds in relation to the literal meanings.

Poems like these of Spenser, Tennyson, and George show a powerful musical suggestiveness. They are in fact more musical than poetry needs strictly to be, for which reason they illustrate the musicalization of poetry. They are types of musical verse. There are many such poems showing great refinements of art and composition. But there are also all those that come under the heading of lyrics of feeling, or simply "lyrics", a word which itself indicates by origin and tradition a kind of poem meant for singing. We recall folk songs, the interspersed lyrics of Shakespearean plays, like 'Come unto these yellow sands', and numerous others in English, whilst poets like Goethe and the German romantics, or Verlaine in France, have a great and even extraordinary reputation for this kind of composition. These vary in degrees of sophistication and in many cases a certain artlessness and simplicity of feeling, in strong contrast to the ingenuities of Spenser or Tennyson, contributes to the lyrico-musical effect. But the common link between simple and studied types is their use of well-tried modes of auditory imagery, sound, rhythm, and the repetitions or echoes that give cohesion and induce incantation.[1]

But if the quality of the poetic is modified in such verse by the musical, we observe that musical here means 'lyrical-musical'. Lyrics are said to be musical, but their "music" is, in its turn, of the *lyric* variety. It is confined to certain ranges of sentiment, tone, and mood. It is not a dramatic or rhetorical music. What degree of musicality there is in dramatic or rhetorical verse will be discussed later, but we may here say that these styles do not, on the whole, give rise so immediately and naturally to the musical analogy. The preponderance of the view that lyric poems are normally the most "musical" is justified in the sense that although "lyric-ism" is available to different arts—Giorgione, for instance, is a lyrical painter—we feel that music gives the most intense and appro-priate expression to it. Hence the musical analogy presents itself naturally.

Milton's is the music of rhetoric, showing a less intensive musicali-zation than the above examples of the truly lyrical, and yet insistent and convincing. His form is epic narrative, but a governing factor in his style is an unrestrained and powerful, even tyrannical, emotional attitude towards the subject under treatment; and if it is in the first place a mark of the poet narrating, it is also transferred to his characters speaking. This attitude, though emotional, depends, of course, on intellectually determined judgements and knowledge, and few passages in Milton run for more than two or three lines without the sensuous presentation being interrupted for some admixture of high thought and scrupulous adjustment between life and theology. Moreover, Milton's descriptions tend on the whole to establish a vague and general sensuousness rather than pictorial definition; they indicate and enumerate the broader features of the scene, and are sparing with the vivid detail. The senses are not often nakedly exposed to the immediate impact of sharp and particular impressions; one is more often asked to survey the scene and be reminded of the appropriate responses:—

> High on a throne of royal state, which far
> Outshone the wealth of Ormus and of Ind,
> Or where the gorgeous East with richest hand
> Showers on her kings barbaric pearl and gold,

Satan exalted sat, by merit raised
To that bad eminence; and, from despair
Thus high uplifted beyond hope, aspires
Beyond thus high, insatiate to pursue
Vain war with Heaven; and, by success untaught,
His proud imaginations thus displayed . . .

                              In this pleasant soil
His far more pleasant garden God ordained.
Out of the fertile ground he caused to grow
All trees of noblest kind for sight, smell, taste;
And all amid them stood the Tree of Life,
High eminent, blooming ambrosial fruit
Of vegetable gold; and, next to life,
Our death, the Tree of Knowledge, grew fast by—
Knowledge of good, bought dear by knowing ill.
Southward through Eden went a river large,
Nor changed his course, but through the shaggy hill
Passed underneath ingulfed; for God had thrown
That mountain, as his garden-mould, high raised
Upon the rapid current, which through veins
Of porous earth with kindly thirst updrawn,
Rose a fresh fountain, and with many a rill
Watered the garden; thence united fell
Down the steep glade, and met the nether flood,
Which from his darksome passage now appears,
And now, divided into four main streams,
Runs diverse, wandering many a famous realm
And country whereof here needs no account;
But rather to tell how, if Art could tell
How, from that sapphire fount the crisped brooks,
Rolling on orient pearl and sands of gold,
With mazy error under pendent shades
Ran nectar, visiting each plant, and fed
Flowers worthy of Paradise, which not nice Art
In beds and curious knots, but Nature boon
Poured forth profuse on hill, and dale, and plain,
Both where the morning sun first warmly smote
The open field, and where the unpierc'd shade
Embrowned the noontide bowers.

There are thus two streams in Milton's verse running towards abstraction: the diminution of immediate sensuousness in generalized terms of description, and the constant intellectual statement; and this abstraction, set amidst a full flow of circumambient general emotion, creates his particular musical effect, expressed in ample and stately paragraphs of broad rhythmic design in which pictorial definition is sacrificed to rhetorical suggestiveness. Here again we observe the inseparability of sound and sense. The meanings are inseparable from the emotional attitudes; together they govern the emergence of a sound-rhythm imagery. But rhythm in Milton is more subtly organized than sound. Or rather, more attention is bestowed on the details of rhythm, which is moulded with the greatest variety and flexibility according to the immediate needs of the story and the thought, whilst the sound effect lies less in verbal detail and more in a broad and general rise and fall of tone coincident with the architecture of the narrative or dialogue.

All the examples examined so far oblige us to recognize, within the whole extent of poetry, possibilities of musical quality of a specific kind. The notable feature is that these are achieved by certain combinations of imagery, and certain kinds of feeling and thought. They are, above all, carefully organized sound and rhythms, images and metaphors of a largely non-visual kind, suggestions of the immaterial and the ideal, fleeting evocation rather than plastic pictures, and certain kinds of intense feeling predominant.

V. MUSICAL EFFECT THROUGH METAPHOR AND SYMBOL

Auditory and motor imagery offer the most easily apprehended link of poetry with music. But since poetry exploits oblique expressiveness effects akin to those of music accrue where words and images carry an emotional meaning not through what they obviously denote or connote but through their function in a complex pattern. Thus we find a type of verse in which musicalization depends on metaphor and symbol as much as on auditory imagery. Take, for example, Ariel's song:—

> Full fathom five thy father lies;
> Of his bones are coral made;
> Those are pearls that were his eyes:
> Nothing of him that doth fade

> But doth suffer a sea-change
> Into something rich and strange.
> Sea-nymphs hourly ring his knell.
>
> (Burthen)   Ding-dong.
> Hark! now I hear them,—ding-dong, bell.

This poem, like *Come away, come away, Death*, or *Take, O take those lips away*, is a lyric, interpolated in a play, and sung to music. All three are very "musical". But are they so in the same way? The two latter we should call musical for reasons similar to those alleged for our previous examples; and we note explicitly that logical statement is preserved within the musical suggestiveness. But what of *Full fathom five thy father lies*?

> The ditty does remember my drown'd father . . .

says Ferdinand, indicating a dramatic appropriateness which, nevertheless, still leaves it a mysterious poem. It is no simple dirge; it has no clear-cut sentiment which the images and metaphors illustrate in a straightforward way. On the contrary, metaphor here assumes a primary role. It is not a support to logical meaning or narrative or description, but itself absorbs the meaning of the poem, which exists only in the metaphors, taken separately and as a whole. Direct statement in this poem (like the first line, or lines four to six) is seen to be simple only in a syntactical sense, and to be otherwise indirect and metaphorical. The images are of sea, coral, pearls, and there is the total image of wondrous transmutation, of fanciful creatures, sea-nymphs, that ring a knell, which has become, with the progress of the poem, ambiguous; scarcely a knell, but a celebration of something admirable and exquisite.

This poem has emotional but not logical definition. Logical statement, and direct description of observed things, are refined by being assimilated to an order implicit in metaphorical relations between images. The images are not presented as things that are real, existing in the pictorial world we observe, and claiming our interest in themselves alone. The bones of a drowned man turning into coral; his eyes into pearls; nymphs ringing bells under the sea; who ever heard of such things? These images, external to the order of "reality", are evocative and symbolic. Their meaning lies not in the objects the words stand for, but in their relations to each other. They are used as a formula—a complex one, but nevertheless a formula—which is largely esoteric in character, as music is esoteric; and it expresses a state of mind, or, to use the simpler term, a feeling.

When a group of images is constructed in this manner, the importance of each one tends to become purely *functional*; and as the pattern is elaborated, images that at first did not seem necessarily to be figures of speech become clearly metaphorical by their new function, their place in the pattern. I do not, of course, mean that the images used are so absorbed into a function that their content does not matter at all. In this poem the coral, the pearls, the nymphs, the transformation, although finally they refer to something else, are important for their content, in the sense that only these particular objects, with all their strangeness and richness and suggestions of wonderful happenings and feelings, evoke in our minds the proper responses. *These* images, and no others—not just any set of images —are necessary for the effect desired. Nevertheless, their significance lies predominantly in their function in a pattern, and they indicate a withdrawal from the world of external reality into an inner world of thought and feeling.

Using images in this way a poem approaches music. Music uses melodic images, harmonic images, powerful in themselves through the colour and the dynamics of sound, and with them it develops an elaborate pattern, adding to this first significance that of expressive relationships. The language of music is esoteric, it has its own syntax and vocabulary, which cannot be transcribed into ordinary speech, and it speaks directly to our imagination about our "feelings". When a poem relies on a structure of metaphorically functioning images, and so circumvents ordinary syntax and straightforward statement, like the poem we have considered, it moves us directly and immediately without our knowing why, in a way analogous to music.

In the example we have used, rhythm and sound no doubt play their part; a subordinate one, however, by contrast with our earlier types of poem, in which the musical element arose primarily from sound and rhythm.

This is the second important pattern of musical effect in poetry. It is, as the example from Shakespeare intentionally shows, much older than Symbolism, but that movement developed the method with special refinements, and under the influence of idealistic trends of thought.

vi. INFLUENCE OF SUBJECT AND THOUGHT ON MUSICALIZATION

We observed above that musical quality never derives only from one feature of a poem but from a certain emphasis and functioning of the imagery, in relation to the total effect or idea envisaged. By virtue of this functionalism the subject-matter or thought, as distinct from a content of feeling, may also contribute to musical effect. A remarkable though well-known example is to be found in *The Merchant of Venice* at the beginning of the fifth act, where Lorenzo and Jessica are waiting for the arrival of Portia:—

LORENZO:
How sweet the moonlight sleeps upon this bank!
Here will we sit and let the sounds of music
Creep in our ears; soft stillness and the night
Become the touches of sweet harmony.
Sit, Jessica. Look how the floor of heaven
Is thick inlaid with patines of bright gold;
There's not the smallest orb which thou behold'st,
But in his motion like an angel sings,
Still quiring to the young-ey'd cherubins;
Such harmony is in immortal souls,
But whilst this muddy vesture of decay
Doth grossly close it in, we cannot hear it.—
                    (*Enter musicians*).
Come, ho, and wake Diana with a hymn;
With sweetest touches pierce your mistress' ear,
And draw her home with music.
                    (*Music*).
JESSICA :
I am never merry when I hear sweet music.

LORENZO :
The reason is your spirits are attentive;
For do but note a wild and wanton herd,
Or race of youthful and unhandled colts,
Fetching mad bounds, bellowing and neighing loud,
Which is the hot condition of their blood—

If they but hear perchance a trumpet sound,
Or any air of music touch their ears,
You shall perceive them make a mutual stand,
Their savage eyes turn'd to a modest gaze
By the sweet power of music. Therefore the poet
Did feign that Orpheus drew trees, stones, and floods;
Since nought so stockish, hard, and full of rage,
But music for the time doth change his nature.
The man that hath no music in himself,
Nor is not mov'd with concord of sweet sounds,
Is fit for treasons, stratagems, and spoils;
The motions of his spirit are dull as night,
And his affections dark as Erebus.
Let no such man be trusted. Mark the music.

The general effect of this passage is extremely musical, and it is so also in translation, for instance in the German of Schlegel-Tieck. But in the English original the language does not show the elaborate orchestration of verbal sound that we find in Spenser, or in Stefan George, or the examples considered earlier. There is a sufficiency of assonance and near-alliteration, and an adequate avoidance of harshness, to produce general melodiousness, but falling short in this case of any lavish degree of sweetness. On the other hand, the whole dramatic scene, in its context in the play (after the harsh intransigence of Shylock and the saving of Antonio by Portia's skill) contributes to the creation of a special mood. There is the warm night atmosphere, the moonlight, Jessica and Lorenzo in love; the trial of Antonio is over; and there is a general expectancy of a tranquil and happy end to the events. The words compass the impressions of the scene and the feelings of the persons, reaching out with a gentle nostalgic idealism to thoughts of nobility and immortality, to knowledge and feelings that transcend life. Then, music having been played, it is made the subject of comment, and the scene culminates in the pointed linking of the power of music with gentleness of spirit and alienation from base or savage nature. Thus the colours of life are dimmed; the remnants of light, the sleeping moonlight and the patines of bright gold, are no more than pointers to something distant, obscure, and alluring, feeling is intensified, but at the same time refined, and the mind withdraws into a condition of desire at once intimate and strange.

This scene, with its theme of love, of the spirit of Orpheus, and its idealizing tendency, is an example of how an exquisite musical effect arises from the intricate interfusion of many elements of poetry, including an explicitly stated subject-matter. And it is especially interesting because music itself is part of that subject-matter. But it is also a metaphor, so subtle here is the play of ideas in the imagination. The poet focuses thought and feeling on music because music is a symbolic key to the situation. The scene is not musical merely because music is heard, nor because music is talked about, but because the mood is one that music expresses best and so all the images and thought—the dramatic scene, the persons, the words, the figures, the accompanying music—are assimilated to the spirit of music. By "spirit of music" we mean ultimately the power to resolve the discords of life in an ideal harmony.

This is an example of how the subject, explicit thoughts and declared feelings may influence musical values in poetry.

vii. PARTICULAR TENDENCIES OF THE NINETEENTH
CENTURY; ROMANTIC POETS AND THE MUSICAL
IDEAL; MALLARME

We have distinguished two approaches to a music within poetry. One is through acoustic features, verbal sound and rhythm, together with a tendency to avoid concrete or pictorial images and withdraw from visual reality into a kind of idealizing suggestiveness. The other is achieved mainly by an organization of symbol-images so as to secure a precise emotional reference. But here, too, we observe usually, at least where the effect is intense and concentrated, a withdrawal from the pictured world and from propositional statement. The images used may be of visual objects, but their meaning lies not in the reference to objects but in the emotional effects occasioned by them and their association in a particular passage. These two approaches, seemingly so different, appear to be fundamentally similar if we view them in the light of our principles of imagery and the metaphorical functioning of all art-images. For in both cases we observe the expressive formula-image brought into play, the auditory images being immediately parallel to the formula-images of music, and the symbol-images being examples of the visual or object image that is a formula-image by function.[2]

It is essential to pursue this subject a little further because, although all poetry, of whatever period, has some relationship with music, some romantic and symbolist poets of the nineteenth century affected a so-called "musical" ideal of particular cogency and virtue, so much so that for many decades the whole idea of the "poetic" was profoundly modified if not disturbed and restricted. The ideas involved have a certain general application but also, as we can now better see, a decided period significance. For this reason, and also because they are complex, I shall review them from a historical point of view. Moreover, we shall for the moment restrict ourselves to lyrical-musical types of poetry, leaving the question of a *dramatic-*musical type until later.

The determining influence in this development arises from certain well-marked and recurrent features in romantic poetry of the early nineteenth century : its pantheistic leanings, its philosophical idealism, its cult of the life of sensibility, feeling and inwardness, its interest in the irrational, with consequences both for good and evil, its transcendentalism, its search for spiritual ecstasies, for perfect Love and Beauty, in all of which there is an implied depreciation of the homely and real world, made of the familiar scenes and sentiments of nature and man, except in so far as these, endowed with an ennobling lustre, can be visioned as types of perfection. Through all the varieties of romanticism there is diffused a profound nostalgia for some kind of perfect consummation for the human soul, called variously God, the Absolute, the Infinite, the eternal oneness, supernal beauty, Heaven, the Ideal, Perfect Love, each of these names vibrating with echoes of the others. This sentiment of "something beyond", the ineffable perfection and ecstasy of which may only be apprehended in fleeting moments of anticipation, makes romantic poetry fluid, musical, and suggestive by contrast with the plastic visual qualities of the realistically or pictorially-minded author. The seeing eye yields to the listening soul, the sense of the particular and diverse to that of the enveloping spirit. Romantic poetry uses images to indicate, in mysterious and hieroglyphic fashion, Ideal Beauty (Novalis would say "Poesie") and the response to it. And indeed it may be said to be at its best when the force of the emotional impulse towards the ideal succeeds in creating an imagery which, distanced from the real and therefore in a way incredible, makes itself acceptable as the sign of a transcendent world and the desire for it. From the same source proceeds the reason why romantic poetry is not so much a constructed, completed thing, as for instance a renaissance sonnet, which takes its place in the world of created objects, with a willed shape and character, but rather a symbolism of initiation, or of inspiration, with the Aeolian harp as its appropriate emblem. Nowhere, not even in Shelley, is this aspect clearer than in Novalis, whose poetry and beliefs focus more strikingly than any other the quintessential nature of the romantic impulse. Such poetry, which caresses the infinite, may be continuous, or fragmentary, but never of finite or centralized shape. And not only is the distinction between verse and prose thus rendered insignificant, but one feels also that the language is not the poem, which is rather the condition itself of "inwardness", or of "otherness". It is the infinite desire to transcend, the leap to Heaven, the fleeting apprehension of paradise, the momentary benediction of mortal senses, and the enduring desire. "Poetry" is in fact a condition of soul; ideally speaking, it is the consummation itself, an attempt at the mystical; as a linguistic creation it is a token of the higher state.[3]

Music, also, is such a token and is used with the most urgent symbolic suggestiveness in this connexion. It was a favourite symbol of Novalis, though, significantly enough, he had only a superficial knowledge of music proper. His poet-hero Heinrich von Ofterdingen sums up the rapture and ultimate significance of his beloved and his love for her with the words: Sie wird mich in Musik auflösen; words which catch their meaning from the larger pattern of recurrent ideas and symbols in the poet's work, and the central clue to which is the sense of an ultimate realm of great spiritual consummations. With these affiliations the word, or idea, "music", undergoes a characteristic process of subtilization. Like other phenomena, or realities, it may offer a pretext for being taken as a symbol. Poe, for instance, enumerates 'a few of the simple elements which induce in the Poet himself the true poetical effect' :—

He recognizes the ambrosia which nourishes his soul, in the bright orbs that shine in Heaven—in the volutes of the flower —in the clustering of the low shrubberies—in the waving of the grainfields—in the slanting of tall, Eastern trees—in the blue distance of mountains—in the grouping of clouds—in the twinkling of half-hidden brooks—in the gleaming of silver rivers—in the repose of sequestered lakes—in the star-mirroring depths of lonely wells. He perceives it in the songs of birds—in the harp of Æolus—in the sighing of the night-wind

—in the repining voice of the forest—in the surf that complains to the shore—in the fresh breath of the woods—in the scent of the violet—in the voluptuous perfume of the hyacinth—in the suggestive odour that comes to him, at eventide, from far-distant, undiscovered islands, over dim oceans, illimitable and unexplored. He owns it in all noble thoughts—in all unworldly motives—in all holy impulses—in all chivalrous, generous and self-sacrificing deeds. He feels it in the beauty of woman.

(*The Poetic Principle*).

Just as some things are here selected, whilst all others are passed over, so music is selected by romantic poets as a symbol because of certain appropriate qualities; its withdrawal from plastic reality, its esoteric structure, its nostalgic suggestiveness, its emotional intensity. Definite compositions are not relevant; in fact, it is not so much music that Poe, or Novalis, or Verlaine, or any of their romantic colleagues, or symbolist admirers, have in mind at all, but an idea of music, an idea of a music transcending all music.

When things become symbols in this way they lose their identity in a new function. Music is caught up in the devices of romantic sensibility and made to contribute to its imagery of the ideal and the infinite. We observe at this point the limits of the romantic claim upon music. Music, as an orthodox continuing art, arising like all art from experience, is more extensive than romanticism, as the "music of poetry" must also be more extensive than any one romantic poet's conception of it, and than all romantic conceptions together. For it is not so much that nineteenth century romantics sought in music an ideal for poetry; they sought really an ideal of transcendence for each of the arts, none of which was content to remain within the finite limits of its proper identity. Poetry made a cult of musical effect; music sought an alliance with the world of poetic fancy, as we see in the programme music and literary motifs of Weber, Schumann, Chopin, Berlioz, Liszt and many others; painting took literary subjects or explored poetic mood in landscape; whilst in the work of Wagner, the great artistic idol of the mid and later nineteenth century, we find aesthetic promiscuity prosecuted on a grandiose scale in the confidently styled *Gesamtkunstwerk*. The ambiguous significance of music in all this was that it presented itself amongst the arts not necessarily as the *ideal* art but as the happiest symbol of *transcendency*, of the plain triumph of spirit over matter. In this ramification of sensibilities and ideas the four words ideal, romantic, poetic, musical, entered the close fraternity from which they have never quite escaped to this day. This does not mean that the romantics did not value the simpler musical qualities of verse, but only that these were associated with a larger symbolism as well.

In a poetry dominated by the cult of inwardness, and by the mystical or near-mystical sense of unseen life and powers, representational images give place to symbols, which, in romantic poetry, are important both philosophically and aesthetically. Moreover, the much discussed phenomenon of synaesthetic effects depends on the same process. It is not that the sensuous particular is capriciously negated; none of the sensuous features mentioned in the passage from Poe, quoted above, can be arbitrarily replaced. Yet they are all endowed with a second, and higher, meaning, to which their meaning as references to particular sensuous phenomena is subordinated. From such ambiguity it is but a step to the next stage where an object loses its literal reference entirely, or almost so, and is pure symbol of emotion. It was their pantheism, or whatever other sense of mystic Unity the romantics possessed, that made particular images of reality unimportant and opened the way for their use as counters or signs for something not themselves; and opened the way also, by a natural consequence, for the sense of "correspondences" or equivalences in symbolic function. After all, Baudelaire's famous lines only propose a theory of sensuous correspondences as part of a hymn to the mystic and infinite One:—

> La Nature est un temple où de vivants piliers
> Laissent parfois sortir de confuses paroles;
> L'homme y passe à travers des forêts de symboles
> Qui l'observent avec des regards familiers.
>
> Comme de longs échos qui de loin se confondent
> Dans une ténébreuse et profonde unité,
> Vaste comme la nuit et comme la clarté,
> Les parfums, les couleurs et les sons se répondent.

Every word and idea in these lines is a note or phrase in this hymn to the cosmic All.

These developments bring the liberation of the image, functioning metaphorically, from its illustrative place in picture or statement, and

give it independent constitution as an analogue of feeling; and the
style emerging as a result is one suited to the expression of feelings
or states of sensibility in which description of scene, or thoughts, are
no longer important as in eighteenth century poetry, and certainly
not the basic structure of the poem. The point appears with sufficient vividness in a remark of Mallarmé's, in whose work these tendencies are focused, epitomized, and systematized with a greater rigour and exclusiveness than in other poets. 'J'ai enfin commencé mon
Hérodiade. Avec terreur, car j'invente une langue qui doit nécessaire-
ment jaillir d'une poétique très nouvelle, que je pourrais définir en
ces deux mots : *Peindre, non la chose, mais l'effet qu'elle produit.*

'Le vers ne doit donc pas, là, se composer de mots, mais d'intentions et toutes les paroles s'effacer devant la sensation'. (Letter to
Cazalis, 1864). Another passage runs:—

'Décadente, Mystique, les Écoles se déclarant ou étiquetées en
hâte par notre presse d'information, adoptent, comme rencontre,
le point d'un Idéalisme qui (pareillement aux fugues, aux sonates)
refuse les matériaux naturels et, comme brutale, une pensée exacte
les ordonnant; pour ne garder de rien que la suggestion. Instituer
une relation entre les images exacte, et que s'en détache un tiers
aspect fusible et clair presenté à la divination. Abolie, la prétention,
esthétiquement une erreur, quoiqu'elle régit les chefs-d'œuvre,
d'inclure au papier subtil du volume autre chose que par exemple
l'horreur de la forêt, ou le tonnerre muet épars au feuillage: non
le bois intrinsèque et dense des arbres. Quelques jets de l'intime
orgueil véridiquement trompetés éveillent l'architecture du palais,
le seul habitable; hors de toute pierre, sur quoi les pages se
refermeraient mal.
'Les monuments, la mer, la face humaine, dans leur plénitude, natifs,
conservant une vertu autrement attrayante que ne les voilera une
description, évocation dites, *allusion* je sais, *suggestion*: cette ter-
minologie quelque peu de hasard atteste la tendance, une très
décisive, peut-être, qu'ait subie l'art littéraire, elle le borne et
l'exempte. Son sortilège, à lui, si ce n'est libérer, hors d'une
poignée de poussière ou réalité sans l'enclore, au livre, même
comme texte, la dispersion volatile soit l'esprit, qui n'a que faire
de rien outre la musicalité de tout'.

(*Divagations. Crise de Vers*, the second paragraph being
extracted from *La Musique et les Lettres*)

This indicates the decisive shift of interest from the representational effort to the responding sensibility, from the sense of the external object to the exploration of the reaction to it; in which process the responding sensibility becomes the active focus, the centering reality, whilst the signs and images of the external world become the occasion of sensation-patterns.

According to the principles of imagery elucidated in this essay such images are termed expressive formula-images by function, because their literal meaning yields to a functional metaphorical meaning. We can also bring synaesthetic effects under the same heading. For this tendency was a symptom that poetic expression, once become sensitive to the image as feeling-analogue, realized the logical consequence that images would re-group themselves on a new basis. They would detach themselves from their affiliations in the ordinary world of perception, to form new associations according to the kind of feeling they evoke, and this process would involve images formed from the various kinds of sense perception. In other words, synaesthetic effects are the discovery of cognate expressiveness in differing sensuous realms, given the aesthetic process whereby images are valid not by content but by their functioning as expressive formulas.

Thus the development of romantic, and post-romantic, poetry produced a double technique of imagery that was novel. On the one hand it required symbols, at once emotionally saturated and having esoteric implications, for its rarefied ecstasies and mystic apprehensions of a super-reality; and on the other it exploited an imagery to express its expanding ranges of feeling and also its own sensibility reacting to external objects and events, as something interesting and valuable in itself. These two aspects of imagery interfuse both in the same works and also as influences operating in various degrees and at various points in the poetic production of the second and third quarters of the nineteenth century.

In this process, a historical one, we observe the gradual refinement of the notion of a poem as a perfect analogue of feeling, the simplest contrast to which would be Dr. Johnson's ideal which still included "thoughts" and a moral substance. Clearly it is not a narrative, or dramatic, conception, nor one for a meditative or didactic form. It is a quintessential lyric form, which has the closest affinity with music because language, its conventional semantic extensively limited or modified, is made to function as pure imagery.

A particular significance of Mallarmé's poetry derives from its being an example of this poetic method applied with such rigour and system that every part of the texture, every sound, rhythm, and nuance of word and evocation, becomes an analogue of feeling, or sense, or intellectual quality. For the point of view of this chapter it shows the simultaneous use of the two musical approaches analysed above, that of auditory imagery and that of metaphorical obliquity. To the key observation quoted just now the following may be added:—

'Sa très rare originalité c'est, procédant de tout l'art musical de ces derniers temps, que le vers, aussi mobile et chantant qu'il peut l'être, ne perd rien de sa couleur ni de cette richesse de tons qui s'est un peu évaporée dans la subtile fluidité contemporaine. Les deux, vision et mélodie, se fondent en un charme indécis pour l'ouie et pour l'œil, qui me semble la poésie même . . . ' (1887, to Ernest Raynard).[4] These words illumine Mallarmé's conception of what makes poetry. Language as thought, as logic, as affirmation, as syntactical and grammatical nexus, loses its importance. 'Il faut toujours couper le commencement et la fin de ce qu'on écrit. Pas d'introduction, pas de finale.' This maxim of composition has no doubt a restricted meaning, but the principle it embodies, the reduction of logical explicitness, is Mallarmé's most precious belief and may be applied legitimately far beyond its initial scope; that is, not merely to the general design of a poem or passage, but to the whole linguistic pattern. Language suffers, from the point of view of its normal use, a fragmentation, to be reassembled with the utmost degree of freedom by the imagination, working towards an expressiveness that lies in the interaction of rhythm, verbal sound-conformations, and evoked images: 'vision et mélodie se fondent en un charme indécis pour l'ouie et pour l'œil':—

> Quelconque une solitude
> Sans le cygne ni le quai
> Mire sa désuétude
> Au regard que j'abdiquai
>
> Ici de la gloriole
> Haute à ne la pas toucher
> Dont maint ciel se bariole
> Avec les ors de coucher

Mais langoureusement longe
Comme de blanc linge ôté
Tel fugace oiseau si plonge
Exultatrice à côté

Dans l'onde toi devenue
Ta jubilation nue.

Poetry of such a kind is characterized by the avoidance of realistic representation and by systematic deletion of ordinary verbal meanings, in favour of a metaphorical tissue of sounds and images. One can look at it in two ways. Either language as communication is put into a crucible and refined to the point of poetry where it appears anarchic in relation to its ordinary character; or one can think of it as a correspondent or organically cognate expressiveness of sounds and image evocations which exist in the poetic imagination as something not linguistic, but intra-linguistic. This is 'le vers qui de plusieurs vocables refait un mot total . . .' (Œuvres Complètes, Pléiade edn., 1945, p. 858).

In connexion with Mallarmé's conception of poetry it would be idle to disregard the powerful sentiment of the Ideal driving him on to create something ineffably pure. He wrote to a friend: 'Mon Dieu, s'il en était autrement, si le Rêve était ainsi défloré et abaissé, où donc nous sauverions-nous, nous autres malheureux que la terre dégoûte et qui n'avons que le Rêve pour refuge? O mon Henri, abreuve-toi d'Idéal.' Much of the idealism of romanticism was impregnated with copious sentiment or emotion or love which kept it broadly and generously "human"; so that, to take only one example, we do not feel gross inconsistency between Shelley's metaphysical nostalgia and his social Utopianism. In Mallarmé, on the other hand, pessimism is more pronounced, and nihilism is casting its shadow before. But energy is not dissipated in the shows of despair. It is concentrated instead on the Ideal Poem. The romantic sentiment of the ideal, developed without orthodox belief but with religious fervour, suffers here a degree of intensification that converts it into a specialism. The poet renounces the world, renounces materialism in all its forms, and cultivates with a sacerdotal sense of dedication the most exquisite idea of inwardness, of spiritual ideality in opposition to the world; but this ideal is its own object. Mallarmé saves the sense of the Ideal by conceiving it as the ideality of the perfect poem, a spiritual nostalgia merging into an artistic ambition. The mystic quality of vision that in earlier poets, Traherne, or Vaughan, for example, makes poetry otherworldly he incorporates into the imaginative process. Thus, instead of allowing poetry a refulgence that comes from reflecting, imperfectly and fitfully, a transcendent and divine radiance, he works on the ambitious assumption that the imaginative creation, the poem, when perfect, can itself ignite the mystic flame.

The ineffable beauty, the ideal nature of the perfect poem, is thus intended to indicate an order of experience remote from reality. To this end language, which is a part of practical reality, is negated and reconstituted, undergoing self-transcendence. Mallarmé's remark, that poetry is made of words, is always quoted in connexion with his poetry, and in isolated quotation it always acquires a more absolute meaning than its original use in Mallarmé's conversation with Dégas warranted; for it was a simple retort to Dégas' comment that he had no "ideas" for poetry. The quotations given above point more accurately to Mallarmé's way of conceiving "words". For the whole meaning of Mallarmé's style lies in his challenge to language —words—in their ordinary prosaic reality, the stiff conventions of practical communication. A poem by Mallarmé is a system of auditory and visual evocations in which the merest residual element of propositional statement remains caught. Language is refined systematically towards imagery.[5]

The extraordinary significance of Mallarmé for poets and poetry lies in the degree to which he insisted on this conception of poetic language. It does not produce necessarily 'great poetic works'. The work of many great poets, and of the greatest, has elements that were eschewed by Mallarmé. Nor did he discover the true essence of the poetic for the first time; the Shakespeare poem referred to earlier in this chapter works with fundamentally similar aesthetic means. But Mallarmé's conception, applied as an exclusive method, does isolate in the most radical and spell-binding way an indispensable element of the poetic process in the medium of language. Deprived of all beliefs except that in poetry, imbued with a sense of the Ideal that had lost all object except its own necessity, Mallarmé devoted his imagination to expressing the pure functioning of the imagination—i.e. of images and their evocations in relation to a sensibility—in language. In all his poems one hears, beneath the primary voice, a second one announcing continuously the identity of this poetry, drawing attention to the perfect assimilation of language to the Poetic. The Poetic, in Mallarmé's inner sense, was not simply words, nor music, nor the audible music of words :

'Certainement, je ne m'assieds jamais aux gradins des concerts, sans percevoir parmi l'obscure sublimité telle ébauche de quelqu'un des poèmes immanents à l'humanité ou leur originel état, d'autant plus compréhensible que tu et que pour en déterminer la vaste ligne le compositeur éprouva cette facilité de suspendre jusqu'à la tentation de s'expliquer. Je me figure par un indéracinable sans doute préjugé d'écrivain, que rien ne demeurera sans être proféré; que nous en sommes là, précisément, à rechercher, devant une brisure des grands rythmes littéraires (il en a été question plus haut) et leur éparpillement en frissons articulés proches de l'instrumentation, un art d'achever la transposition, au Livre, de la symphonie ou uniment de reprendre notre bien: car, ce n'est pas de sonorités élémentaires par les cuivres, les cordes, les bois, indéniablement mais de l'intellectuelle parole à son apogée que doit avec plénitude et évidence, résulter, en tant que l'ensemble des rapports existant dans tout, la Musique.' (*Crise de Vers*).

Here is indicated the haunting image of a transcendent dream, hovering beyond both poetry and music in their ordinary forms. With his *préjugé d'écrivain* Mallarmé felt that the light of this image might be caught in a poetry made of *l'intellectuelle parole à son apogée* but impregnated with music. For the texture of such a poetry this means a wonderfully intricate mutual adjustment of its imagery, of its rhythms, sounds and evocations "orchestrated" around an initial motive, so as to create a poetic presence that is, paradoxically, both *in* the imagery and infinitely beyond it. Such a texture, or image-structure, borrows for the evocations of language the structure of music, achieving thereby a similar symbolic suggestiveness.

viii. DISTINCTIONS AND CONCLUSIONS

From all these observations about the imagery and symbolism of language and music it is apparent that poetry can approach the condition of music in more than one way, though it is difficult to establish precise definitions of "musical" effects since so many factors interact. But in this atmosphere we note how the unity of the arts asserts itself in spite of their differences. By virtue of a principle common to them all we can say of a poem: this is poetry, this is art, this is a kind of music; or of a piece of music, it is art, it is a kind of poetry; of a painting: this is a painting, it is art, it is poetic, or it is a symphony of colour; and so on. And indeed these analogies chase each other constantly in critical writing. The paradox of medium is laid bare; to the artist it is everything, and yet it is but an instrument of the imagination. All-important as the *condition* of imagery, it must never be taken literally. Art in every form is finally a kind of thought, and the seeming barriers of medium are seen to be unimportant amidst their importance. Such paradoxes are to be accepted, not explained away.

Another factor always to be taken into account is the nature of what we have called "intertexture", which, as we saw, means that the effect is always in the complexity and not in separate elements. Rhythm, for example, is not, in the poem itself, a separate imagery but is merged into the words and their evocations. This principle of complexity applies in multifarious directions and clearly influences the "musical" quality of any given poem in a number of ways.

Summarizing our conclusions on the topic of music and poetry, we can single out in particular four distinct conceptions: (1) a poem, (2) a musical poem, (3) a particular symbolism of music in the romantic and symbolist phase of poetry, and finally, (4) a general idea of "the poetic" which need not be tied to verse.

By "poem" I want in this context to indicate a norm, however theoretical, against which certain poems may be judged to be especially "musical". This norm would cover narrative and dramatic poetry, and meditative, philosophical, or didactic poetry. In all such poetry there is, as we said above, a "music of poetry", by which we mean that some aspects of poetic language and its evocations almost always show affinities with the processes and effects of music, but not a particular and deliberate musicalization. The degree of such implicit musicality varies extensively, and above all it varies within the composition; and in the present context, of course, we conceive it as a non-dominant factor. To illustrate this "norm" of poetry, take Shakespeare's sonnet 113 and compare it with the Spenser sonnet quoted earlier. They are both on the same theme.

> Since I left you, mine eye is in my mind;
> And that which governs me to go about
> Doth part his function and is partly blind,

Seems seeing, but effectually is out;
For it no form delivers to the heart
Of bird, of flow'r, or shape, which it doth latch ;
Of his quick objects hath the mind no part,
Nor his own vision holds what it doth catch;
For if it see the rud'st or gentlest sight,
The most sweet favour or deformed'st creature,
The mountain or the sea, the day or night,
The crow or dove, it shapes them to your feature.
 Incapable of more, replete with you,
 My most true mind thus mak'th mine eye untrue.

No essential poetic quality is lacking in this sonnet. Moreover, its emotion flows powerfully, and the style cannot be said in any way to be austere, or rugged, or harsh, or otherwise opposed to lyrical smoothness. But its "music" is of the subdued or underlying type and not the dominant musical effusion of Spenser. In the same way the following poem of Hölderlin, though saturated with feeling, is not of the special musical type:—

Mit gelben Birnen hänget
Und voll mit wilden Rosen
Das Land in den See,
Ihr holden Schwäne,
Und trunken von Küssen
Tunkt ihr das Haupt
Ins heilignüchterne Wasser.

Weh mir, wo nehm' ich, wenn
Es Winter ist, die Blumen, und wo
Den Sonnenschein
Und Schatten der Erde?
Die Mauern stehn
Sprachlos und kalt, im Winde
Klirren die Fahnen.
   (Hälfte des Lebens)

The second category shows within the framework of poetry generally certain kinds of lyrical-musical intensification of which we have given examples. The analyses have demonstrated various sources for this which it is not necessary to recapitulate.

The third conception emerging from the preceding examination is that the relation between poetry and music in much romantic poetry and thought has peculiar features of its own. The same general processes are to some extent involved but in addition the romantic outlook is influenced by a particular kind of musical symbolism for which the ordinary realities of, and distinctions between, the arts were of little significance. When invoking music the romantics had in mind a music that was poeticised. They meant one that expressed the themes they themselves were putting into poetry. Hence the relations between music and poetry here imply a unity of particular style resting on a common spiritual complexion. They sought the musical phrase in language in order to express their subtleties of feeling. Music, on the other hand, sought the "romantic", or romantically poetic, subject. Its "programmes", the *Wald-* and *Kinderszenen*, the *Frühlingssymphonien*, the Oberons and Faust symphonies, the ballads and nocturnes, were not simply literary subjects, but particular kinds of them, romantic kinds. This period style makes it dangerous to generalize about music and poetry on the basis of romantic poetry alone. On the other hand it confirms amply the theory of music advanced in this essay, namely that, like all other arts, it is closely linked with experience, and therefore with historical circumstances and period sensibility.

The fourth conception is that of a quality, "the poetic", which is not necessarily a feature of verse compositions alone but recognizable in various forms. Usually, work that evokes this epithet has features that suggest one or more of the romantic themes, the world of dream, of childhood and innocence, of nature, of love and the ideal. Thus we use it of the paintings of Christopher Wood or Stanley Spencer, of the late plays of Ibsen and those of Chekhov, of the novels of Hardy and Virginia Woolf, all post-romantic artists, as it was used of the music of Schumann and Chopin and Berlioz. But I think the epithet now carries another meaning. For the romantic writers, as we have seen, concentrated on the independent poetic potency of every image that is an analogue of feeling, converting all the sights and sounds of nature into a notation of signs for their inner sense, using language and its suggestiveness to the same purpose, and exploiting the synaesthetic correspondences. This left a heritage for poetic expression, whether on romantic themes, or on others. Romanticism created the prose poem and paved the way for *vers libre*, both of these being aspects of the same discovery, that poetry lies in the expressive power of the metaphorically functioning image, the rhythm and sound of *verse* being only one such imagery amongst others.

Mallarmé and his symbolist disciples, working to the same essential principle of metaphor via linguistic images, produced a specialized form of lyric that was restrictive on poetry. Its very power, concentration, and consistency made it so, for it sought a quintessence of poetic form which in its turn suggested that all other ideals of expression were inferior. So long as this ideal dominated European poetry, as it did for decades, narrative and dramatic poetry, satire and didactic forms, languished under a cloud. But the principle of a poetic imagery outside verse set free an immense compensating force, so that drama and narrative especially, working with the imagery of dream, myth, and allegory, with a finer exploration of compositional rhythms and forms, and with the constant sense of the potential symbolism of apparently realistic surfaces, and of the saturation of images from life with individual feeling, were to recover some at least of the metaphorical and poetic power they lose when deprived of verse.

What limits, we may finally ask, are set to the music of poetry? The terms of Pater's passage, quoted at the beginning of this chapter, lack the sharpness, not to say "scientific" discrimination, of later aesthetic criticism. Yet in the language of his age, and inspired by its enveloping poetic ideal, he defined a central feature of art, and this inspiration came to him in writing of a painter, Giorgione, of great lyrical power and musical suggestiveness. But since his dictum is often misquoted, it is worth noting that he did not say that all art aspires *to be* music, but simply to the *condition*, or "principle", of music, 'music being the typical, or ideally consummate art', because it obliterates the opposition of content and form. It is true that in the course of the essay he almost forgets the subtle distinction implicit in his phrasing, to fall temporarily into the error of making high musicality the first criterion of art. This error must certainly be avoided in connexion with poetry, whose richness would suffer were it to acknowledge only the lyrical-musical ideal. Coleridge's formulation, though not worked out, does cite the musical sweetness as one quality in a compound, and the ambiguity of his terms leaves his definitions closer to the heart of poetry as a linguistic medium. And, indeed, in an art of words a peculiar power must still reside in logical meanings. As we said in an earlier chapter all the uses of words are available to poetry, and to reject any of them is to impoverish the medium at your disposal. Direct statement is one use of language, metaphorical implication another, and they intertwine to the advantage of expression. Every poem, and poetry generally, moves between the poles of music and plain statement; tempted in each direction, it knows that neither is its only or true goal. If it becomes too musical it is at variance with one main function of language and thus the medium is at war with itself. It falls consequently into a weak position compared with music, the great power of which derives from its perfect self-consistency. It is a complete notation, a language with an ordered syntax, a perfect co-ordination between its signs, an impeccable grammar of their relations and their metaphorical function. Apart from the natural origins of music in singing, this power is based on a consistent elaboration in history of the medium as something esoteric, for which reason we now have the esoteric experience by which to judge its products. Poetry, linked inseparably with logical language, has never achieved an esoteric self-consistency of this kind and is not likely to. Beyond a certain limit all attempts at extreme and exclusive musicalization will fail for lack of a perfected grammar or harmonic theory of the system. There is no certain means of knowing the "meanings" involved, or of knowing whether there are any at all, much less of achieving a judgement, and the general uses of language would always prevent such developments. Some degree of music is essential in poetry, too great a degree inimical to its own possibilities. Its ideal is not another art but its own kind of inter-texture, which blends meditative statement with the imagery of feeling and sense.

CHAPTER TEN

THE ART OF DRAMA

i. DRAMA AND THE THEORY OF IMAGERY

EVERY ASPECT OF ART touched upon in these chapters may be illustrated from the form of drama. It is an art; it is imagery for eye and ear and mind; it shows a characteristic intertexture. There are in it elements of representation and of expression. It incorporates the visual images of scene and persons, it uses words in dialogue, which may however include many uses of speech, emotive, analytic, declamatory, exclamatory, rhetorical, descriptive, lyrical, musical, and so on. It may express moods, emotions, subjective conflicts. It springs from experience and reflects it; it is clearly and intensely a re-enactment. And finally, it resembles all other forms in that it exploits many kinds of imagery and expressive tones whilst maintaining its typical character. As a branch of art it is an interpretation of experience by means of images and words in which the representational and the expressive intermingle and in which, indeed, the law of functional assimilation holds in respect of all the kinds of image used.

In the following chapters we shall reconsider some major problems of dramatic form in the light of our theory of images and image-intertextures.

ii. VARIETY OF DRAMATIC FORMS

The question: what is drama? admits of two answers, one historical and complicated, the other theoretical and by comparison simple, and each complementary to the other. Drama is all drama as we know it in a multitude of historical examples; and it is also a type of

157

art, the concept of which we construct by generalizing from recurrent features.

The first meaning is complicated because so many varieties of the form have existed, each with a different significance and function in extremely diverse cultures and in more recent times showing increased elements of personal idiosyncrasy as against drama based firmly, like religious plays, on communal cults or beliefs. Greek tragedy and comedy, the mysteries and moralities of the medieval Church, Elizabethan drama, French classical plays, the comedy of manners, the *commedia dell' arte*, *comédie larmoyante*, Ibsen, Claudel, expressionists, romantic and symbolist plays, to mention only a few types, have each an original way of associating dramatic form with a view of life held by a society or an individual, and from them we learn forcibly that "drama" has been many things to many people. It can be the handmaiden of a creed, a simple but moving story, an analysis of character, a portrayal of manners, a declaration of subjective feeling, a vehicle of the acquisition or loss of faith, a fairy-tale or fantasy, a "proverb", a history, an allegory; every drama is either a common type, that is, one of the predominant historical kinds, or, drawing on several of the features associated with drama, it is a mixture.

The second, theoretical, answer to the question about what drama is appears simple by comparison because it is easy to enumerate a set of characteristics necessary to the form. There must be an action; that is, events and situations must be presented with accompanying tension, sudden changes and a climax. Persons must be portrayed with sympathy and truth. The conception must embrace possibilities for the actor's art. And there must be some central meaning, whether religious, moral, emotional or psychological, which strikes home to the spectator's head and heart. These ingredients, present in the simplest and most intricate, the most ritualistic and the most sophisticated, the most tragic and most comic, drama, arise from the aesthetic conditions of the art. Starting from the fact that a play— life depicted by acting—gives pleasure, it is natural to seek those actions that are best for the purpose; they are the tense and exciting ones that keep the spectator interested. From this initial simple condition everything else flows; the art of subtle dramatic construction, of portraying persons to the life, and of drawing on every means of intensifying the expression. But let us not anticipate a more detailed treatment; it is only necessary here to indicate in the briefest and most general terms what drama is, reserving more precise analysis for the following sections. It is moreover appropriate, before embarking on the oretic statements about aspects and types of drama, to tabulate the many possible sources of pleasure in plays. We enjoy the story, the character-drawing, taking a sympathetic interest in the fortunes and misfortunes of the persons, their problems and feelings. We enjoy the unfolding of an idea in dramatic situations and the release of feeling that it occasions. We take pleasure in the skill of the dramatist, in his construction, his sense of the theatre, the opportunities he gives his actors. Another source of delight derives from the style and language, whether prose or verse, the eloquence, poetry, wit, epigram, rhetoric, the sentiments and ideas expressed *en passant* or as the immediate product of the situations. And finally we enjoy the décor, the production, the acting, and the personalities of actors and actresses which are inseparable from their art. This immensely rich and varied arsenal of delights lures us perennially to the theatre and it is a poor play indeed that does not offer one or the other. Some of them constitute a snare, as purists always point out, since the superficial sensuous attractions of décor and acting may degenerate into gratuitous and vulgar spectacle. On the other hand the harmonious use of such varied means of expression can secure effects so intense and moving that they bestow a particular aura on the form.

In the following pages of analysis and definition we shall try not to forget this simple view of the pleasures of going to the play.

iii. THE IDEA OF "THE DRAMATIC"

Our notion of the dramatic derives in the first place from exciting things observed in nature and human life, but it has been refined by the art of drama itself, with the result that life and the art form are inextricably intertwined in the idea. The word "dramatic" has a natural meaning in relation to any events of a sudden, surprising, disturbing, and violent kind, or to situations and sequences of events characterized by tension. Thunderstorms, high seas and floods, animals pursuing and killing their prey, are dramas of nature. Accidents, sudden death, battles, rescues, crimes, quarrels, politics, adventures, failures, triumphs, constitute the natural dramas of human destiny, winning a place in the columns of the daily news-papers. It is usual to denigrate these as sensational but they are a touchstone for what strikes men and arrests their interest, and it was no accident that Ibsen pored daily over his newspaper. It is commonly held that conflict makes drama, but surprise, and particularly tension, are the truer symptoms. They both arise from conflict, of course, but not always, and conflict is only dramatic when they do. A cricket match involves a conflict, yet with most variable tension, as foreign spectators are apt to observe; it is only a dramatic conflict at particular moments when the pace increases and puts the game in the balance. On the other hand what is more dramatic than a train moving at speed towards a broken viaduct? Yet there is only tense expectation here, no conflict.

When the imagery of art incorporates such features we ascribe to it "dramatic" quality, and clearly this process is not confined to drama and theatre alone. The baroque style in architecture, the sculptures of Michelangelo, the paintings of Delacroix and Picasso, offer examples of the dramatic in the plastic arts, whilst many features of music—rhythms, change of tonality, tempi, in fact all its "dynamics"—and of ballet, which approaches close to drama, come under the same head. Sonata form is commonly looked upon as a structure of dramatic quality. Masks, although fixed in a single immobile expression, are charged with dramatic effect.

In drama proper the basic formula is that persons make decisions and act on them, which has consequences involving other persons, and complications and crisis follow. Some events and actions have always occurred before the start; the beginning of a play implies that a certain situation exists between a group of people, the play showing the further evolution. In other words a past and a future are always implicit in the opening scenes. And indeed this may be said of any subsequent moment in the course of the play; it constitutes the essential feature of a *plot* in which all hangs together in tense relationship for a short space of time. When we speak of dramatic situations we mean such as spring from cross-related human characters and their circumstances, and in which destiny and fatality inhere. One of the distinctive and most powerful effects of drama, as against the narrative or the film, is to show a *group* of people, present simultaneously on the stage, held together in this way by the embrace of fate. The events and actions and cross-currents of human living are then felt, one might even say "seen", as presences amidst the group.

The Greek drama established very early this general pattern, though according to Aristotle (*Poetics*, III, 1) the name itself appears originally to have meant simply that kind of poetry which "imitated" by representing the characters as real and employed in the action itself. Obviously characters and actions not exciting or tense may be represented in this way, so that if drama had done no more it would never have become "dramatic". Hence the importance of exciting complications and crisis. The form of enactment requires, in order to be successful by nature, and hold the emotions of spectators, a concentration of effects, which is derived from the increased tempo of events, from involved situations, and from the gravity of the issues at stake in the action represented. The non-literary drama of entertainment (comedy-thriller, for example) cultivates only the external excitements. The literary drama derives its excitements from serious subject-matter.

The practice of the great dramatists has followed these natural requirements of the form of representation. They have always cultivated the good "plot". Some, like Sophocles and Racine, have been more skilful than others; none have denied its importance. And they have learnt from the suggestions of life itself what a good plot is. In other words, they exploit for dramatic art the dramatic imagery generated by life.

Thus it comes about that our notion of "the dramatic" is influenced constantly by the interplay of the two ideas of drama in life and the cultivated dramatic quality of art. And as the word assumes a technical meaning in connexion with the drama it suggests the possibility of concentrating various modes of the dramatic. In this way a stylization occurs which involves a *sustained* complication and intensity not in fact usually found in real life. When we judge a play not dramatic enough we mean that it falls short of this stylization.

Many things, functioning sometimes alone and sometimes together, can be dramatic about a play; the action, if complicated or tense or impetuous; the speeches, revealing personal dilemma and confusion and a range of emotions and passions explosive or tempestuous; surprises of every category, such as confrontations, discoveries, confessions, turns of thought and situation; rhythms of various kinds, the modulations of which, apprehended in the anguage and the developing action, are amongst the most powerful dramatic elements; the dialectic of ideas, scenes and situations. No play uses all forms of the dramatic all the time but it will use them

sufficiently to establish the feeling that the dramatic is predominant. Even so "a drama" is any variation of dramatic form that lies
within two limits, the one being the greatest concentration con-
ceivable, the other the point at which the dramatic is altogether
negated. Racine and Ibsen are near to the one, Chekhov sometimes
near to the other, limit.

None of these features should be taken, however, in an external
or superficial sense. In good drama the sensuous appearances are all
related to meanings, to thought, beliefs, philosophies, religious
feelings, moral judgements. Indeed it must be categorically stated
that the intensest dramatic quality will be realized where the most
vital meanings are involved. This can be illustrated even from non-
literary drama. Melodrama depends, with all its falsities, on the
actuality in the audience's minds of the conflict between "virtue"
and "vice" as embodied in the stock hero and villain. It flourished in
England particularly in Victorian times when the sense of this conflict was acute. The thriller, playing on the whole gamut of nervous
shock, relies by implication on a moral sense of horror at murder.
The "fatalistic" drama of the early nineteenth century (in Germany
especially), mechanical in its use of theatrical clichés, and devoid of
poetic quality, rested nevertheless on an appeal to the genuine sense
of fatality and the supernatural. These examples show sufficiently
that the images of drama, all the vivid sensuous experience that is
thrust upon the spectators from the illuminated stage or arena, the
persuasive illusion of violent and catastrophic action, are impregnated with human thought and judgements. In such cases the latter
are stereotyped or conventional, since the writer of a thriller does
not reveal anything new about human nature. But they are present,
incorporated in the raw material of the story. They may in fact be
called agents of the form because they release the dramatic element.

The sense of meaning is important however for action itself, the
element so universally invoked as indispensable in drama. In the
"action" of a play people are expected to "do things" and thus
create a concatenation of actions, situations, and events. We perform
daily innumerable actions that are not in the least dramatic since they
belong to a peaceful routine. But when actions are fraught with
consequences, they become dramatic. 'To be fraught with consequences' is a phrase we can only use in relation to the meaning of
an action and its possible effects. Into that enter all the beliefs and
principles by which we live and all our general interpretations of

experience. The peculiar prestige of "action" for the drama is not simply the result of the material sense of something happening, or people creating a commotion, but it derives from the general sense of fate and fatality in actions that have important consequences. "Destiny" has always been a well-worked topic in discussing drama; and no wonder, for they are by nature linked. There is, it is true, an undramatic form of destiny, as when we say of a man that 'it was his destiny to live a long and uneventful life in the village of his birth'. On the other hand destiny emerges often as an almost tangible presence, with the force of a personality, from the inter-action of events and people ; and where this interaction appears most striking, where man seems to be the plaything of forces quite beyond his control, the notion of destiny becomes most pregnant. A situation in which a man is subject to reversal of fortune, or unprecedented success, or persecution, and so on, shows destiny in command, generating drama.

Just as actions are dramatic by the fatality in them, so, too, tragedy is highly dramatic because its meanings are complex, profound, and sublime, involving our sense of divine purpose, of order and justice in the universe and in human life, and our beliefs in good and evil. The moments in the course of a play when these meanings are clari-fied are always of great emotional intensity. For this reason, no doubt, tragedy has by tradition been especially associated with the dramatic form, whilst tragic elements in another literary form, as for example the novel, almost always induce dramatic quality.

In a similar way the dramatic force of ritual depends entirely on the meanings involved. Rites belong to religion from which they derive all their mystery and significance; they are intense and dramatic because they pertain to gods. Emotions are keyed up in their performance because of this sense of significance, and the formalization of ritual is a fixing of the ceremonial pattern found most adequate to evoke the highest emotional response to the religious meanings invoked.[1] The same principle applies to trials and arraignments which are dramatic in life and have in consequence always been a stock device of the theatre ; trial scenes always warm up plays. It is not merely that they represent an obvious example of "conflict"; the conflict in any particular instance is heightened and the suspense raised because of all the meanings associated with law, with right and wrong, crime and punishment, because the fate of a person depends on the issue, and because justice is re-affirmed or contaminated by the judgement. One might also mention a situation like a royal abdication. This is dramatic, as Shakespeare knew, because of the institution of kingship and all that it implies in a religious, political, and social sense. When a king abdicates kingship itself is in question and is seen to be.

From these examples it may be concluded that to define drama simply as "action" or "conflict", as so often happens, is to rely too much on a narrow abstraction. Physical incident and conflict provide something dramatic, it is true; but the dramatic quality of any moment or situation in a play is directly commensurate with all the meanings involved. These include of course the "conflict" of ideas or beliefs as represented in the persons of the play, but extend also to all the meanings operative in a given social context. Human situations only stand out in relief against such a background of spiritual and social meanings, as we immediately apprehend in the subjects and plots of Elizabethan plays, or, equally strikingly, in Ibsen's plays, with their later nineteenth century period atmosphere.

The force of this point about meaning in drama may be gathered from the effect created by over-statement. Meaning very deliberately pointed produces the effect we call theatrical. What constitutes legitimate emphasis, and what impairs the quality of this by exaggeration, provides a nice problem of balance. All the best drama carries with it a sense of the scene being set, which in itself adds an emphasis to the drama that is to come, pointing deliberately to its meaning. Sometimes this is implicit in the exposition, as in the opening scenes of *Hamlet*, or *Macbeth*, or *Antony and Cleopatra*, where secondary characters both help to initiate the action and also, being secondary, are a preliminary audience wondering at events and scanning them for their significance. But sometimes a dramatist sets his scene with still greater deliberation. An eminent example is the opening of Hofmannsthal's *The Great World Theatre*, where God distributes parts to souls about to enter life. Here the image of the "theatre of life", embodying the quality of the theatrical, is itself used to lend force to the scene. It sets the tone, grandiose and solemn, warning the spectators that something is to be enacted, and with significance, something full of consequence. A play is beginning, its meaning hidden at first but progressively to be revealed. The sense of the dramatic and theatrical radiates from this image, by means of which the poet determines his aim, and doubles his effect.[2]

Wagner, constantly singled out for praise—sometimes a little ambiguous—by Nietzsche and Thomas Mann as a genius with the deepest theatrical instincts, was a master of the "magic" that emanates from an elaborately pointed scene. One of the best examples is Act III, scene 5, of *The Mastersingers*, which leads from the homage to Sachs to the contest between the singers, the foreseen but demonstrative victory of Walter, and then, at the very crest of the huge and wonderful theatrical build-up, the exaltation of *deutsche Ehre* and *deutsche Kunst*. All the power of music, here incorporated in the theatrical texture, is lavished on the expression of the expectation and *Ergriffenheit* of the crowd, on meaningful ceremony and the triumph of an idea. The great scenes of Wagner's operas are all "staged" in this way; they all have a meaning which is not only shown in an action and in characters, but is exhibited with grandiose stress in the whole apparatus of theatrical and musical imagery. Wagner's *Leitmotive* were a device to help this purpose and they fit aptly into the scheme. They are a set of pointers with which Wagner constantly and solemnly draws attention to the central meanings of his fable or myth. They share in the ambiguity of the theatrical quality in that they are sometimes sounded with beautiful discretion and suggestiveness, and sometimes appear blatant. Thus they strike one now as a wonderful invention, and now as a device so obvious as to be rather childish. But all these features of Wagner make him a superb example for the specific quality of the theatrical, the essence of which is dramatic meaning set in relief, over-stated, deliberately exhibited, and washed round with feeling, excitement, awe, and exaltation.

This theatrical quality, in its purest forms, strengthens the fabric of drama, and in its debased forms impairs it. On the one hand it heightens the sense of the dramatic image, stirs the spectators to excited participation, and thus enhances the enactment of a play in its social liaison. The *scène-à-faire*, the 'big scene', the 'great aria' in opera, Ibsen's framed discussion scenes, as well as the incorporation of trial scenes, arraignments, and ceremonies, "naturally" dramatic scenes with crowd effects, constituting plays within plays, theatre within theatre—all these show the subtle interweaving of dramatic and theatrical, the legitimate conjuring up of the sense of dramatic import in the audience, a positive theatrical enhancement. Brecht's technique of distancing (*Verfremdungseffekt*) derives also from this process of making one conscious of the theatrical *image*, though his method is rather crude. On the other hand this process can be so mismanaged that the mark is overshot. Instead of heightened and more impressive effect we get artificiality, affectation, and exaggeration; there is either too much emphasis of meaning or a large effort at emphasis on a non-existent meaning. Many works of the baroque style in sculpture and architecture, with their ample and agitated gestures and forms, stand uncertainly on the narrow frontier between the positive dramatic and the negative theatrical. The histrionic, we should note at this point, is the personal form of the phenomenon, the theatrical quality bursting out of the individual. The last degradation is the resort to the cheap tricks that show the hollow shells of the dramatic-theatrical, as when, to take simple and obvious examples, an author makes easy points with actors, or better still actresses, and their histrionic behaviour, amongst his *dramatis personae*, or introduces too often inset scenes of acting and mimicry. This is relying on effects, mere empty forms, on the theatrical not as an over-emphasis on meaning but emptied of meaning. It is a weakness Anouilh is prone to.

Opera in general, apart from what has been said about Wagner, presents a curious footnote to this problem. It is notoriously productive of theatrical effects, so much so that "operatic" is sometimes used as a disparaging synonym for theatrical. There is no doubt that this arises from the feature of over-emphasis here referred to. But it is inherent in the texture of opera. The musical structure changes the dramatic and, above all, the character of the acting, which has to be much more conventionalized or stylized. This produces inevitably the effect of over-emphasis in gesture. Wagner's genius turned this weakness into a measure of triumph because his mythical and heroic subjects were well served by an enhanced style of gesture.

iv. SPEECH AND DIALOGUE OF DRAMA

After the general observations of preceding sections one might expect now, following conventional precedents going back to Aristotle, a discussion of plot and action. But the argument of this essay calls first for a statement about the *characteristic imagery* and *intertexture* of drama, the sensuous terms that give it its distinctive character as an art. Hence we shall consider next speech, impersonation, and gesture as the chief focus of dramatic form, leaving plot till later.

Drama, as one of the arts of theatre, is a composite form, because it presses more than one "medium" into its service. The dramatist, actor, producer, stage-designer, and others each contribute something; and even if an austere taste or rule would eliminate the producer and his team as of secondary significance, one is still left with an inescapable union of dialogue and acting, an enactment and an impersonation, which places drama somewhere between the literary arts and the arts of mime and dancing. In a drama actors play and speak parts in a localized setting. Even the most cosmic or mythical settings, of Aeschylus, or baroque allegory, or the Faust plays, are localized, and supernatural beings appear anthropomorphic. And this acting and speech, or action and dialogue, present themselves not simply as a harmonizing of different media, or adjustment of two separate things to each other, but as a complex imagery of art based on a complex imagery of nature. For speech and correlated gesture form a natural intertexture of imagery; their association is not fortuitous but essential and organic.

Speech takes many forms, since it exists wherever words are used for communication or expression, and every kind of speech is accompanied by some degree of gesture, either in the changing expression of the face, or in gesticulation, or even movements of the limbs and body. Thus our idea of an academic lecture, or a speech at a conference of industrialists, or an oration in Parliament, or a sermon, or a harangue by a mob orator, or an informal talk by an instructor, or the speech of conversation, is determined always by two things. On the one hand there is a voice which conveys meanings and all kinds of supporting emotion in its own inflexions ; and on the other hand it finds a natural and correlated accompaniment in physical gesture. Each of the above types of speech shows a different style of physical behaviour. This applies *a fortiori* to excited kinds of speech which we use in giving way to emotion and passion. Physical actions, including facial expression, of varying violence accompany the words uttered, both together making up a total expression of our state of feeling. Not the words only, not the gestures only, but both together show how angry, or joyous, or ill-tempered, or aggressive we are at a particular moment. This intimate alliance between two natural modes of expression, acknowledged in manuals of acting from Elizabethan times onwards, is the basis of drama, which, as we said above, represents persons in a relation of crisis to each other. The sort of language that is spoken in the course of such a relation, uttered under the influence of all varieties of feeling, emotion, passion, and will-power, and in consequence a language that is always part of a physical-mental excitement, is the characteristic speech of drama. It is the agent of the action, the plot, the tensions. It is an activated language, implying constant movement, development, and changes in the feeling and the relations of persons. It is a language that makes explicit both the external action and the driving motives. Dramatic speech is thus the complete and adequate realization in dialogue of a tense situation between people. Expressing the matter in terms of the principles of imagery we may define it as an image-intertexture of co-ordinated speech and gesture (acting) which makes apparent in sensuous terms a vision of life and human behaviour. In dramatic art this complexity is, like all art, a construction or creation, in the sense that the dramatist constructs a system of speech and acting to express a particular conception; but it is based on a natural complex imagery, as we said above.

For examples of this characteristic speech it is only necessary to recall the openings of plays by Shakespeare and Racine. It is remarkable how consistently and with what certainty they establish from the start the sense of momentous situation. Every word spoken is already a participation in events and at the same time big with prophecy. Think of the curtain rising on the pack of mutinous Roman citizens who within a few seconds have declared Coriolanus chief enemy of the people and called for his death. Lear speaks straight off words which compass with terrible irony the action that follows:—

> Meantime we shall express our darker purpose.
> Give me the map there. Know we have divided
> In three our kingdom: and 'tis our fast intent
> To shake all cares and business from our age,
> Conferring them on younger strengths, while we
> Unburthen'd crawl toward death.

We remember the intricate and excited first speeches of Iago, bristling with all the main traits of his character, hatred, cynicism, ambition, greed, and dissimulation as the instrument of his perverted self-assertion—Iago telling of his new post with Othello and inciting Roderigo to help him to begin to stir up trouble with Brabantio on account of Othello and Desdemona. *Antony and*

Cleopatra opens with words of Philo in which his indignation forces
from him a vivid description of Antony's situation. In this speech
the violence of the feeling is paralleled by a force of expression that
reaches towards hyperbole but remains nevertheless simply and
extraordinarily precise. A situation of tragic dimension is indicated,
a reaction expressed, and with that the drama has already started.
As Philo speaks Antony and Cleopatra enter and we are given a
view of the sublime "dotage" of Antony, whilst immediately afterwards comes "news from Rome". Racine, with a quite different
style, is nevertheless comparable in mastery of dramatic speech at
the opening of a play. We remember how *Britannicus* begins:—

ALBINE:
    Quoi! tandis que Néron s'abandonne au sommeil,
    Faut-il que vous veniez attendre son réveil?
    Qu'errant dans le palais, sans suite et sans escorte,
    La mère de César veille seule à sa porte?
    Madame, retournez dans votre appartement.

AGRIPPINE:
    Albine, il ne faut pas s'éloigner un moment.
    Je veux l'attendre ici: les chagrins qu'il me cause
    M'occuperont assez tout le temps qu'il repose.
    Tout ce que j'ai prédit n'est que trop assuré:
    Contre Britannicus Néron s'est déclaré.

It would be tedious to quote further examples, though we should
mention that they may be found in the modern prose drama of
Ibsen, Sartre, Cocteau and others, no less than in Shakespeare and
Racine, and indeed my reason for quoting so many already, and
moreover from the beginnings of plays, is to emphasize the singu-
larity of this kind of speech and the way in which the great dramatists find the note at the outset. For plays are not simply dialogue or
conversation with actions and tense events added or interspersed.
They are something more athletic and compact. They seize upon
situations of conflict and dilemma as they are focused, or may be, in
the form of speech-plus-gesture.

Faulty dramatic speech is well illustrated in Byron's works; we
will take an example from *Manfred*. We remember, of course, that
the poet himself described his work as 'a kind of Poem in dialogue

(in blank verse) or Drama' but boasted that he had 'rendered it *quite impossible* [sic] for the stage, for which my intercourse with Drury Lane has given me the greatest contempt' (Letter to Murray, 15th February, 1817). But Byron is referring no doubt to the flights of fancy in the setting of the poem, as for instance 'The Hall of Arimanes—Arimanes on his Throne, a globe of Fire, surrounded by the Spirits'; and such things do not exclude dramatic quality, though they make a play difficult to produce. There is in *Manfred* a good deal of acceptable dramatic surprise and effect. A Gothic gallery at midnight, with a magician conjuring spirits, is not an unpromising beginning for a play. It is also true that a private emotional drama is going on in Manfred himself. Nevertheless the dramatic is not established as the unmistakable type of form. This may be seen in Manfred's mode of speech:—

> The spirits I have raised abandon me—
> The spells which I have studied baffle me—
> The remedy I reck'd of tortured me;
> I lean no more on superhuman aid,
> It hath no power upon the past, and for
> The future, till the past be gulf'd in darkness,
> It is not of my search.—My mother Earth!
> And thou fresh breaking Day, and you, ye Mountains,
> Why are ye beautiful? I cannot love ye.
> And thou, the bright eye of the universe,
> That openest over all, and unto all
> Art a delight—thou shin'st not on my heart.
> And you, ye crags, upon whose extreme edge
> I stand, and on the torrent's brink beneath
> Behold the tall pines dwindled as to shrubs
> In dizziness of distance; when a leap,
> A stir, a motion, even a breath, would bring
> My breast upon its rocky bosom's bed
> To rest for ever—wherefore do I pause?
> I feel the impulse—yet I do not plunge;
> I see the peril—yet do not recede;
> And my brain reels—and yet my foot is firm:
> There is a power upon me which withholds,
> And makes it my fatality to live;
> If it be life to wear within myself

This barrenness of spirit, and to be
My own soul's sepulchre, for I have ceased
To justify my deeds unto myself—
The last infirmity of evil.

The self-conscious thoughts in this passage spoil the sense of emotional urgency and produce make-believe. This is not the dramatic language of suicide but of a vain character full of complacency and self-pity, striking dramatic attitudes for himself as audience. It is a language of thoughts, of introspective reflection, and is typical of the whole poem. So that although there is often an air of drama and much attitudinizing the true characteristic tone is absent from the dialogue. Manfred's words are not action-in-speech but agitated meditation. Byron lacks the sense of dramatic dialogue and of how it incorporates character and action. His talent is for haughty narrative, coloured, it is true, by a narcissistic and histrionic trait.

The particular character of drama is thus determined by a form of speech; there is always an "action" or "plot", but it must be carried on in the main by dialogue. Gesture accompanies speech; the relations between people are embodied in speech. The characteristic intertexture of the imagery of drama, deriving from the basic feature of *enactment* and impersonation, lies in a speech-gesture unity in which an action or plot is made manifest. This delimits drama against forms that use some of the same features. Persons, situations, events, actions and crisis all belong to narrative poetry, the novel, and the film, as well as to drama; impersonation and enactment, on the other hand, belong to other forms of theatre, such as opera and ballet, which have a dramatic aspect but are not drama. The alliance of these two sets of characteristics produces the special and distinctive form we call 'a play'.

The speech-gesture feature, as conceived here in terms of an image-intertexture, is the pivot of the whole idea of dramatic form, because it is the focus, in the process of dramatic development, both of the immediate point in time of that development, and of all the implications. For this form is particularly distinguished by two things in close relation to each other: an unfolding of a situation of crisis, which is keenly felt, from the rise to the fall of the curtain, as a *process* in time, with before, and present, and what next?; and the sense also that any given moment is capable of being isolated and seen as a focal centre for the whole action. The situation at any moment is completely interlocked with the whole action, deriving all its meaning from its precise place in a series of events. This gives to speech its specific dramatic quality. The events and actions explode in it or prepare for explosion. It is always either expressive of passion, will, and feeling, or suspense-inducing; either demonstratively giving utterance to the feelings involved, or full of reference, information, and implication, contributing to the tension generated by a concatenation of events and circumstances.

The main features of the form, persons, situations, action, crisis, gesture, dialogue, thus find their point of adjustment in the speech-gesture imagery. It is an organic interfusion. Persons imply action and dialogue, dialogue implies something that occasions it, situations imply decisions and behaviour, crisis implies events involving persons. The characteristic image-complexity of drama appears where all these features realize completely the implications they contain for each other, as is best seen in the three greatest masters of the form, Shakespeare, Racine, and Ibsen. Shakespeare includes more in his schemes than the two latter, and in consequence, whilst his texture is always, or nearly always, perfectly dramatic, his design includes luxurious outgrowths. Racine and Ibsen, by a severer restriction in composition, suggest the perfection of the type more potently, though not without a touch of the artificiality that often lies in the shadow of perfect art.

V. MALADJUSTED DIALOGUE AND ACTING; INDEPENDENT EFFECTIVENESS OF THE ACTOR

The ideal of speech-gesture unity, belonging to and circumscribing the particular form *drama*, both in its texture and its architectonic design, implies also an ideal type of actor. He is the man who can realize in his speaking and acting the full contexture of imagery implicit in the dramatist's scheme, and of which the text is the clue. Three sets of meanings—words, voice, and gestures—coalesce in his rendering in such a way that one feels equally strongly that the actor has subordinated himself perfectly to his author's meaning and that the author has conceived his play perfectly for the actor's art. This may be expressed in another way by saying that a good dramatic text itself suggests or even imposes the appropriate acting and in these circumstances the excellent actor knows quite well that he has sufficient opportunities for his talent without adding extravagant and personal frills.

But it is also true that two of the actor's instruments, his voice and his gesture, can be given great independent significance. Mime can be made into an imagery of the most explicit kind. Plays in this manner, usually farcical and depicting scenes from everyday life, were known in the ancient theatre of Greece and Rome, and the art of mime is still cultivated to-day, though on a restricted scale. A mime may be described as a system of gesture-imagery conveying pre-linguistic dramatic meanings. This aspect of the actor's art can become obtrusive in straight plays, developing in opposition to the author's intentions and giving the actor prominence over the play.

The voice cannot achieve the same independence because it must still speak words. But even here we are compelled to recognize the enormous part played in expressive acting by the quality of the actor's vocal powers. As we said in an earlier chapter, the music of language is the music of the voice speaking and the most mellifluous words may be delivered as raucous sounds. Words are but abstract signs and in order to unfold their full dramatic meaning they have to be realized in the sensuous context of vocal sounds in which the meanings of emotion and feeling inhere by nature. If frivolous words are spoken sadly, or vice-versa, a common trick of humour, we recognize at once the discrepancy between vocal expression and sense; which emphasizes the independent expressiveness of the voice. This power can join hands with mime and become in its turn a force helping to disrupt the speech-gesture unity of drama, unless, of course, special effects of parody or comedy are intended.

On the other hand we have in these facts the reason why undistinguished plays can be made to appear tolerable or even successful pieces for the theatre, or why characters in quite commonplace plays may, when the actor has great imagination, be invested with poetry. In such cases we recognize that we are seeing a poor play; but we are then analytically aware of the specialized effort of the actor. It is not that he is showing especially *his* art, the art of acting, because, as we mentioned above, he can do that quite well and still serve Sophocles or Shakespeare. It is simply that he is throwing an emphasis on to one or two aspects of his art, drawing on their resources to compensate for poverty in another direction. A poorly-written part thus becomes enhanced, and an initial failure of imagination in one form is converted into a triumph in another. Perhaps the same powers of compensation help the process of transplanting plays, giving them an easier international viability than poetry enjoys. The independent efforts of voice and acting endow plays with imaginative life, redeeming the deficiencies of a possibly prosaic or faulty translation.[3]

vi. STYLIZATIONS OF DRAMATIC SPEECH

To investigate the various problems of dramatic speech in any detail would require a separate treatise, but one or two comments arising from the preceding observations are appropriate at this point.

The argument here put forward emphasizes that action is incorporated in speech and dialogue, and does so deliberately in order to counteract a customary loose way of calling theatrical "action", or business that is extraneous to dialogue, the real nerve of drama. Accordingly we should remember, in further support of the argument, that such theatrical business is itself part of the larger context that includes the actor with his speech and gesture. A pistol shot or a blow are not isolated; they are preceded and followed by the participants' dialogue and exclamations. When Caesar, in Shakespeare's play, is struck dead by the conspirators, he has just uttered a speech that lays him open to the charge of overweening personal authority and provocation, and though there is doubtless a momentary pause as he dies, and though any act of dying is in a sense dramatic, the real drama of that moment is pointed by speech, when Cinna cries:

> Liberty! freedom! Tyranny is dead!
> Run hence, proclaim, cry it about the streets.

An equally cogent example is Shakespeare's use of ghosts. Nothing is so dramatic or theatrical as a ghost, but only so long as someone sees it and reacts. A ghost in a play is not a ghost if only seen by the audience. It is an extension of the characters who see it, a part of the context of behaviour and dialogue. This is strikingly illustrated in the banquet scene in *Macbeth* where Banquo's ghost, "entering" and sitting in the chair placed for Macbeth, is seen only by the latter and its presence only apprehended in consequence in Macbeth's agitated cries and interjections. Even if this scene is played with an actor actually appearing as Banquo's ghost the dramatic focus lies in what Macbeth does and says, and not in the mere wondrous apparition. The ghost of Hamlet's father gives still more eloquent proof of this view, proceeding from mere appearance and mysterious signs seen by Hamlet's friends to its long communings with Hamlet himself. These examples represent how in fine composition the theatrically effective incidents are in no way external but form part of an intricate dramatic plan essentially based on speech.

My second comment concerns the *tirade* and stichomythia, two well-established conventions of the French and Greek theatres respectively. Both are examples of the stylization of natural dramatic forms. The speaker of a *tirade* marshals the arguments and ideas that justify his feelings or actions or desires in a given situation and he utters them with all the weight of which his feelings make him capable. This happens in real life, but of course the concentration, eloquence, and rhetorical purposefulness of a *tirade* transcend in their formal skill anything that real situations normally produce. They concentrate, however, the meanings of a situation and hence intensify the sense of drama, a certain amplitude adding to, not detracting from, dramatic significance. For such a speech is not conversational and tranquil; it is both an action and a move in a larger action. The failure, exaggeration, indiscreet use, or decadence of the style of the *tirade* should not blind us to its real nature, which is essentially a mode of speech in which action inheres. Shaw exploited the drama of the *tirade* brilliantly for his comedy of ideas.

In contrast to the forceful and insistent assertions of the *tirade* stands the equally natural thrust and counter-thrust in the heated argument of antagonists, or the tense eliciting of information, of which stichomythia is the stylization within the framework of verse. Like the *tirade*, though not in the same degree, it departs formally from reality, but only to express the dramatic meaning more vividly. For that reason both these conventional forms illustrate the idea of the dramatic apart from the particulars of any given dramatic situation in which they are used.

vii. STAGE-SETTING AND DECOR

Since drama depicts persons it must also show their habitat, the places where they enact their fortunes. The first function of stage scenery and décor, which includes costumes, is representational; we may conceive them as an extension of persons. In so far as these are also representational the décor belongs to the imagery of the fable, for which reason plays are mostly set and costumed either on realistic or historical lines, whichever is appropriate, and no particular difficulty or aesthetic problem arises except in special cases (e.g. a "pre-historical" or "mythical" setting where the details of costume are unknown). But setting and décor fall also under the law of expressive, as well as representational, imagery, which means that they can be made to serve, often with impressive force, the emotional and affective aspects of the play. What we said in earlier chapters on simultaneous representational and expressive function holds here, too. The most sublime example of expressive setting is in the heath-scenes of *King Lear*. Here the heath with its exposure to the naked elements is the physical place to which Lear, in his domestic deprivation, is driven, to become the butt of nature, too. The wilderness and its tempest, however, are also made to match symbolically the disturbance in society and Lear's own rage and suffering, and, with an additional subtlety, to offer a challenge to his moral pride.[4] The witch scenes in *Macbeth* are one of the most obvious cases of a setting in which the creation of a dramatic atmosphere arises with the physical scene itself. Another example is Faust in his Gothic chamber, which, together with its contents, he feels as one of the things conspiring to intensify his spiritual malaise and sense of frustration. An example of the most finely-pointed kind is the setting of Racine's *Bérénice*: *à Rome, dans un cabinet qui est entre l'appartement de Titus et celui de Bérénice*; a small space the location of which reflects the whole drama of proximity and separation in the fate of the two lovers.

Costume, either in a realistic setting or in association with symbolical décor, plays a prominent part in adding to expressive meaning, especially in respect of colouring. But it is rarely possible to draw a dividing line between the representational and the expressive. Costumes, like the setting, pertain to the persons, and like them are both pictorial and emotional, and beyond that part of a general idea or feeling. They serve the story and also the directive symbolism of the play as a whole or of particular scenes with their predominant emotional mood. The costume artist uses historical costume for representation and art for expression, taking account both of the common psychological responses to colours, and of traditional colour associations (green for magicians, red for devils, white for chastity, etc.)

The imagery of scene and décor can, like all images in art, displace a representational emphasis and assume purely, or at least predominantly, expressive or symbolic functions. This happens, for instance, in Yeats's Plays for Dancers. *At the Hawk's Well* begins with Musicians unfolding 'a black cloth with a gold pattern suggesting a hawk', whilst a 'square blue cloth' represents a well. The Guardian of the Well wears a black cloak, and underneath it a dress 'suggesting a hawk'. She dances, "moving like a hawk". The persons of the play move like marionettes. In this technique Yeats exploits images of language, music, painting, dancing, and sculpture, interwoven harmoniously in a single direction of emotional meaning. Décor used in this way is still an extension of the persons, since they enact a drama, but it is symbolic as they are. Cocteau, in *Orphée* and *La Machine Infernale* especially, exploits objects of décor and stage furniture for dramatic symbolism without over-musicalizing them as Yeats tends to. Jocasta's scarf, over which she constantly trips up, and with which she finally hangs herself, receives a "rôle" of sharp theatrical effect to play. The mirror through which *Orphée* gains access to the underworld is also a forcibly dramatic symbol with mysterious overtones. These are just a few examples, chosen at random, to illustrate, first, how scene and décor are an extension of the *dramatis personae*, and secondly, how their symbolic expressiveness is always assimilated to the dramatic meanings, which they enhance thereby.

viii. DRAMATIC IMAGERY AND ITS SPECIAL PROBLEM OF
REPRESENTATIONAL REALISM. TWO ASPECTS OF
EXPRESSIVENESS IN DRAMA

Our earlier distinction between representational images and expressive formula-images comes in useful when we turn to the question of "realism" in drama. We justified the element of representation on the grounds that some kinds of feeling and idea in art are occasioned by objects of the external world, scenes of nature and human life, and not to be separated from them. But we were careful to mark the difference between the aesthetic representational image, which is always expressive as well, and the scientific copy-image.

These distinctions will help us to deal more adequately with a special problem arising in connection with the dramatic form, that of representational "realism". As a form requiring enactment and impersonation, and the actors being living people, drama conveys very powerfully a sense of "reality" or of real existences. The dramas of real life can always be used as models for drama, as may be seen from historical plays, and amidst all the changing fashions of the literary drama we observe a constant reversion to an elementary type of play, as in O'Neill, or a writer like Rattigan, made of strong emotions and passions as they exist in reality, which is but evidence of the pull exerted towards realistic illusion in this form. And when drama tries to evolve symbolic or abstract styles, as in the last thirty years, it cannot, like painting and sculpture, work with rarefied abstract forms but must still use persons, who, even if to some degree depersonalized, must move and speak like human beings. Thus the relationship between the dramatic image and real human life offers peculiar difficulties to which we must devote a special comment.

The problem I have particularly in mind may be stated best by the common contrast with lyric poetry and narrative. Quite simply, the latter forms are more malleable from the subjective point of view. Reflective poets may choose freely according to their personal bias the ideas they express in their poems, and all the works of nature and man feed their imagination in its search for words and symbols. Novelists, also, though nearer to dramatists by their use of a fiction, can be equally restrictive and subjective by manipulating their principal character, or by playing down the plot of characters and situations in favour of other features such as description of landscape, of historical periods or social conditions, by introspective meditations, by lyricism, and so on. A dramatist, by contrast, working with impersonation and actors, is compelled to make his play live by its persons; and not by *one* of them, but by *all* of them. This applies, moreover, even when the persons concerned are the fictions of fairy tale, myth, or fantasy. Drama, in fact, can only emerge when the imagination functions in a quite special way, showing sympathy for all the innumerable and above all conflicting aspects of human character. For only then can it create the *dramatis personae* with interest and vividness, and lay the foundations for the dialectic of drama, in which people react on each other, with all the situations arising in consequence. Whatever is said about life, philosophy, religion, morals, man, or nature, whatever subtlety of spirit or feeling the poet proposes, has to be said in these terms.

178

In a very general way this sympathy may be called a love of human life; of one's own life, of the fact of being alive and what that involves; of human life altogether, its excitements and variety. It implies particularly a love of the complexity of human nature and an acceptance of its contradictions. It begins with the simple appetites of the individual and the conflicts that arise from them in the self, but extends then to all the complexities of the moral life in the individual, and that unavoidably involves the desires and moral life of others. Thus, given the initial sympathy with human nature, life appears inevitably as a vast and continual conflict and reconciliation, in which the nature of man shares both with pleasure and remorse. Upon this profound sense of relationship and antagonism with others, expressed in sympathetic re-creation, the dramatic vision of life is founded. To this sense life appears as a drama at every turn, and no man is a good dramatist without it.

What I want to clarify here is that this sense is primary in dramatic creation. I mean that it precedes any specific philosophical or moral beliefs that the dramatist may imply. It makes his play, his dramatic medium, possible as such, whatever philosophy he may be declared to hold in the long run or whatever ideas influence his view of life. It can perhaps be exemplified from the attitude Ibsen took up in relation to admirers who looked on his works as propaganda for particular ideas. He used to protest that he was a poet and not a preacher, that he was clarifying life and not dogmatizing about it, nor, we may add, just writing about himself. This was the voice of the dramatist—not the moral critic—in Ibsen, speaking with a universal sympathy for the rights of all individual desire; of the dramatist who, like Shakespeare, could conceive his characters with all the vital self-centredness of real people, each in turn holding the stage as though he were the centre and law of life. The primary dramatic interest of Sartre's plays also lies in this feature, derived brilliantly and inevitably from the existentialist moral sense of "les Autres", those "others" whose freedom restricts one's own. Sartre's plays are illustrations of a philosophy, doubtless, but it is a philosophy with the acutest sense of the dramatic substance of life and human society. Dramatists may adopt particular moral judgements or at any rate imply them, as Ibsen himself certainly did, but their vision is made possible by an antecedent intuitive self-identification with many possible variations of human character. Drama contains always this expression of universal sympathy with the desires of men and the possibilities of living. You must love Iago, or you must have him prefigured as desire in yourself, to be able to portray him. Only by virtue of such sympathy can the *dramatis persona* be brought to vivid life in the imagination.

Thus we have to recognize in the elementary conditions of drama something that makes and keeps it a highly "representational" and pictorially descriptive form, just as portraiture, or landscape, though art, must remain representational. A play must be acted, and the dramatist must disappear behind characters who borrow a persuasive existence as of "real life". It is the anthropomorphic form *par excellence;* and also inveterately humanist in the sense that it is a mirror of men for themselves. Whatever other forms drama assumes, however allegorical or symbolical its method, however didactic or devoted to a cause it may be, this belongs to its basic character. Hence the sharp criticism it draws upon itself if it strays too far from a solid foundation of "characters" and situations, a nostalgia for which infallibly arises where non-realistic forms are too prominent. Hence the success of Bertolt Brecht, whose real power lies not in his novel-sounding techniques but in the orthodox dramatic gift of portraying with simplicity and humanity types of the common people. Perhaps one can expect drama never to deny this basic structure just as we said poetry would tend to modify an excessive symbolism by return to propositional statements. The tendency will always be supported by the actor's desire to impersonate, based as it is on a similar sympathy with character and its variety, and a desire for self-identification with others in human situations that are interesting and moving. The audience must also be mentioned, as sharing these interests and sympathies.

ix. MORAL AND PSYCHOLOGICAL THEMES NATURAL TO DRAMA

Implicit in this attitude of the born dramatist, in his comprehensive sympathy for and knowledge of human beings in all their variety of character and fortune, is a keen moral sensitiveness; without such discrimination and the sense of quality and nuance in personality human beings would appear reduced to a few crude and simple physical types. The dramatist's love of life, of all its impulses, to wickedness as well as to virtue, to liberty and licence as well as to a solicitous order, is in no way divorced from morals; it is simply a greater capacity to sympathize on all sides. And indeed his moral sense is more irritable and tender precisely because of his own sense of the conflict springing from the primary tensions of instinct, will, and passion. The effects of love, of egoistic ruthlessness in all its evil forms, the effects of remorse, all belong to the complexion of human nature and only in their range and alternation is the true and complete character of human life, in its more than individual meanings, to be found. The dramatist's peculiar power issues from this comprehensiveness which, as we insist, is so intimately linked with impersonation and enactment. And it makes possible all the complexity of great drama in which the bursting, throbbing sense of life asserting itself dynamically is counterpointed with the vision of goodness and the ideal, the response to all the values, emotional and spiritual, of living. Drama is sustained by these two things; by the primal sympathy with all human beings and their right both to existence and idiosyncrasy, which makes a play implicitly an act of piety for humanity and human kind; and, secondly, by a moral sensibility which, inflamed by the conflict between egoistic assertion and idealism, the one evoking the self-love and self-indulgence of men, the other their dignity and despair, passes a general judgement on the human condition.

The form of drama being thus tied to impersonation and enactment, its natural themes relate to psychology and morals. It is, of course, like all art, an imagery; not living, but made; not reality, but symbol. But persons belong to its imagery, and where persons carry the meanings, the meanings best carried are those concerning persons. The images of drama can only be expressive by being representational first; and therefore only certain kinds of expression can be achieved by them. The visions and feelings of dramatic art must always in a quite obvious way concern human beings and their ways. And if they extend to religious or philosophical ideas these also will be shown, if the form is not to be offended, as aspects of psychology and morals. Thus, though every interesting play embodies a "meditation", it is only one of such a kind that it can lie implicit in the images. It must be, in short, one about human nature. For people, situations, and relationships are the material in which the dramatist works, and if we consider him as a subject meditating about life, his meditation is particularized as about human relations. A lyric poet may meditate on his relations with God, or the universe, or nature. To a dramatist these subjects are not forbidden but their simple subjective presentation is. They must be seen in terms of human relations, and what emerges in drama is not the relation of the individual to any god, or ideal, or idea, but the relation of the community to these things, because a play must always be a statement of relations between men. Eliot shows himself aware of this when he speaks of the "human drama" within the "divine drama", and we observe in general about religious plays, which most often deal with martyrdom (*Polyeucte*), temptation (*Murder in the Cathedral*), miracles (*L'Annonce faite à Marie*) or Bible story, that they are based not on an individual's idea or feeling about God, or a mystic experience of God, but on the intervention of God in the human community. They invariably bring home the significance of religion for social relations. Even a play like Claudel's *Partage de Midi*, which concerns a man's sense of religious vocation, is a play only because the main character suffers an agonizing conflict between sacred and profane love. It is a relationship with another person that occasions the drama. The same may be said of his *L'Otage*, an even better example of the necessity of the "human drama". Sygne, the main character, accepts the duty laid upon her by the priests, interpreting God's will and meaning to her, although she finds it so outrageous that her faith is jeopardized. Thus the issue is one between Sygne and God. But the duty, and the drama, pertain to terrestrial life and human society, involving her in love and broken faith with her cousin Georges, and a humiliating marriage with their common hated enemy, Toussaint, the son of their family servant, a parvenu of the post-Revolution age.

In this the natural character of drama, the poet's idea, his vision, his feeling, his "meditation", his particular motive for expression, is always inextricably intertwined with the picture of life and the illusion of reality. The dramatic writer must use images that in the nature of the medium are close to life, and so he is compelled to seek always the situation, the event, the complication, the person, the detail, that forms the axis of moral insight, or psychological illumination, or of his emotional response to life. Thus the picture-of-life, and the poet's declaration, are concentric. The story is convincing in itself simply as a portrayal of people and events, but in addition it has been so apprehended and constructed that it is impregnated with the symbolism of the poet's own meanings. The point at which we perceive most easily the functioning of this concentricity is often the main character. In a play like *Hamlet* or *Othello* the material is organized around a central person, who appears as the single centre, first, of an illusionary picture of life and, secondly, of a meditation on life. The greatest dramatic art appears where this concentricity is perfect and therefore doubly convincing. If we accept the idea that Hamlet is a meditation on corruption, it is one made apparent in the particular terms of plot and persons that make Hamlet a play. These are the necessary foundation of the idea of corruption; they are the life in which corruption inheres. They have to be shown in order to show the corruption. Hamlet himself is the focus and the conscience of that life. In a similar way Othello and Iago are magnetic poles for ideas and feelings about nobility, jealousy, and dissimulation. The fifth act of *The Duchess of Malfi* shows the most vigorous moral pointing in dramatic construction, whilst examples of concentricity from the modern prose drama are the finely conceived plays of Gabriel Marcel (*La Chapelle Ardente, Un Homme de Dieu*).

Thus, in the natural conditions of dramatic form, the meanings of the author, everything we sum up in the words "vision" or "meditation", must appear implicit in a convincing situation. Or, to put it more forcibly still, when situations are visioned with the acutest sensibility and liveliest imagination, so that they are given complete detail and transparency in relation to human feelings and values, then the image contains the meditated idea, the fiction is the metaphor, the illusion is the symbol. The achievement of this perfect adjustment throughout a play is the sign of the masterpiece. The faults that inevitably go with the nature of the task are that sentences and epigrams, which are natural to the moral atmosphere of drama, are stuck on unskilfully, and that the moralizing harangue is also introduced too obviously, forming a lump in the texture. The speech of Tecnicus to Orgilus on honour, in Ford's *The Broken Heart* (III, i) illustrates this point.

The period that shows the most perfect unfolding of this natural character of dramatic art, in which poetic expression is only achieved in conjunction with a full illusion of personal reality, is the late sixteenth and seventeenth centuries in England, Spain, and France, when a number of circumstances were especially propitious to the form. It is not necessary to enumerate them in detail, but undoubtedly the rise of drama reflected the general liberation from medieval society and culture by its implicit sense of the importance of individual character, of the impulses of natural man whether expressed in heroic or diabolical forms, and its sense of the conflict between natural or pagan man and the ethical tradition deriving from orthodox religion. The earlier drama had been didactic, consisting mainly of religious allegories or moralizing farces serving the purposes of the Church. The new development transformed drama into a comprehensive humane expression of the heights and depths of human behaviour, and it has in fact never again equalled this assertion of its natural character in the Renaissance period. Within this period Shakespeare is pre-eminent because he had the greatest range of psychology and situation at his command. Since the eighteenth century it has been a commonplace of Shakespearian commentary that in his power to create living characters he is as "universal" as nature herself. But this power cannot be separated from his sense of situation, for only the latter reveals character. The really astonishing thing in Shakespeare is his power to conceive the dramatic shape of a seemingly endless series of human situations and the moral dilemmas arising with them, from the most far-reaching and tragic to the most comic or light-hearted. From this point of view it is the whole of Shakespeare, not parts, that tell us what he, and drama, are; and to see all separate plays, including Shakespeare's, in the whole context of drama as an imaginative form is our present purpose. In him we see in perfection how thought, comment, and poetic idea are simply the proper amplification of situation (though we are speaking generally, of course, and admit in some plays, like *Troilus and Cressida* or *Measure for Measure*, particular problems concerning precisely these relations). All the great speeches on set themes, like Richard II on kingship, Portia on mercy, Macbeth on guilt, Hamlet on suicide, all the sentences, epigrams, and general observations on life, are embedded in a context, a plot. The philosophic thought growing out of the play always circles back into it, and the poetic power is not something added to the play but is released by the context, made possible by the antecedent dramatic form.

Shakespeare, showing many patterns of interfused picture-surface and implicit symbolism, is paradoxically both the best criterion of what dramatic form can achieve and a hindrance in the assessment of other authors, who are one and all dwarfed by the comparison, but, being in the majority, represent what we may usually expect. That, normally, is a narrower range of themes. With most authors the picture of life may be sufficiently convincing at the story level, but we observe the same theme, or a small group of themes, recurring in a succession of plays, from which we derive the clues with which to interpret each work separately and illumine the nature of their imagery. In other words, the repetitions and variations of basic features determine the "figure in the carpet", making it clear, first, that there is indeed a figure, and secondly, what it is. Sometimes, though not necessarily, these predominant figures show the authors in tune with characteristic interests or feelings of their age. Marlowe's heroes display Renaissance grandeur, heroism, exuberance, sensuous splendour, achievement, pride, and excess. Corneille's recurrent theme concerns the conscience and will-power of the man of honour. Racine derives tragedy repeatedly from the exacerbated passions of men and women in love, or in search of power. Schiller is attracted by the fate of historical personages in whom he perceives a conflict of duty and passion, moral idealism and egoistic desire. Ibsen inculcates the free personality or analyses the cankered hero. Shaw pivots his plays on some incarnation of the Shavian hero, Eliot his on the elective martyr. These are but a few examples of the common rule that in most plays a directive symbolism is woven into the central fabric, more often than not through the principal character, constituting an addition to, and modification of, the primary picture-of-life layer of drama. Ibsen offers the best example of a dramatist who, having a wonderful command of psychological variety, combines great power of character creation and consequent representational quality with an insistent theme conveyed through the main characters of numerous plays.

In the twentieth century the new psychological knowledge and the conception of the unconscious have changed completely the view of personality and character, with consequences of great importance for drama. A progressive development can be seen from the later plays of Ibsen, those of Strindberg, and the very disagreeable ones of Wedekind, through the intellectual analyses of Pirandello, the symptomatic though somewhat bowdlerized psycho-analytical approach of Lenormand, to the surrealist fantasy and symbolic realism of Cocteau and the existentialist neurotics of Anouilh. In this series we observe how a new kind of drama is derived from the exploration of the person itself, and not simply from clashes between persons, or from a conscious dilemma of the person facing issues of conduct. At the beginning of the series, characters like Rebecca West, Hedda Gabler, Borkman, and Rubek, the sculptor of *When*

We Dead Awaken, are conceived with an imaginative subtlety that is devoted in the first place to a pessimistic psychological analysis, which displaces the moral optimism of Ibsen's previous militant period. They are persons in whom outer action and circumstance do not correspond to inner desire, who never discover their true selves or do so too late, or discover an undesirable self beneath the conscious social appearance. In Ibsen, however, these analyses are presented still in terms of realism and with the older ethical temper, though with a significant use of symbols or symbolic motifs to suggest a surging unconscious life of the will. Lenormand and Cocteau, on the other hand, represent post-Freudian sophistication, in a bad and a good form. The former, deliberately applying psycho-analysis, though in a clumsy and muddled manner, pivots his plays—for example *À l'Ombre du Mal*, or *Le Mangeur de Rêves*—on the revelation of the unconscious desire as the climax to events and behaviour inscrutable, mystifying, and wicked by the old simple moral standards of right and wrong. Cocteau, however, with a finer and more relaxed imagination, seizes on the pattern of symbols in gesture, action, dream, and circumjacent objects, and makes that into the structure itself of his play, so that all, including the surface, is symbol and the unconscious shines through the sensuous appearances. Thus, combining psychological sophistication with a poetic sense of pregnant theatre imagery, he externalizes the inner world of desire, in the myth-fantasies *Orphée* and *La Machine Infernale*, or the symbolic realism of the novel and film *Les Enfants Terribles* and the play *Les Parents Terribles*, which also develop the quality of myth. In this kind of dramatic writing the long tradition of psychological illumination in drama continues, though transformed in accordance with a modern knowledge and viewpoint. Here a very different view holds of character, of what a "person" is, and there is an acute apprehension of the shaping world of unconscious motive behind the illusionary world of actions; nevertheless persons and their actions and suffering are the central interest. But, above all, the free poetic movement draws the spectator into the sphere of a tragic ritual, in which, piercing appearances, he is in contact with the forces that are in the "person" but uncontrollable, creating him, his actions, and his Destiny. In this way drama is derived again, not from social or external moral conflicts, but from the depths of passion, appetite and the unconscious.

In the older tradition the picture-of-life imagery, and the thematic symbolism implicit in a leading person, are a harmonious alliance. The symbolism is effective without being obtrusive. Or, to put it another way, literal and symbolic meanings lie close without mutual negation or restriction. But sometimes the symbols can be accentuated, reducing the immediate persuasiveness of the pictorial or literal element, though not necessarily falsifying the general truthfulness of the vision. Heinrich von Kleist's plays, vivid illustrations of this point, show distorted forms in the plot and persons which destroy literal validity and throw into relief symbolic expression, producing—the idea has its genesis here—"expressionism". The actions and conflicts in Kleist's plots run to extremes, the persons behave with maximum irrationality, propelled by trances or trance-like states of mind, by dreams, by contraries of violent passion, particularly by alternating hatred and love, so that they appear "abnormal". They are, however, still persons and they are best read as accentuated symbols of psychological tendencies in human nature generally. The distortion is not an untruthfulness or inaccuracy (Kleist probably believed firmly in the objective reality of his characters) but an emphatic lighting, a way of throwing analysed aspects of behaviour into sharp relief. It is a distortion not of the individual person considered as a "case" (a pure example of a pathological type) but of the more normal breadth and variety of personality. Kleistian heroes and heroines are admissions of Kleist's personal conflicts, so that the symbolism is forceful but restricted. They put his drama near to the dream image that is less than the best art because it is too near to *natural* dream. Too much in Kleist is documentary in the sense of being evidence of dream, trance, or the unconscious, and not sufficiently integrated, as art requires, into a controlled vision and commanding idea. It is only in *Prinz Friedrich von Homburg* that the Kleistian speech of the hunted victim yields to a more comprehensive view which acknowledges the values of a social and extra-personal world.

Dramatic art has not always confined itself to what I have in this chapter called its "natural" form, the image that carries equal conviction in two ways, both as a dramatic picture of life, and as a symbol for an author's interpretation, judgement, and feeling. It has explored allegory, frank and bold symbolic forms, expressionism, myth-revival, all of which, to be touched on again later, establish very different relations between the real world and the author's expressive purpose as embodied in his dramatic picture. Some of the attempted forms, as we shall note, bring drama to the limits of what it can legitimately do, where an author's private ideas or feelings or beliefs are more important to him than his respect for persons, for the idea and the necessity of the *dramatis personae*. Drama then breaks down. It fails to hold the stage, and the audience is either bewildered or bored.

For, concluding this section, we reiterate that the basis of a play is impersonation and acting. This demands particular human sympathies shared by author, actors, and audiences, and imposes naturally a firm loyalty to the representation of persons, and therefore to life-like appearances, to a certain kind of objectivity, a close intimacy with "man in general". These are conditions the dramatist must fulfil. What he wants himself to say, his own message, the vision that is his and no one else's, for this he varies the form of drama, but without dissolving its initial conditions.

Thus we are always aware of two aspects of expressiveness in drama. There is the primary layer of illusion, of fiction, of the story that might be true, about persons who remind us of ourselves and our neighbours. Such fictions are representational and not free fantasy; but they are not copies of actuality, not records of historical events. Their relation to "reality" is not a scientific copy-imagery but a general truth to nature that persuades and carries conviction. "This could be true" is their silent motto and working assumption. Closeness to truth and reality in this sense belongs to the expressive quality, which is here not simply the result of an individual uttering his message, but of a number of factors socially shared. Sympathy with people, curiosity about human affairs, about the ways of destiny, the impulse to share in a life larger than one's own, to identify oneself with others, the urge to imitate, to mimic, to recapitulate, to impersonate, the pressing desire to clarify and illumine what is normally only half apprehended in the flux of sensation and activity;—all these, felt by authors, audience, and actors, help to make drama a spectacle and a ritual, a performance and an art. In this aspect of its expressiveness the author's voice merges with that of the community.

In the other aspect it is the author alone who speaks. Dramatic writers, like others, have their vision, their sensibility, different conflicts, different philosophies, which find expression in a new variation of the dramatic form, in theme and implicit symbolism, always making a play its author's poem. This idea need not be laboured, for it is a commonplace of the present time. What is not commonly accepted is the power of the primary expressiveness implicit in the form as such, in its very existence and continuity.

X. DRAMA AND THE COMMUNITY; NATURAL TYPES OF DRAMA

It is appropriate at this point to comment briefly on the social relations of drama because these also have some influence on its subjects and forms. It relies very much on an intimate relation to society for its vitality. One of its greatest glories is that it is always in an exceptional degree the product of community, not merely in ultimate or indirect ways, which applies to all art, but in the obvious sense that it brings people together, men and women, the old and the young, and for the space of a few hours holds them spell-bound in an all-comprehending emotion. The moments in which, by the power of a poet speaking for many, an audience feels suddenly as one, when it is no longer a conglomeration of separate individuals and appetites but simply humanity enveloped by a human vision, are a peculiar social achievement of this art. No other forms reach such a degree of communal power except the ceremonies of religion. For this reason no doubt religion and drama have often gone hand in hand, and do so still.

In the midst of more intricate details of aesthetic analysis it is well to state a simple truth. Drama must be one of two things: either comic or intensely moving. All ingenuity and lavishness of art or spectacle or "poetry" or ideas or problems are useless if the play fails to strike one of these chords, whilst on the other hand they are not missed in the simplest, plainest play that does find the note. It is relevant to emphasize again the link connecting the world of a play with the world of "real" experience. A play is a work of art, and has its integrity. But it does rely on an appeal to general experience by which we can think of it as in fact springing from human experience and saying something about it. Nothing is so misleading as the fashionable dogma of the "words on the page", a queer phrase in any case to use in respect of drama, where the words are in the air and are only one element. One can take almost any of the plays of Shakespeare or the Greeks or Racine, indeed, any good play, and state in brief, simple form its "story" and it will be found to be moving, even in its barest outlines. No dramatist has ever worked successfully without this hard kernel of ultimate human reality, of the fiction that could be fact, and, if it were, would move us. Drama never reaches out to the audience or transforms and transcends its artificial habitat the stage unless it stirs deep and strong emotions, or, alternatively, evokes the spirit of comedy, which is also social and simply human in character. These insistent requirements of the form account for the popularity of mad scenes, deaths, funerals, processions, ceremonies of various kinds, love-scenes, drunken scenes, trials, and stock conflict situations of particular pathos (father-son, husband-wife, mother-daughter, brother-brother, and so on). All these are *clichés*, but they show the stuff of theatre and drama, and can always be revitalized. The use of the term "drama" as a descriptive category in theatre and cinema advertisements, for plots with strong and gripping emotional scenes, is also a symptom of the primary effects in which drama is rooted.

These simple facts have influenced profoundly the growth of drama, which has tended to fall into well-marked types. Four in especial may be clearly distinguished, recurring with great persistence through the centuries and in widely separated cultures: tragedy, comedy, romance, and allegory, using this term to cover all didactic drama. A fifth should perhaps be added: the historical play as "dramatized narrative", though in Shakespeare's elaboration it is not so much a separate type as an amalgam of two or more of the others. They are all represented in Shakespeare, significantly enough.

The vigour of these natural types flows from the forcible conjunction of several factors, some aesthetic, some social. The sense of what is tragic or comic, the sense of romance, the impulse to convert, all rest on common feelings or commonly held beliefs. They do not exist in the purely private world; they appear only in social contexts. Tragic and comic situations occur in relations between human beings or depend on judgements connected with human values, human implying society. Moreover they are used to describe real situations before they denote aesthetic categories. "Romance" and "allegory" may be included as natural types because they also have a well-defined social appeal. The former, which usually takes the form of a moving story of love or heroism or successful adventure, expresses universal desires which are hailed and reaffirmed as such by the communal emotion of the theatre audience. Allegory emerged in the first place from the emotions of religion. In the mysteries, moralities, miracle plays, in the Jesuit and baroque drama and later forms of religious play, it has a long history as a mode of focusing the feelings on ideas and symbols that are spiritually elevating and fortify both the real and the mystic sense of community.

Two powerful socio-aesthetic factors have contributed especially to the persistent vitality of these types. The first concerns tragedy and comedy. Tragedy involves events which are felt to be terrible and catastrophic, as well as unexpected and often of rapid evolution; it is dramatic by its nature. In a similar way an element of dramatic surprise is always inherent in comic situations. But the tragic and comic, being always "seen" in connexion with persons, have in consequence a powerful impact both as meaning and as something sensuously experienced. We cannot experience catastrophe, or a comic incident, without a precise sense of it. When it is before us we recognize it. It has a meaning in itself as a phenomenon; in its being catastrophic, or comic. Our reaction to the situation together with its meaning is immediate. Such force of impact on the senses and the mind is of the essence of drama. Thus, although the tragic and comic as categories may transcend drama as an art-form they are naturally allied to it, social and aesthetic features reinforcing each other.

The second factor is the singleness of effect, or unity of tone, which all the types mentioned create with a sure purpose. This could no doubt be viewed as an aspect of art-works of any kind. In the theatre, where the reaction of a numerous audience has to be reckoned with, it is essential to establish unmistakably the right key and keep the audience attuned to it. In this way the play is understood, the same emotional mood envelops players and audience, and the performance takes on a ritualistic colouring from the implicit participation of the community in the play. When a play fails in this respect the audience are at sea; the loss of social unity follows on that of aesthetic unity.

Within its predominant character each type of play can of course draw on a variety of feelings; singleness of tone is not the same as repetition or a monotonous uniformity. This is especially true of tragedy. We are here affected by the externally dramatic features, the violence and suspense in events. We find our moral feelings and judgement brought into play. There is a metaphysical element always present, since the events show men affected by forces beyond their control, by Destiny or by "the gods". And since life and death are involved, heroism and failure, success and ruin, good and bad impulses, the commonest human fears and emotions are evoked. It is not one or the other of these things, but all of them, that give rise

191

to our being profoundly moved, for they reverberate through the depths of the life of individuals and of the whole human community. And all of them together, familiar in a recurrent pattern, create the clear and unified tone. In comedy the appeal is to other faculties, with a different range of emotional undercurrents, but the effects are as immediate and compelling as those of tragedy.

These persistent forms of drama are natural and organic because they pertain to its profoundly communal character, and are based on salient general features of experience. We touch here not merely on the cultic significance of some kinds of drama in their association with particular religions but above all on the element of ritual that inheres in all drama because of the conjunction in it of the features considered. We might say that each of the four types indicated above has its own ritualistic colouring. Tragedy is a ritual of piety; comedy a ritual of reason and moderation; romance a ritual of optimism; and allegory a ritual of faith. And we speak of ritual because every dramatic spectacle commands an assent from the audience-community which by its presence and participation re-affirms the profound human and social impulses that find expression in the form. Suffering and evil, unreason and absurdity, aspiration and enchanted desire, truth and faith, each of these has had a major influence on a type of drama.[5]

In thus suggesting a few salient forms of drama I do not of course wish to overlook the numerous types and combinations that the history of the art shows, but simply to clarify what would seem to be essential tendencies of drama in connexion with the conditions of its existence. The simplicity of the basic types has been overlaid or complicated innumerable times, but one feels their presence, and the undercurrent of ritual, wherever drama and its performance are vital and successful. I think this applies also to the middle-brow class of play like Terence Rattigan's. Rattigan hits off perfectly the average English middle-class view of life and morality in its contemporary phase, and so, based solidly on the conventional, he is in complete accord with a given audience, who help his plays to success. This is the ritualistic and communal side of the theatre operating in a secular mode and without great art.

The tendency over the last century or so has undoubtedly been more and more for the pure type to disappear. Twentieth century dramatists no longer tell us that their play is "a tragedy" or "a comedy". At the most it may be "une pièce rose" or, more probably, "noire". Neither do they always tell us that their plays are allegories or parables. But that in fact is what a large proportion of good plays since Ibsen have been. It is the common bond between the social problem plays, Shaw's "parables", Kaiser's expressionism, Pirandello's metaphysical essays, Giraudoux' free adaptation of myth, Sartre's existentialist parables, Hofmannsthal's frank re-creation of religious allegory, and Brecht's social plays, to mention a few of the most prominent examples. The didacticism may be grafted on to a basic type, of course. This is seen in the comedy of Shaw and Pirandello, for instance, whilst with Giraudoux it may be tragedy (*Électre*) or comedy (*Amphitryon 38*) or sardonic romance (*La Folle de Chaillot*). Indeed a didactic drama is likely to be success-ful only if vitalized by such grafting.

It is often said that the audience of the modern cinema, by contrast with the theatre, is heterogeneous, atomized, and passive. Yet we may note in this context that the salient types of drama have tended to reconstitute themselves in the film, both in art and enter-tainment. Under tragedy we can include the common type of "human drama", a kind of para-tragedy, strong emotional drama potentially tragic; and if we add comedy, romance, and history ("period" or "costume" film), a fair proportion of film production is covered. Such evidence emphasizes the powerful social factors involved in the actual life and being of a theatre form.

xi. PLOT CONSIDERED AS IMAGERY

Having established the particular importance for dramatic art of both the picture-of-life illusion and the social context, we must now turn towards an elucidation of its varied image texture, observing the range of metaphorical imagery and symbolism. To begin with, let us look more closely at the uses of plot and persons.

As we noted above, persons acting in certain ways, reacting on each other, producing a series of situations further complicated by impersonal events, provide the model in life for the "plots" of drama. The dictionary defines plot as 'the series of incidents, situations, etc., invented by a writer, upon which play or story is built, es-pecially series of complications in such a work solved or explained by a dénouement'. In practice, over the whole field of drama writing, plot construction becomes a minor art in itself, performed by some indifferently, by others with great care, every link being scrupulously forged and made convincing. These differences make us aware of an abstraction, the concept plot, as a separate feature which may be handled with diverse degrees of skill. Some dramatists develop this feature, according to a trick of their own talent, in a disproportionate way and end with something quite artificial, either divorced from all probability, or stereotyped according to a few well-tried formulas, as may be seen from Scrife and the *pièces bien faites* of the later nineteenth century. This brings the idea of a good plot into disrepute. Other writers find the construction of a plot irksome and belittle that aspect of their work as a matter of "technique" or "machinery" which is less important than the ideas or emotions they want to express. Such impatience is either ephemeral irritation or the result of real deficiency. For the core of the matter is that drama is based on relations between persons and not on their introspective meditations or on a separate "message" of the author. If you choose drama as your form, you accept its evocation of life, with consequent obligations.

For the argument of this essay a plot is part of an intertexture of imagery and words. It belongs by function to the vision being expressed and does not, aesthetically speaking, exist separately. All plot-making, in fine dramatic art, is a manipulation of meaning; and plot and persons go hand in hand in this respect. Which persons, which situations, which predicaments, which fortunes and misfortunes, and which arrangement of them, says the dramatist, consciously or unconsciously, embody my ideas and feelings? Even a simple handbook on play-writing will exhort the novice to have some idea in mind with his play. This is the basis of the concentricity we remarked upon in good plays. They show a harmonious union of the primary picture of life-as-drama and of the dramatist's own theme and symbolism. In this way they satisfy both our desire for dramatic spectacle and for an author's particular vision. They satisfy, irrespective of subject-matter, the deep-rooted response to the form of drama, fulfilling our ritualistic desire for this kind of art or re-enactment, and also our interest in an original interpretation or view of life. "Plot" has thus two aspects. It is a concept of dramatic construction, and also a device for the pointing of vision or meaning. By producing the convincing evocation of life and the concentration we recognize as "dramatic" it serves the primary expressiveness of all drama as an art; whilst by structural counterpointing it creates a symbolism for the author's meanings and feelings.

It is the requirements of the general expressiveness of the form that give rise to certain general principles of construction and, more narrowly, to "rules" like the notorious Three Unities. Amongst the former come the demands that opening scenes must embody an exposition, that these should be followed by complications, leading to a climax which is best placed slightly beyond the half-way line, at the end of act three, if a five-act form is used, and towards the end of act two in the three-act structure. Such requirements are natural, and most dramatists satisfy them or try to. Under this head comes also the technique of writing effectively "for the theatre", acquired by experience.

The three unities are an example of stringent rules laid down at a particular period and in a certain climate of taste. Both in the history of drama and of critical theory they have raised startling clouds of dust, to which no one need now add. But it must be admitted that they were highly important conceptions. In principle they arise from profound intuitions of the nature of the dramatic vision and of the natural form of drama as described above. They are fully explicable as conditions helping to make the illusion of life convincing, and the form concentrated, by avoiding any diffuseness, as of narrative, that would impair the natural sequence of scenes in sustained tension. Thus far they could be looked upon as both natural and reasonable, and intimately in place in the French society and audience of the seventeenth century with its developed sense both of social and moral man, and of rationality. Applied with absolute rigour they lost their reasonableness and degenerated into a stultifying mechanism.

The attitude adopted by Corneille to "les règles", besides showing eminent good sense, illustrates very well the ambivalence of the terms "plot" and "rules". They are grounded in the nature of the form, giving it a set of "basic conventions", codifying the principles most likely to secure the powerful effects peculiar to it; but applied too rigidly as an exclusive dogma they impede other modes of expressiveness that would add liveliness and variety to the form, extending its possibilities. These oppositions may be discerned in the *Examens* of Corneille, as for instance in the opening of the *Examen du Cid:*

Ce poème a tant d'avantages du côté du sujet et des pensées brillantes dont il est semé, que la plupart de ses auditeurs n'ont pas voulu voir les défauts de sa conduite et ont laissé enlever leurs suffrages au plaisir que leur a donné sa représentation. Bien que ce soit celui de tous mes ouvrages réguliers où je me suis permis le plus de licence, il passe encore pour le plus beau auprès de ceux qui ne s'attachent pas à la dernière sévérité des règles; et, depuis cinquante ans qu'il tient sa place sur nos théâtres, l'histoire ni l'effort de l'imagination n'y ont rien fait voir qui en ait effacé l'éclat.

Or again a little later:—

Cette même règle presse aussi trop Chimène de demander justice au roi la seconde fois. Elle l'avait fait le soir d'auparavant, et n'avait aucun sujet d'y retourner le lendemain matin pour en importuner le roi, dont elle n'avait encore aucun lieu de se plaindre, puisqu'elle ne pouvait encore dire qu'il lui eût manqué de promesse. Le roman lui aurait donné sept ou huit jours de patience avant que de l'en presser de nouveau; mais les vingt et quatre heures ne l'ont pas permis: c'est l'incommodité de la règle.

As craftsman Corneille distinguishes between "subject", "conduct of the action", and "brilliant thoughts", a convention of "regularity" and the liberties he takes, and he notes an inconvenient pressure of the rules on a more natural development of the subject. But we detect also the dramatist-poet in these observations, claiming implicitly what we easily concede nowadays, that poetic power transcends rules and narrow conceptions of regularity, appearing in the imaginative movement of the whole rather than in the nice articulation of mechanical parts.

The essential issue here lies between factors of general expressiveness in the dramatic form and the particular expressiveness of each individual play. All plays must share in the former in order to be dramatic, and in the latter to be original and interesting; and a certain antagonism must arise if the rules are made so specific as necessarily to exclude numerous possible subjects. Rules, even those of good pedigree, embody a theoretical ideal of perfection which tends to restrict, whilst vision seeks always particularity of expression which may conform in general but deviates in detail, as Corneille's position shows.

This brings us back to the aesthetic idea of the total image in which are harmonized the various demands on the form: the convincing evocation of persons, the concentration and order that we recognize as "dramatic", and the expressiveness particular to each author and play, to *Antigone*, to *Othello*, to *Phèdre*, to *The Master Builder*, to *Partage de Midi*. The abstraction "plot" is then re-immersed in the sensuous forms of vision. As we said earlier, good drama is always an enactment of meanings. The disposition of the scenes through exposition, climax, and dénouement shows the author making his points, investing the dramatic imagery with a particular symbolism of idea and feeling.

In this context the significance of irony as a weapon of the dramatic imagination appears with great clarity. Irony, in Greek usage, meant dissembling or dissimulation. It indicated pretence, a deliberate disparity between what was said and what was meant, and the practice of Socrates, who feigned ignorance in order to provoke argument, is the usual example of its use. An ironist is always a species of actor. Irony is a mode of oblique statement. You use words in such a way as to direct attention to a real meaning which lies behind, and is opposed to, their literal meaning. It is the sly evocation of implied meanings. Its commonplace forms are the everyday greeting of the English in a downpour: Lovely weather, Mr. Smith! Or the stock manner of gentle reproach: You're a fine fellow! Debased, it becomes heartless sarcasm. Its effect depends on a reference being made, by the whole statement, to something not actually mentioned, so that where irony is involved the meaning intended arises always from a context larger than that of the literal statement. To create and convey the irony in the above simple examples, speaker and spoken-to know that it is raining, or that X is not a "fine" fellow but the opposite. The meaning is often clarified or reinforced by the inflexion of the voice running counter to the straight sense of the words, which is a form of communication by vocal imagery.

Irony has many refined uses in literature which we cannot here explore. In drama it is immensely fruitful, because, by the arrangement of his action and the way in which his characters are placed in the sequence of events, or come face to face with each other, the author can communicate his meanings—the real sense of his play and the purpose of his expression—to his audience. Sometimes this occurs in localized places, as in the scenes in *Othello* where Iago works his poison on Othello (III, iii), or later (IV, ii), where in her distress at Othello's attitude Desdemona turns for help to "good

Iago". Sometimes it is an effect built up through an entire play, as in *Oedipus Rex*, where Oedipus in pursuing the search for the scourge of Thebes is fulfilling unknowingly his own tragic destiny.[6]

Irony is thus one of the ways in which the dramatist shifts the plane from illusion of reality to that of the symbolic image. It places the actual image on the stage with dramatic emphasis into a larger framework of meaning. Ironical focusing always expresses feeling and judgements of the dramatist; it is an instrument of imaginative construction and not of simple illusion. All the great dramatists have been masters of irony: Sophocles, Shakespeare, Corneille, Racine, Grillparzer, Ibsen, Molière, Cocteau. Yeats was alive to its importance. Eliot knows about it but in practice suffers from a lack of invention in regard to *peripeteia* and ironical sequences.

At this point it is essential to extend the discussion to the persons of drama. It is not in any case easy to separate plot from persons, since it is they who carry it on; it is still less so for the argument we are pursuing, which holds expressly that both plot and persons are an imagery functioning in relation to an expressive purpose. They are just as metaphorical as the metaphors of the text.

xii. PERSONS CONSIDERED AS IMAGERY

The persons, like the plot of which they are the agents, belong to the total imagery of a play, the interpretation of which as a whole determines the view taken of the persons. The illusion of reality necessitated by impersonation is consistent with extremely varied presentation of persons, as may be seen at a glance by comparing Oedipus, Macbeth, and Tartuffe, or any similar set of characters from Sophocles, Shakespeare, and Molière. In each of these cases we are given sufficient information, and an adequate personal speech, to establish a credible person, or rather an image of a person, that is true in a general way to our experience of persons. But how different they are! Oedipus has none of the psychological complexity unfolded over a period of time in Macbeth, whilst Tartuffe is an intellectual simplification, his person appearing as the incarnation of a single predominant trait, hypocrisy. All the circumstances of the action make Oedipus credible; all the motives Macbeth; and Tartuffe is credible because people are indeed often dominated beyond all reason by a commanding trait of character, and because Molière secures in the person and his relations with others a sufficient vital complexity and depth to correct the over-abstract simplification and make it ring true.

What precisely a person is in a play thus depends on the interpretation in which the dramatist is engaged. There is no one standard of life-likeness, and we must resist a use of the word "character" for person which always confuses its conventional meaning of "personage in a play or novel" with the suggestion of native idiosyncrasy of character, or of fully developed psychological detail. For the sake of comparison, consider the figures of painters. Botticelli, Jan van Eyck, Rembrandt, Cézanne, in their treatment of human persons, all maintain a persuasive "truth to life" but with greatly varying methods, because each sees the human face and figure in a different aspect and with a different expressive purpose. The non-realistic styles of art in this century have made it easy for everyone, after the first unfamiliarity, to see in all pictures a selective imagery that speaks not for an absolute, fixed, fully identified "nature" but for an "artist-seeing-nature". The same principle holds for drama. Its persons are images, defining not "reality" or historical particulars but selected interpretative and expressive meanings.

Dramatic criticism in the past, not to mention the teaching of literature, has made great play with the distinction between individual characters and "types", the former being "good" examples of character-drawing, and the latter "bad". This sort of judgement rested on false assumptions. Type characterization is not necessarily bad; it is one sort of character presentation and may be highly appropriate. At least the stock types of drama—the villain, the heroine, the stage parson, the stage Irishman, or, more subtly, traditional types such as the dissembler (Iago)—reveal the processes of art since they are excellent examples of images, which always, as we have said above, are partial references to reality and have in addition, when incorporated in a work of art, a new function. A stage parson, for example, corresponds to a phenomenon familiar to us in life. We often say "he is a typical parson" and when we make such an observation in real life we mean that a few typical traits are so predominant in our impression that we generalize instinctively and say we have a good example of the "type" before us. I think such an impression in real life constitutes an image because it is a highly selective impression, a profile which we endow with meaning. Moreover, we *wish* to see the type in such instances, and in consequence we "see" the image as we in fact make it for ourselves. We know perfectly well on reflexion that the individual person behind the image is ambiguous and complex, but we exclude the complexity from our interest. What we apprehend in such a moment is not "reality" but a part of it, a rigorously limited bit of the potential real which to explore fully would demand of us a thousand more images and their correlation. All the stock types and conventional figures of drama in its various historical phases emerge from this process of image-making, ubiquitous in life and exploited by art. They come in for criticism usually when they have become purely imitative and stereotyped, and appear amidst deficiencies of other kinds.

The detailed realization of character, on the other hand, as we find it so often in Shakespeare and Renaissance drama generally, conforms with the humanistic interest in human and natural truth, truth here meaning the faithful portrayal of character in its intricacy, with a considerable documentary or scientific motive. The same tendency appears in portrait painting at that time. As we said above, this ideal suited the natural conditions of dramatic art.[7]

The success of truthful psychological portraiture beguiles people sometimes into speaking of the characters in a play as though they were real persons. But a dramatic character remains always an image in a pattern of imagery. The point can be put best in connexion with a much discussed feature of dramatic characters, their self-explanatory nature. Macbeth, for instance, is portrayed in a cultural milieu of a relatively undeveloped kind, which we certainly do not believe equal in refinement and subtlety to Shakespeare's own. Macbeth himself, although not savage, is at least no philosopher-king or sophisticated Renaissance prince, but he describes his feelings, his situation, his state of conscience with a precision and poetic felicity which they might envy. A sense of realism prompts the question: can Macbeth "know" all this about himself? Is he conceivably conscious of it in so lucid and exact a way? The answer from "reality" is a plain no. One might concede that he must, being human at all, have some sort of knowledge of himself; he knows his ambition, his deeds, and their consequences, as his career proceeds. But a "real" Macbeth would not speak in the way Shakespeare does. For it is the *poet* who is so verbally explicit. What he says is potentially there in a hypothetical object (a "real" Macbeth), but it is only actually there in the image he creates.[8] It is quite mistaken to read dramatic characters as though the lucid insight they show of their own emotions and its concentrated, not to say poetic, expression in speech is a fact of a real person. There will always be certain characters who have peculiarly vivid self-knowledge, but even with these it is a question whether, in reality, they would utter it; and in any case no one ever speaks poetry in real life, where the most that is achieved does not go beyond precision, force, clarity and eloquence. The poetic order in a speech by a character of Racine or Shakespeare at important junctures of the action is an imaginative order created not by the "character" but by the poet. Characters do not talk thus because they have 'moments of intuition', 'of sudden insight into their own feelings'. It is the poet who makes them talk thus, having himself gathered together analytically distinguished elements in the story and the people scattered, in a potential reality, over a considerable area, and unelaborated. He amplifies into a structural order what in real persons would be fragments of self-knowledge and declaration, potential intuitions, incipient or imperfectly realized feelings. It is thus that the form rests on suggestions of nature, but is finally an ordered creation of the imagination, which is a dramatist's idea.[9] The poet's role here is exactly parallel to that of the composer in opera. For in the music, in the singer's melody and still more in the orchestral accompaniment, he can draw on any of the leading themes of the music and therewith of the ideas of the whole conception. And thus the song of any character always presents two aspects of expressiveness in one utterance; it shows the person in a situation, giving voice to his emotions, but it is always simultaneously the composer defining, musically, his image of the person in relation to the whole dramatic-musical sequence of the work. He is both inside and outside the person through the music. He creates the drama of the persons within the envelope of the music. So, too, with the dramatist, and especially if he uses verse. The drama of substantial persons, the illusion of reality, is contained within the envelope of poetic statement, of the poet's vision and idea.

When we speak of the "reality" of the great characters of fiction and drama what we mean is that they are convincing images. The quality that makes them convincing derives from the imaginative fusion of various elements; the just observation of sensuous appearances, accurate psychological and moral judgement, and the presiding purpose, the predominant idea or feeling embodied in the play as a total unified image, and to which the former are assimilated. The elements, however, vary greatly in degree and balance, and this in itself confirms that the power of such characters inheres in their image-nature, and not in a normalized objective reality. Hence the simpler mythical characters like Prometheus, Don Juan, and Faust have as much persuasive "reality" as the complexly developed characters of Shakespearian tragedy, or the persons of Corneille, so conscious of motive and will.

The tragic, and the comic, character as image have a sharply different relation to the real world. Tragedy is based, as we said above, on certain emotional and moral responses to life. In consequence its effects, in all their poetry and sublimity, are inseparable from a picture of human destiny, a mimesis, that carries conviction by its general truth. In such a scheme the persons, too, have a high degree of "reality", as of life ; we always have to feel that they are like ourselves, that we might easily be in their place. But tragic drama, though necessarily faithful to truth in this way, is implicitly an interpretation. It embodies and expresses not simply a picture of life but one view of it, one feeling about it. It is thus an imagery, of which the tragic hero, however vividly realized with the sense of life, is but the centre and focus. To put it sharply: the characters in tragic drama must first seem to be not images, but real, before they can contribute effectively to the total tragic image.

The character in comedy, on the other hand, is more obviously an image, an artefact, part of an aesthetic game played openly by the author and also by actors and audience. Comic personages, always near to caricature, appear as schematic human beings built up on one or two outstanding traits of physique or moral character or intellectual complexion, as with Falstaff, Dogberry, Aguecheek, Belch, Volpone, the Alchemist Subtle, Mrs. Malaprop, Tartuffe, Harpagon, Doolittle, and so on. Even a more finely conceived character like Benedick we find activated by a powerful predominant passion, his hostility to women. An external symptom of this deliberate simplification of a substantial person into a profile-image, an accentuated and abstracted caricature, is the firm tradition of proper names that give the cue as to the main feature involved.

The world of comedy develops when such a simplified "person" impinges on his surroundings. Being unreal he propagates unreality. Or, to put it in its strictly aesthetic form, a comic *fantasy*—a concentrated unrealistic image—unfolds as the natural sequence of "characters" propelled only by one governing trait. Thus comedy no doubt starts with, and remains linked with life by means of, the natural idiosyncrasies of men, but by setting highly simplified characters in motion it dissipates the normal complex relations of living people and puts in their place a comic complication which is disordered in comparison with normality but logical by the laws of its own imagery.

The impulse towards comic creation, the recognition of foibles, absurdities, eccentricities, and the incongruousness of vice, is as "natural" to man as any of the serious passions and emotions rooted in the will and the unconscious, but once the comic imagination has launched its creation everything is calculated and artificial, whether in the action or the dialogue. The effort of the actor then contributes also to the transparent fantasy. He is not required to sustain a convincing picture of a possible human situation, but to be effective, as an exaggeration or a caricature, vis-à-vis the audience, and thus set the mechanism of comic effects in motion. Unlike the tragic actor, who must seem to be real in order to function as an image, the comic actor must from his first entry be a calculated image.

xiii. VARIED TREATMENT OF THE PERSON-IMAGE

We have not yet mentioned a large field of drama, besides comedy, in which the image quality of the person is plainly obvious. In all mysteries, moralities, and allegories, as well as in fantasy and fable, symbolism is overt. It no longer half conceals itself in a "realistic" picture. It provides a main structure of calculated symbolic types—types of person and situation—with a fragmentary and diffused realism in the detail as the necessary representational support. From our point of view all this class depends on the standard poetic figure of personification applied on a large scale. The representational needs of drama are satisfied in such cases by adding anthropomorphic appearances to human portraiture; gods and goddesses, angels and devils, spirits and fairies, and other creatures of myth and legend are let fabulously into the pattern of human dramatic speech. Human persons, on the other hand, retain the semblance of human beings when they are symbols standing for abstract ideas or concepts (as Everyman, Beauty, Fellowship, Discretion, etc. in morality plays).

In the twentieth century, after a strongly naturalistic phase of drama, there has been a reversion to symbolic, allegorical, mythical, or parable forms, in which the person as a profiled "expressive image" predominates over the fully-developed, psychologically detailed person of Renaissance humanism or of Ibsen. In this respect we remember how modern dramatists have deliberately modelled themselves on pre-Elizabethan plays; Eliot goes to the morality *Everyman*, Yeats to heroic legends and fairy tales, whilst many others have joined in the exploitation of old myths, and Shaw and Pirandello openly call their work "parable". We have referred above to the ubiquity of allegory in modern drama if only one looks a little beneath the varied surface. And there is a clear division between orthodoxy and heterodoxy, between those who use the didactic form for traditional beliefs, like Claudel and Eliot, and those who use it to propagate new secular philosophies, like Shaw, Giraudoux, or Sartre. In the last fifty years of development interest and originality of idea have to a large extent gone hand in hand with decisive stylistic change in the treatment of persons. The fruits have been the break-up of a stereotyped or faded "realism"; in its place we have seen the expressive image triumph. Yet this general movement has often brought drama to the verge of the impossible, where the balance between the primary substance of drama, with convincing persons and the pressing sense of life, and the expressive idea of the poet, becomes too precarious. To follow this process in full would require a history of modern play-writing; let us be content with a few examples.

The point is illustrated well by the frequently used idea of the "marionette", a comparison which makes clear the simplification of purpose in presenting persons. Dolls are costumed and painted with one fixed expression, and persons in a play can be reduced to the same kind of simple unity. This in itself marks their denuded aspect by comparison with the potential richness of human personality. Beyond that they are enveloped with emotional suggestions of pathos because they can seem so human but are manipulated, which reminds us of men's helplessness against fate, or their ignorance of the larger purposes of the universe they belong to. The word occurs with Maeterlinck's earlier poetic plays—*La Mort de Tintagiles*, *Intérieur*, *Les Sept Princesses*, etc.—which express the frailty of human beings facing the terrors of death, love, and destiny. The persons in these plays have human reality, and the plays are bathed in strong human emotion. But the simple aim makes the persons unindividual; they are humans and nothing more, images of men reduced to one or two primary feelings.

Yeats also had recourse to the term marionette to suggest something of what he wanted in the *Plays for Dancers*. Under the same symbolist influences as Maeterlinck he aims at something not dissimilar, the expression of those 'profound emotions that exist only in solitude and in silence.' His symbolism and play technique are more elaborate than Maeterlinck's but his persons are equally stripped of detail and tuned to a single chord of feeling.

The comparison turns up again in the very different context of expressionist drama. Toller said that you can see people as "realistic human beings" and also, in a flash of vision, as puppets, showing a single aspect of themselves. This applies to his own handling of persons, but still more to certain much stronger plays of Kaiser, like the *Gas* trilogy, or *Von Morgens bis Mitternachts*. Here, in accordance with a remorseless analysis of a technocratic society, and an explosion of revolutionary emotion, people are deprived of their human roundness and whittled down to profiles corresponding to their social function. The image of the person is simplified to a dominant aspect or generic idea: worker, industrialist, beggar, prostitute, brother, and so on. It becomes a symbol with a double function; on the one hand in an abstractive scheme of pointed social analysis, on the other an emotional symbol helping to express in the cumulative pattern of the whole a mood of protest. Though partial and "abstract" such images are not untrue, nor do they fail in conveying a sense of "reality"; on the contrary they reflect a very real social process of this century by which the function of a person has not only more and more out-valued the person but stunted him. Thus this kind of image can in fact be evaluated in two different ways. Measured against a humanistic conception they are abstractions; set against twentieth century conditions in the industrial proletariat and the depressed "black-coated" class they come closer to realistic images. This ambiguity helps to keep such *dramatis personae* within the proper sphere of dramatic impersonation. Nevertheless the degree of rarefaction is considerable, diminishing the interest for the actor; which is a sign that this type moves towards the periphery of what is possible in the form. It is not surprising that the style did not prove attractive for long.

Giraudoux's plays, in contrast to the foregoing, are full of characters who partake very clearly of human nature, yet his treatment of persons illustrates a very subtle kind of adjustment between image and idea. It depends initially on his myth-allegory form, used in a series of plays of which perhaps the best are *Électre*, *La Guerre de Troie n'aura pas lieu*, and *Judith*, though others are hardly less good. Although using subjects from myth, the method of Giraudoux is not, like Cocteau's, to realize old myths anew as archetypes of human experience. He appropriates the old myths, then expropriates them, using the fictional vestige to express in images of persons certain ideals of virtue, and convey an acute apprehension of contemporary problems facing society as a whole. Thus on the surface we are met with poetically attractive creations imbued with fantasy and capricious wit, whilst beneath the surface we distinguish a powerful examination of ethical and social principles.

Giraudoux makes his principal characters the instruments of his ideas and feeling for values, and reserves for the secondary ones the role of enlivening the picture-of-life. This is seen very well in *La Guerre de Troie n'aura pas lieu*, where the members of Hector's family give reality to common life whilst Hector himself is reserved for a more exalted and spiritualized function. Not that such primary persons are mere abstractions or mouthpieces; they always have substance enough to exist as part of a story. But they are idealized representations, personifying an unfolding of some fine human quality or desire, and, projected in a crisis which focuses their aspiration, they develop into forcible centres of feeling. Électre, for instance, derives from the Greek myth and appears with the general semblance of a human being like ourselves. But she is neither historical, nor an archetypal myth-figure, nor a transcript from our own entourage, but a newly-conceived image expressing a certain group of feelings and thoughts the author has about life and the place of justice in it, and the modes by which the higher values reveal themselves in human person and action. If these feelings and thoughts were hers, as a realistic character, she would be a simple representation; since they are the author's, existing in his sensibility and imagination, and then embodied in her nature, she is an expressive image, functioning like the images of metaphor. Giraudoux treats in this way Hector, Judith, Alcmène, Ondine, and others, in all of whom some generalized problem of ethical or social behaviour, based on idealizing nostalgia, is focused, both rationally and emotionally. Giraudoux's form is thus an allegory or didactic fiction evolved from myth and used as a vehicle for contemporary and public meanings.[10]

If, in Giraudoux, we find the real, that is, the contemporary human situation, abstracted, analysed, and diffused through a myth-fantasy or fiction, in Eliot we observe a myth generated from the real contemporary situation. His plays have a literal, realistic, very contemporary surface, 'ourselves of this present time and year, upon the stage', but they develop, as they progress, into poetic rites. He portrays the scene from familiar life—the family in the country house, the barrister with wife, mistress and social circle—through which an underlying mythical pattern diffuses its meanings to the surface; so that the "real" becomes, without being negated or displaced, transparent, and through it the myth appears as the immanent meaning. The treatment of persons corresponds. They have, in character, psychology, and action, more "reality" than the profiled persons of many modern symbolic styles; yet the principal characters, Becket, Harry, Celia, are also profoundly symbolic, whilst all contribute to a symbolic pattern of events. In a drama based on such a view both realistic and mythical form are authentic; the one is more than a preoccupation with limited aspects of social reality, and the other more than a modern aesthetic device. The symbolism of Eliot's characters is implicit because the personal form contains the meaning. Similarly, the mythical power inheres in the real human situation, since people like Harry and Celia, unlike figures from past myths, begin as ordinary persons leading ordinary lives and remain human even after the assumption of their distinctive functions. The incorporation of elements from primitive or ancient ritual, though not uniformly successful, is at least relevant, since it fortifies the endowment of the whole situation (especially in *The Family Reunion*) with its complex meaning. Eliot's considered technique of verse also makes an appropriate and organic contribution, pendulating between the realistic surface and the underlying myth, the verse that is very close to the prosaic, and that which draws on all the expressive sources, ancient and modern, of poetry.

Eliot thus, following his own insight into the mutual balance required between realism and ritual in the drama as a form, renews the ritualistic strength of drama at a moment when it had been dissipated by the realist style, but without betraying the individuality of personal life. His drama is not only of ideas or feelings but of persons. Yet he links it to a spiritual theme and makes it also an instrument of belief and catharsis and a poetic image for the inner life.[11] His success may have been unequal; his aim, which for our argument in this essay amounts to a profound recovery of a natural form of drama, was true.

These brief comments on a few outstanding examples of the treatment of the person in contemporary drama illustrate the constantly shifting relationship between descriptive and expressive imagery, the picture-of-man and the symbolism of thought and feeling. The forms considered spring from the double functioning of the imagination. On the one hand, applied to the realities of human situations, the imagination interprets and gives meaning; on the other, applied to feeling and thought, it constructs expressive forms; and these two functions coalesce in the vivid and conclusive imagery of the whole drama, so that the representation of realities is suspended in expression, and the expressiveness is emergent from representation.

Thus, in all these types, we observe a variation of imagery taking place within certain limits. The analysis emphasizes the central aesthetic fact that we have to do with an *imagery*, that is, sensuous forms constituting an expressive interpretation; but also with a feature particular to the art of drama, arising from its being an enactment, viz. that this imagery can never become "abstract" in the way of abstract painting, nor extremely symbolistic like symbolist poetry. It can never consist solely, to use the term we used in an earlier chapter, of expressive formula-images, as music and abstract art do. Its images must always tend, or revert, towards persons with representational likeness to life.

We may sum up the subject of this section, and perhaps throw a last gleam of light on it, by distinguishing between the *detail* of the action in a drama and the *whole* conception in its unity of idea or impression. The former will in the main show the representational element at its strongest. For in the moment-to-moment dialogue and action we find the expression of passion and feeling, and apprehend the contour of human situations, all of which, when the art is fine, yields a clarification, illuminating the opaque masses of the "real" with the light of imagination. But, on the other hand, as the drama unfolds before us and the sense of a unifying impulse gradually establishes itself in our mind, to be fixed there as the final curtain falls, we are affected by some general idea or emotion which is embodied in the creation, not to be detached, it is true, from the persons and their action, and yet felt as the determining factor and ultimate purpose of the whole.

In the former of these two features we see the sensuous detail of representational art from which the sense of *life*, indispensable in art, and of *personal* life, indispensable in drama, disengages itself. In the latter lies the imaginative aura of the whole as a whole, its expressiveness, the impression its imagery conveys of tragedy, pathos, joy, romance, pessimism, ideal striving, aspiration, or any other of the commanding emotions that life evokes; and from this feature the sense of the *dramatist*, of the poet himself, disengages itself. Nevertheless, all is image, and poetic quality may be in both.

xiv. REALISM IN LATE NINETEENTH CENTURY DRAMA

In previous sections we have tried to define to what extent an element of simple representation, or in other words, how much illusion of "reality", is essential in drama. But throughout we maintained the point of view established at the beginning of this essay, that representation in art, however realistic, is always an imagery; its realism is always aesthetic, always imaginative, always interpretative and expressive. As such it does not pertain to "reality" as against poetry, but belongs, like poetry, to art.

Nevertheless the term "realism" has lent itself to various uses at the expense of clarity. In dramatic criticism it often describes the descent from poetry to something more documentary; Ibsen himself, abandoning the freer, poetic style of *Peer Gynt* and *Brand*, spoke of getting nearer to reality in *A Doll's House* and similar plays. Or it has indicated the drop from heroic to domestic tragedy, as in Lillo and Diderot after the age of Dryden and Racine. It is also common to contrast the realistic tone of comedy with the poetic one of tragedy. The word is used almost invariably to characterize a less intense imaginative effort, a work in which the imagination comes down to earth again, when one feels nearer the familiar world than on the rarefied heights of poetry. It means the non-idealized, the non-spiritualized, the anti-noble.

Such usage obscures the true issue, making the word carry the sense not only of qualifying the degree of art or poetry in a play, but of negating the aesthetic image altogether. For the opposition often drawn between "realistic" and poetic style is after all inaccurate. There is plenty of the plainest psychological realism in Shakespearian tragedy amidst the most splendid poetic statement. On the other hand even in comic plays the "realism" clearly functions within the aesthetic purpose of comedy, which illumines it with its own light, a light of criticism and intelligence.

Apart from these unclarities further confusion arises from the novels and plays of the second half of the nineteenth century written in the mode of "realism", sharpening later into "naturalism". As a consequence of this phase realism added to its general meanings a historical one; it became one of the broad inclusive words that sum up a whole phase of writing and art. Realism in this sense was a post-romantic phenomenon, appearing as a reaction against romanticism and its exaggerations. It answered an insistent question: what do we see, when we forget dreams, the Ideal, and the beautiful solitudes of nature, and open our eyes upon men and the conditions in which they actually live day by day? And its particular flavour, by which it was marked off from previous kinds of realism, derived from the new social realities. They showed an increasingly powerful, but progressively more materialistic bourgeoisie, governed by hypocrisy and decadent conventions rather than by faith and genuine idealism; and alongside it the grimy and increasingly oppressed proletariat of the industrial era, becoming articulate, militant, and revolutionary. The realism of the drama in this period, observable in Hebbel, Dumas *fils*, Ibsen, Strindberg, Hauptmann, Sudermann, Tom Robertson (followed by Pinero and Jones), Brieux, and others, pertains to subject-matter and ideas in the first place; it is anything but a merely stylistic reaction against high-flown romantic verse. It follows on the rejection of the ideas and beliefs of literary romanticism and philosophical idealism, of the pantheism, meta-physics, and *Schwärmerei* of every kind that had characterized so much work of the first half of the century. It is a sober confrontation of man with the society that had been slowly maturing and had at last realized its particular character.

This confrontation was on the one hand documentary; it produced a new picture of social life and conditions. But it was animated also, and very urgently, by a spirit of protest sometimes implicit but often openly expressed as social criticism. It embodies an appeal to the conscience of society, though this specific conscience was still at that time awaiting precise recognition and consecration.

It is not easy to assess the aesthetic complexion of this realistic drama. Certainly the problem is least of all solved by blandly referring, as many do now, to the realistic *convention*, which amounts to little more than a play on words. As a first step we should remember that the new realism cannot be divorced from powerful influences and beliefs of the time. It belongs to the age of Feuerbach, Marx, and Comte. In the background we observe a rapidly evolving scientific outlook, with its partner historical knowledge. Scepticism in religion and metaphysics, a secular and humanistic view of morals, faith in the "facts" of science and history and present-day "conditions", and an implicit optimism bred by reliance on the powers of reason and knowledge and human potentiality, were determining factors of a new outlook shared by progressive minds. The character of the new drama was influenced by all these things, which together constituted a cluster of beliefs, determining the focus of vision. In this way a protest in the name of a higher humanity and social idealism was made by the unflinching portrayal of the hypocrisies of middle-class morality or of revolting social conditions amongst the poor. Thus the realistic play was, like other dramatic art, an expressive imagery, taken as a whole; yet its expressiveness is achieved by a partial betrayal of the law of art, insofar as a "truthful", or "normalized", representation replaces the free working of the imagination. "Society" could only be seen through blinkered eyes.

The *drame à thèse* shows best the contradiction between aesthetic and non-aesthetic factors, and how factual truth of description impairs aesthetic quality. For a play with a thesis—some moral or social criticism such as we find in *Ghosts*, or, lower down the scale, in the works of Brieux—is bound by its intention to be completely faithful to the facts of life it analyses and protests against. Its purpose, which is to persuade its audience that something is amiss, compels it to draw a picture of people and society that can be checked as "accurate", so that the protest is properly directed; and this means not imaginative but normative portraiture. The aesthetic issue is of course unimportant in an unpretentious *pièce-à-thèse* or a frank propaganda piece. In plays like *Ghosts* or *A Doll's House*, however, the framework of thesis is in fact disrupted by powerful imaginative elements of various kinds. One observes two plays entangled with each other; on the one hand a thesis play, and on the other an image of individual suffering and predicament with a dominant tone of pathos or tragedy; and they pull as much in different directions as in the same. There are two pivots in these plays. One is poetically alive, a vivid expressiveness conveyed in the vital sensitiveness of central persons like Nora and Mrs. Alving. The other is the picture of a circumjacent society, which has to show, in general terms, that state of affairs against which the central character—and Ibsen—revolts. The milieu is objectively or scientifically analysed, and is represented, in consequence, in typified form; Torvald Helmer and Pastor Manders are purely types in this sense, whilst the basic situation of each play is also socially typical. It is here that we feel a loss of the free movement and organic form of the best art; the ever-moving living image is replaced by analytic or conceptual types, resulting, as far as the persons are concerned, in representative stereotyped figures, and, as far as situations are concerned, in a certain rigidness or artificiality. Hence the realism of such plays is a strange mixture of art and analysis, imagination and factual description, expressive imagery and scientific copy-imagery.

In a sense the *pièce-à-thèse* could be held to correspond to the pamphlet or impassioned essay on a social or moral topic and might be expected to develop the expressive and literary qualities associated with rhetoric. This it sometimes does, in two ways. The simpler and more obvious way is to use a principal character plainly as a mouthpiece, as Shaw does, in which case the play, in the speeches of that character, assumes a style of oratory peculiar to the author, and powerfully expressive in a way in which the dialogue as a whole is not. The prose spoken by the typical Shavian character is very close to that of Shaw's prefaces, energetic, purposeful, brilliant, epigrammatic, rhetorically forceful and winning, whilst the dialogue is often commonplace in quality. The other way is to make a strong emotional statement in terms of theatre, of highly dramatic plot and character with vivid rhetorical implications. Ibsen uses both methods in *A Doll's House* and *Ghosts*. Nora and Mrs. Alving both speak with the voice of Ibsen, whilst the situations in each play, the characters and actions involved and the curtain-falls, are trimmed to an urgent emotional and moral purpose.

Nineteenth century realism in the drama became associated with prose. It is not surprising; verse was inevitably seen linked with romantic poetry which was under attack. We can now see easily enough, however, that the association is not the only possible one. All poetry need not be romantic, and the issue of prose as against verse is not necessarily tied to that of realism against romanticism. It was only apparently so tied at that point in history. At other times there is realism in poetry, as in Chaucer or Shakespeare or Eliot, and romanticism in prose—the "poem in prose" was a creation of romanticism. So that with prose, as with realism, the point upon which judgement should bear is its function; is that aesthetic, or documentary, or scientific, or philosophical? To what degree is it either one or the other? The task is to distinguish between prose as imagination and prose as something else, as thought, criticism, or science. And in this connexion we have also to bear in mind that the dialogue of drama is only one constituent of the play; the total impression is very much influenced by the theatrical production and acting. Nevertheless, just as we have to admit an anti-aesthetic tendency in realism pursued to the point of copy-imagery, so we admit that a prose used in such a development might well tend to eliminate its potentially aesthetic qualities.

CHAPTER ELEVEN

VARIOUS MODES OF POETRY IN DRAMA. EXPRESSIVE FORMULA-IMAGERY METAPHOR AND THEIR RELATION TO STYLE AND POETIC QUALITY

i. THE PROBLEM OF THE "POETIC"; THE CONFUSION OF TERMS; THE CRITERION OF STYLE

WE MUST NOW CONSIDER more particularly various aspects of dramatic expression which involve the notion of "poetic" quality, and we are at once beset by the inadequate terms of English usage, since "poetry" and "poems", losing their broader generic meaning, have come to mean simply compositions in verse. But further linguistic embarrassment arises from the ambiguous uses of the word "poetic", which more often than not suggests romantic poeticality, or lyricism. Thus, of the two terms that arise in connexion with drama, one, "dramatic poetry", excludes plays in prose, calling to mind authors like Marlowe and Shakespeare; and the second, "poetic drama", tends to mean a play written in prose but with a poetic aura or romantic atmosphere, of which the works of Maeterlinck or Synge are notable examples. But even with these clear cases we have an uncomfortable feeling that the terms themselves prejudice our conception. They don't quite fit the examples given, or others we may think of. They indicate categories into which only those works fit that are in fact deficient either as dramatic or as poetic creations, having on the one hand too much poetry, as in Beddoes, and on the other either too little drama or a tainted kind of poetry, as in Wilde's *Salome* or Flecker's *Hassan*. Theoretically, of course, the term "dramatic poetry" proposes, as it did for Aristotle, a subdivision of poetry; but the extension of literary art to prose forms renders it inadequate without any new term having gained currency in English, as the word *Dichtung* has in German.

The usage that deprives us of a generic term provides substitutes, and it cannot be denied that they embody a good deal of common sense, for usage solves problems with rough justice that admit of only very complicated theoretical solutions. Thus, whilst critics and aestheticians argue about the precise nature of poetry and the poetic, we every day speak of a "good play", a "great play", a "beautiful play", and the epithets thus used function not only as descriptions or evaluations but also as indications of *aesthetic type*. The first tends to be reserved for plays of a serious kind, with good themes and various qualities of discreet sensibility, human sympathy, or moderate imaginative power, but not rising higher than the modest lower slopes of Parnassus. If we said that *Antony and Cleopatra* or *Le Soulier de Satin*, or *Phèdre*, was "a good play", we should either be making a joke or we should have a faint sense of sacrilege; or if we heard it put that way we should suspect a lack of literary education in the speaker. But the word does justice to an acceptable kind of dramatic production, to the plays of Galsworthy, for example.

The epithets "great and "beautiful" are most used of plays which show intense imaginative quality irrespective of whether they are in verse or prose, like Ibsen's late works, or Turgenev's *A Month in the Country*, or Hauptmann's *Die Weber*. They give us an opportunity of acknowledging poetic power in forms which do not fall technically into the class "poetry". "Fine" is another hard-worked word, but it is less of a sign-post, conveying most often simply a vague sense of quality. Or the superlative "finest" (his "finest" play) is made to generate special overtones of evaluation.

Comedy being so decisive a category (without prejudice, of course, to incidental comedy in plays of various kinds) the problem of terminology is not quite the same, and other terms, like "high comedy", come to be used, whilst "fine" assumes in this connexion a nuance of meaning—fine comedy—that gives it a sharper profile than in the use noted above. *The Tempest*, or *Twelfth Night*, are no doubt great and beautiful plays ; *The Way of the World*, on the other hand, or *The Rivals*, have to be described differently, "great comedy" being the collocation of words that in this case suggests the high degree of imaginative achievement.

What these various phrases do in a practical way, in order to characterize actual differences in plays, our theory of imagery and complex intertexture must try to do in a systematic way. It has been worked out within the framework of art in general and so it is broad enough to allow of a criterion of *imagination*, an imagination which uses many different instruments and creates many varieties of form. Verse in drama, however important, is but one of these. In this connexion we may add, in order to clear up the question from the start, that the customary opposition between prose and "poetry" is really inept when applied to drama. The reason, at this stage of our argument, should be clear enough. The language of a play is one element in an intertexture of imagery, including stage décor and acting, so that the substitution of verse for prose, although of far-reaching effect, does not imply the same degree of acute contrast as it does, for instance, in narrative, a form for reading only. Moreover the language, whether prose or verse, is dialogue; it is speech. This is also an assimilating factor, since the language in both cases serves the same—a dramatic—purpose, in which the dissimilar functions of prose and verse in other literary forms and usages are no longer of importance.

Next, we must face up to a difficulty arising from the development of poetry since symbolism. In all present-day discussions of the "poetic"—what is it, and where manifested?—there is a tendency to a pronounced rarefaction of the idea of poetry. The "poetic" as a concept has been refined by reference to lyric and reflective poetry, as contrasted with the prose forms of literature; it is exclusive, a highly specialized idea. But in addition, the symbolist movement, led by the hieratic Mallarmé, has had a still more important effect on the over-refining of the notion of the poetic; not poetry, or lyric, but *quintessential* poetry became the established ideal. And the criterion of that, as we saw in chapter nine, is the tissue of imagery. Metaphors, tropes, rhythm and sound are no longer the secondary instruments of story, or ideas, or "thoughts", and their associated feelings, but take control, becoming the primary texture. This is one ground of the contemporary appeal of the later hymns of Hölderlin, alongside the influence of Valéry and symbolism; their texture is densely figurative, thick with symbolic images, into which the ideas have been almost completely transmuted, giving the poems an esoteric quality as of dream or mystic illumination, and comparable to the esoteric quality and poetic-musical ideal of the symbolists.

There is nothing wrong with this criterion insofar as it focuses sharply the feature of metaphor and symbolic transformation central in poetic creation. But it is too easily misapplied. It should not in justice lead to the rejection of poetic styles less concentrated than the symbolist; nor to an implicit depreciation of art in other forms; nor to the view that all poetry depends only on one kind of metaphor or "symbol"—the poetic image in a verse text. (This latter is the error of those who decry Eliot's plays as against his earlier poems; they do not see the transference of metaphorical power from words alone to scene and persons). One has always to distinguish between at least three major current meanings of "poetic". It indicates a text in verse, which meaning derives ultimately from classical times. It means, secondly, the romantically poetic, and this refers rather to certain themes and attitudes irrespective of verse or prose forms, as we observe in fairy tales and in an author like Maeterlinck, whose plays are intensely romantic though in prose. Thirdly, it means lyrical and musical style, primarily in verse, but also in prose. These variants, taken together, show how impossible it is to *restrict* the meanings of "poetic" either to verse compositions, or to romantic ones; the various influences and usages are by now inextricably intertwined. The alternative is to *broaden again* the notion of the poetic. This is what we shall do. We shall associate it, as closely analogical, with the notion of "art" altogether. It is absurd to call Giorgione or Titian "poetic" as if Michelangelo and Rembrandt were not; or Maeterlinck poetic as if Corneille, later Ibsen, Eliot, or Cocteau were not.

In the case of drama it is still more erroneous to apply a poetic criterion with either the romantic or the symbolistic rigour. Certainly imagery is all-important, but what counts for drama is the principle of metaphor and symbol not only in language and verse but in all the varied imagery of which as an art it makes use. A character or characters, the events and actions, the setting, and more frequently still the play as a whole, are all of them in some way symbols radiating their power through all the details of the imagery and creating a unified pattern of metaphor and symbol. Moreover, only such a sense of a metaphorical whole enables drama to assimilate its necessary elements of violence, which are often too harsh in themselves to be made poetic or "musical" even by verse. A character like Ferdinand in *The Duchess of Malfi*, when realized by an actor with the proper sinister ferocity, is in isolation too discordant and ugly to illustrate a phase of the poetic. But the tragic image in which his violence is but a single aspect does as a whole achieve poetry.

This is why we have been at pains to treat drama and its components as an imagery, an imagery sometimes representational, sometimes formula, and always expressive. It is always a symbolism of life seen-and-felt in a single operation of vision or intuition. The truth of the world merges with the truth of the author's feeling and the result is art. A drama showing this effect is art; and such effects are the product, in the dramatic form, of the same essential power which produces, in the verbal texture of poetry, the "poetic image". In this sense Ibsen's *Borkman*, Chekhov's *Three Sisters*, Synge's *Deirdre of the Sorrows*, Giraudoux' *Électre*, Cocteau's *Les Parents Terribles*, to name a few examples of plays in "prose", are, in their character as dramatic wholes, poetic images.

Basing ourselves thus on a criterion of *art*, which is more apposite than a restrictive conception of the *poetic*, we see that differences in dramatic forms should be viewed not in a simplified linguistic contrast of "verse" against "prose", but as variations in *style*, style in this case being the character of all the dramatic imagery and not a partial feature of language alone.

Differences of style pertain to the kinds of imagery used, to their mingling and interaction, and to the power with which they are invested; every play has its own pattern of speech, persons, plot, setting, décor, and incidental imagery. The poetic quality in style depends on the symbolic density and metaphorical interplay of the images and image-kinds. By the former I do not mean aggregation of denotative symbols but the power of images of all kinds—symbols or analogues of sense, archetypal images, symbols of dreams and the unconscious, and what we have called expressive formula-images (auditory-imagery and rhythm)—in their reference to feelings. By metaphorical interplay I mean the process, analysed in chapter three, by which all images in a work of art are by nature metaphorical because functional; their literal or representational meaning is displaced in favour of their evocative effect on the feelings germane to the central artistic idea. As separate images they are not metaphors; they are at the most symbolic. But because they have no independent identity, acting as contributors to the unity of impression essential in all art-works, they partake of the metaphorical.[1]

Some plays achieve this intensity of expression by using verse and the figurative language that goes with it, and the special advantages of these will be analysed in the next section. In others, like Synge's *Riders to the Sea*, which is in a simple prose, the effect derives from the essentially symbolic nature of the subject, which exemplifies human heroism and weakness in its tragic contest with a power of nature. Tragedy, in prose or verse, is always sure of a poetic effect because it stirs profound feelings and, the tragic in life never being hidden for long, any tragic situation is immediately felt to be symbolic of life generally. Some authors, like Ibsen and Chekhov, use in prose plays important symbols which have great affective and also great structural force. Or again, other dramatists exploit myth, allegory, and fantasy to secure the expressive image. And of course any of these forms are used in combination. Within this variety the sense of poetic quality is more easily assured by centralized than by incidental or sporadic metaphor. I mean that, obvious though it sounds, poetry flows freely from a poetic conception, as we see by contrasting Maeterlinck and Brieux, or Lorca and Arthur Miller, whilst sporadic poetic images stuck on cannot redeem a flat conception. The metaphorical key in Maeterlinck, or Chekhov, or Lorca, or Cocteau, or Eliot, is set from the beginning; the symbolic transpositions run through all the imagery, including the initial casting of the line of plot and character, making a fine tissue of inter-acting metaphor. Yeats offers a vivid illustration of this principle, since amongst his plays we find some wholly in verse, some in mixed prose and verse (*The Cat and the Moon*) and some in prose (*The Words upon the Window-pane*, *The Resurrection*), all of them, however, drawing their power from diffused symbol and metaphor. This poetic quality derives ultimately from the disposition of the creative mind, which always blends an image of the world with an image of its own sensibility. "My play is *the world*; my play is *my* world". A play that is only "the world", like so many "problem" plays, is usually an external copy; it is by tendency scientific copy-imagery and not aesthetic, and so fails to reach poetry. The motive is knowledge, not expression. A play that is only "my world", on the other hand, is totally private; it is functional only to the person, like a dream or the aberration of a diseased mind. The same principle reaches into the personal aspects of style in the dialogue, whether prose or verse, by which we distinguish Marlowe from Chapman, Congreve from Vanbrugh, Eliot from Yeats, and so on. All dialogue mingles facets of observed speech with the author's own expressiveness. It is not stylish or poetic if it imitates conventional speech; it becomes style when it incorporates the qualities of vision and feeling.

Supported by this view of style in dramatic imagery as a whole we can admit a scale of expressive quality, or artistic intensity, without getting entrammelled in the snares of the term poetic and its varied meanings, or misconceiving the relation between "prose" and dramatic art. In the centre we keep a steady empirical notion of the drama-poem, the play that generates in one inseparable process the poetic and the dramatic, represented in its verse form by the greatest models Shakespeare and Racine; and here we do feel, as we shall see in the sequence, that verse, though not indispensable and not the one and only source of the poetic, is a powerful weapon in its service. Close beside these, rather as a twin element of the central ideal, we observe prose plays like those of Synge, Chekhov, the latest Ibsen, Yeats, Lorca, or Cocteau. Though not in verse, they are imaginative creations, compositions in metaphorical imagery, which, with their foundation in the characteristic intertexture of dramatic form, makes them essentially related, as art, to the drama-poem. We shall remark later on some details of their metaphorical structure. Then, receding from the dramatic-poetic centre in varying degree on one side, there are all those plays which have had the doors of poetry half-closed, or shut, or slammed, in their faces, but are always serious, often moving, and at the least are interesting and share in that humanity of all drama to which we referred above. From Pinero and Jones, through Galsworthy and Maugham, to Priestley, Morgan and Rattigan, they are always in prose and show a naturalistic surface to the audience. The poor ones fall to a staid and conventional tone. The better are enhanced, as in Granville Barker or Galsworthy, by fine intellectual qualities, by insight, understanding, moral sensitiveness, delicate sympathy, by many qualities which are needed to appreciate art and life; but they remain without the one key to forceful poetic creation, the transposing sensibility of genius.

If this type of play fails in proportion to a diminishing scale of metaphorical power, there are types on the opposite side of the central ideal which fail by reason either of an excess of poetic ingredients, or of irrelevant ones. The chief offenders here are the lyric poets who intrude into drama. They have poetry, but the wrong sort; their failure is in their inability to conceive the right intertexture of the form. Here again there is a scale of recession from the ideal norm, apparent this time in a diminishing *dramatic* force, the lyric meditation strangling the drama. This is the fault in the plays of Anne Ridler (e.g. *The Shadow Factory*) and Norman

Nicholson (*The Old Man of the Mountain*). We feel that they have a tender conscience about certain aspects of the modern industrial and materialistic society, which is in danger of forgetting entirely not only orthodox religions but even the elementary natural pieties, and that they are moved to elegiac protest. Their cast of imagination, and their tone of voice, are lyrical. They do not, like the true dramatist, love and embrace life because they can't resist it. They do not, like Eliot, love what they also hate, the temptation and the sin, the desert and the devil. They are in fact rather vulnerable, more given to wishing the storm did not exist than to riding it out.

An extreme example of non-dramatic verse texture from the nineteenth century is Swinburne, in whom lyric not only swamps drama, but also a false musical ideal vitiates the lyric. The most excusable offenders are such as Byron and Beddoes who, though substituting a virtual monologue for a play, at least do not subside into lyric song.

Finally, we must not mistake occasional excess for a failure of the proper intertexture. This is a characteristic of Elizabethan drama, in which the idea of eloquence played so large a part; the most obvious examples occur in the fine exuberance of Marlowe's style. Whilst we recognise Faustus's famous speech beginning 'Was this the face that launch'd a thousand ships, And burnt the topless towers of Ilium?— Sweet Helen, make me immortal with a kiss . . .' as dramatic and poetic in the same breath, we should feel the need of some apologetic argument to justify the absolute dramatic appropriateness of *all* of Tamburlaine's monologue (Part I, V, i):

> Ah, fair Zenocrate!—divine Zenocrate!
> Fair is too foul an epithet for thee . . .

The monologue in itself is dramatically in place, but what of the following section?—

> What is beauty, saith my sufferings, then?
> If all the pens that ever poets held
> Had fed the feeling of their masters' thoughts,
> And every sweetness that inspir'd their hearts,
> Their minds, and muses on admired themes;
> If all the heavenly quintessence they still
> From their immortal flowers of poesy,
> Wherein, as in a mirror, we perceive

The highest reaches of a human wit;
If these had made one poem's period,
And all combin'd in beauty's worthiness,
Yet should there hover in their restless heads
One thought, one grace, one wonder, at the least,
Which into words no virtue can digest.

This beautiful passage shows Marlowe pushing his character Tamburlaine to one side and making a speech of his own. There are many such flaws in the intertexture of verse plays of that period. Often it would be a nice question to decide clearly the degree of transgression, for rhetoric has in any case an element of dramatic excitement and we accept an added poetic eloquence without demur when it arises within an otherwise secure dramatic context.

ii. VERSE IN DRAMA

Although, as we have affirmed, poetic quality derives from various sources, for all of which we must be receptive, putting prejudice or narrow dogma out of our minds, we must still admit that the use of verse, when successful, as with the Elizabethans or the French classical dramatists, or Schiller and Grillparzer, is a major factor in dramatic expression, which we must take account of.

Our immediate task is not to state over again the main features of poetry, which was done in earlier chapters, but to indicate the special character of verse as it functions in drama. Verse, when appropriate, is the most powerful single instrument of poetic intensification because it adds to language decisive rhythms, and, cultivating more carefully the sound of language, exploits the expressiveness of the voice. Rhythm and vocal sound are both profoundly rooted in our physical nature and therefore intimately linked with feeling.

The first reason for the peculiar fitness and power of verse in drama lies in its being an organization of rhythm, for this makes it congruent with other aspects of the flow of time in dramatic sequences; its function here thus differs widely from that of lyric verse. Everything dramatic is based on an acute time relation; something precedes, something follows; a situation is foreshadowed and rapidly unfolds. Time is folded into a drama from its beginning, since a past is always implicit in any situation from which a drama begins; and the drama, as it progresses, uncurtains a future equally implicit. And not only the whole play, but each scene and each act have their expressive movement with retardations and accelerations according to the mood. Verse, in this context, is simply the deployment of the same instrument, time, in a variant mode. This conforms to the great principle of unity in diversity and adds to the intensity and economy of expression.

The second cogent reason for the power of verse in drama is connected with the fact that intense emotions seek an outlet in heightened speech; and in this respect both rhythm and the figurative language appropriate in verse show greater intensity. This argument is frequently adduced to justify the use of verse. It is essential, however, to distinguish between the psychological reasons for the heightened speech of the *persons* of the drama and those for heightened speech on the part of the *poet*.

It is generally true that when excited we seek relief in speech, and moreover, in exaggerative speech. Psychology is familiar with the fact that intense emotion tends to hyperbolic expression. This clearly has relevance to dramatic situations in life and in drama; but it is also an aspect of the genesis of poetry altogether, of whatever kind it may be. This motive produces the heightened utterance of the characters in a play, this being part of the representational aspect of drama, and an argument from life as the thing portrayed; and it also produces the whole play as a created work of imagination, this being an argument from the need of the dramatist to unburden himself of his vision and his emotion in his vision.

The distinction between them is that in the one case we are dealing with the feelings that are part of an action, and in the other with feelings that are aroused in a poet by some aspect of experience noted, thought about, and elaborated by imagination, and of which the play as a whole is the expression. As between the heightened speech of *real life*, and the heightened expression of *the poet*, the difference is clear. But in the heightened speech of dramatic characters, a speech composed and stylized by the dramatist, there is obviously an overlap.

We may describe the position thus. In everyday life, in the natural situation, the heightened expression of excitement is real but crude; it consists of conventional strong language, vituperation, oaths, abuse, swear-words, hyperbolic epithets, and interjections. The poet, however, does not transcribe the real literally but gives images of it; any speech of a character, although it has the motive for heightened expression from real life, fits into the poet's whole creation in addition; and therefore becomes expression and assumes poetic style. In this way the poet joins his own motive, an aesthetic and emotional one, to the natural motive by which we in real life seek a louder and more violent language for passion; and in this way dramatic speech in heightened poetic form corresponds logically to both the psychology of everyday and the psychology of poetic creation. Thus, although we do not ordinarily speak in verse, and call it a "convention", there is a sense in which it is eminently natural. Just as dancing begins in the natural overflow of intense feelings, so too does rhythm in poetry.[2]

Two points must now, after these general comments, be observed about verse in drama. The first is that there is of course a reciprocal influence of each on the other. What was said earlier about the speech of drama applies also to verse in drama; it is dramatic if it is organically linked with a dramatic structure. If the plot moves, if the characters are involved in movement, passion, or action as they ought to be, the verse is *ipso facto* part of the structure, of the movement, of the excitement; it is, as belonging to the dramatic speech, a form of action. It does not matter, for verse in drama, that people in real life do not talk in sustained iambics or trimeters; but it does matter that it should be verse bearing a relation to what is contained in the dramatic dialogues of real life. Verse in drama becomes a certain kind of verse, distinguishable from the lyric and philosophical tones; and the sense of error, of the false note in poetic style in drama, only arises when the appropriate relationship of verse to action is disturbed, as it is in Byron and Swinburne, or modern experimenters like Anne Ridler and Norman Nicholson.

But the relationship being reciprocal we observe also that an action expressed in verse drama is modified in its turn. It differs from the action of most types of prose play, because the verse allows an unfolding of feeling and passion at once more powerful and more subtle. Thrillers, for instance, have very dramatic plots, and the most unsubtle persons. They are usually framed as an elaborate riddle and a sequence of events tied strictly to a mechanical system of cause and effect. They are at the opposite pole to the verse play. Social problem plays like Galsworthy's *Strife* or *Justice* are full of strong emotions, but they are conceived in terms of social conflict that keep the feelings crude, however sincere, and preclude a finer spiritual insight. Equally the violent emotional and socially-minded drama of a number of American playwrights, O'Neill, Arthur Miller, and Tennessee Williams, depends on the direct realistic impact of rough and primitive, or simple, or semi-articulate, sometimes even sub-intelligent, natures, living in harsh social and climatic conditions, which quite excludes the use of verse. The play in verse, by contrast, however much violent action it retains (we think of the Elizabethans), contains principally an inner drama of feeling and motive in morally and spiritually sensitive persons and develops it in an elaborate and subtle language.

This brings us to the second point about verse, which is that it provides not only through itself an expressive auditory and motor imagery, but it releases other poetic possibilities. Within its framework all the means of expression tend towards greater intensity whilst seeming still to be natural, so that a high degree of figurative language that in prose would be absurd appears spontaneous and appropriate. By seeking congruence in its various kinds of images, or putting it another way, by a mutual reinforcement of the symbolic references to feelings, verse makes available to the material of specifically dramatic vision the more highly organized meanings characteristic of poetry generally. It extends the range of expression over that available to prose, for a subtle instrument follows the subtleties of nature, revealing more of persons, their motives, thoughts and situations than blunter tools could achieve. But everything in art being a matter of mutual assimilation, the extension of meanings through increased poetic power reacts on the dramatic quality; if verse, or poetry, makes the expression of the drama more complete it makes it more dramatic. For all these reasons we find confirmation in the fact, always assumed but rarely stated, that although verse is not indispensable to fine dramatic art the greatest plays have nevertheless all been in verse.

One can find everywhere in the mature Shakespeare examples of this process by which poetry amplifies drama, not by altering or adding to it but by making it more itself in innumerable fine ways. The heath scenes in *King Lear*, which so magnify the drama that many feel it unactable; the love duologues in *Romeo and Juliet*, which determine the scale of feeling and, in consequence, of tragedy; the imagery and sound of Othello's speeches, which alone communicate the emotional complexity of this delicately balanced character and allow us to accept his tragedy in the face of credibility; these are a few examples. To mention the obvious, one may add that the use of verse facilitates also variety and change of mood, when the poetry may lean towards the lyrical, or the meditative, or the philosophical, or whatever, without cutting loose from its anchor in the dramatic scheme. Thus it not only makes possible a more adequate expression of what a person in a given situation has to feel and say, but it also effects a greater range and diversity in composition. The insertion of *lyrics* (songs) in a play is another matter. This introduces a different type of poetic texture; nevertheless it is clearly justified if such insertions have a dramatic function. Often their themes overlap with those of the play, as in Gretchen's songs in *Faust*, or Ariel's songs in *The Tempest*.

All these features are acceptable so long as the verse conforms to the principle of characteristic intertexture. But this does not of course mean that the texture of dramatic verse is maintained at the same density, which would be absurd. Moreover, the various components of expression (metre, sound, figures of speech) are constantly changing their balance in respect of each other; now one, now the other, is prominent; only occasionally are all the stops pulled out; and the contrasts thus available contribute in their own way to dramatic effect. Hence the great force of stark simplicity when it occurs, as in: Ripeness is all. Changes in intensity are not to be confused with faulty complexity; which is evident when the expression is inappropriate or superfluously ornate, as in the elaborate conceits of Shakespeare's early style. Special ideals such as those of "rhetoric" and "eloquence" in Elizabethan drama introduce, of course, complications of detail, about which an abundant critical literature exists. But they do not impair the force of the principle of heightened expression here put forward.[3]

Blank verse owed its great success as an instrument of drama to its being a metre both very simple and very regular, and as near as possible to the natural flow of the spoken language, but admitting the most varied and subtle rhythmic amplification. Quite ordinary things may be said in it in tones almost identical with conversation, whilst on the other hand its extreme flexibility allows rhythmic variations sufficient for all the intricacy of dramatic situations as well as for fastidious demands of poetic invention. Mr. Eliot has pointed out that the employment of blank verse for non-dramatic poetry has spoilt it for drama subsequently; nevertheless Milton's use of it for epic, and Wordsworth's for philosophical poetry, only emphasize the potentialities it possessed.

Mr. Eliot has expressed the problem of variable intensity in terms of an "underlying" rhythmic or musical pattern which keeps the feeling of the spectator so disposed through the lowlands of the play that he accepts the rise into the intense moments without feeling any break or jar in the style or naturalness of the process. When the audience at the first performance of *The Cocktail Party*, before its appearance in print, could not tell that it was in verse Mr. Eliot was glad; he could legitimately feel that his aim had been achieved. However, his style, like that of some of the minor Elizabethans, uses fewer tropes than Marlowe's or Shakespeare's. The highly figurative style of these latter induces the process of metamorphozing the sense of the "natural"; within the framework of such a style we accept, as was said above, elaborate language as natural which would not be so in prose. Eliot's "naturalness" of style, it must be admitted, depends less on this principle. It is not altogether the release of an esoteric "natural" quality within the convention of verse, but the incorporation into verse of the naturalness of tone characteristic of contemporary speech. For that reason it is a plainer, less rhetorical style. But we should not underestimate the remarkable refinements of rhythm and sound (formula-imagery, in our terminology) on which Eliot relies for keeping his poetic undercurrent running and transposing into a higher register when necessary. In this he comes closer to some verse dramatists in France and Germany, for instance Racine and Goethe (in his *Iphigenie auf Tauris* and *Torquato Tasso*), whose verse texture also gains its effects through auditory imagery and rhythm with a comparatively sparing use of metaphors.

Eliot plans circumspectly in his attempt to find a natural and speakable verse for a play. Claudel illustrates the opposite temperament. He is full of high feeling overflowing ceaselessly in an exalted and hyperbolic language, and he conceives his characters and their spiritual activity in the same manner. He is aware above all of the powerful, governing emotional élan in a person, a dynamic urge to the most intense crises of emotion and moral or religious dilemma. These forces in the individual are visioned as part of a mighty pattern of divine activity and governance. His conceptions (in *Partage de Midi*, *Le Soulier de Satin*, *L'Otage*, etc.) are without doubt full of a vitality at once poetic and dramatic. His imagination, haunted and obsessed with the deepest and most sublime reaches of man and his destiny, searches out every turn and degree of feeling and creates an imagery for it in the dialogue, with its versicle rhythms and its range of figures. His great religious themes—the love of earth, the love of woman, the love of self, the love of God—indicate the tensest dramas of human life and, at the same time, requiring symbolic language, flow naturally into poetry. Everywhere in Claudel the theme and conception are so productive of poetry and drama together that he sometimes might seem to be the great answer to Eliot's aspiration for a modern verse drama.

Yet there is a fault in Claudel which has always laid his structure open to criticism. It is common to hear it expressed in the form that he is too lyrical. But I think this is misconceived, even if "lyrical" in this context means an enthusiastic or hymnic poetry. The fault is that the expansive statement of emotion by the separate characters (Ysé, Mesa, Prouhèze, etc.) overflows the discretion of the framework of drama and theatrical performance. The persons are in dramatic situations; their emotions, too, are dramatically potent; but these luxuriate and hold themselves up, checking their flow into action proper. They become static, monumentalized as grandiose expressions of feeling. An essentially dramatic sense of emotional conflict and tension, instead of finding a fluent form of crisis and dénouement, is expressed in monologues of feeling. In *L'Otage* we observe Claudel deliberately trying to correct this tendency and achieve a stricter discipline of character and plot construction.

Looking at the relation between drama and poetry as we have done in this section, we are not, of course, formulating prescriptions but simply analysing the effects of genius. When poets try their hand at drama and fail it is beside the mark to exclaim: If only they had done that instead of this, used blank verse instead of trimeters, omitted their lyrical effusions, and so on. They fail, quite simply, not in verse technique, but in breadth of psychology and humanity, and in their feeling for speech as action. Examples of such failure were examined in the earlier section on dramatic speech.

In concluding this section we may add a note on opera. We said that verse brought with it a more intricate organization of rhythm and vocal sound, producing a more intense expressiveness and heightening the dramatic quality. Opera is really based on the same principle. We saw in chapter nine how in lyric style a point is reached where the effect relies to the utmost on the "music" of language, in rhythm and vocal expression, the poem, beyond this point, passing over into song. Similarly, in the relation between drama and opera, the vocal expressiveness attached in drama to words can be so intensified that song displaces words, song here being dramatic in character. For opera is the still higher heightening of the emotional and passionate aspects of dramatic meaning; its structure depends on the greatest intensification of a very few chosen moments in an action. Words are still used, but with a change in intertexture. A libretto, as we call it, is a brief for the singer, a skeleton to be clothed with the flesh and blood of music; it is a scheme no longer for the voice-in-words, as poetry is, but for the voice-in-song. It stands in contrast to the fully endowed text of dramatic poetry, which incorporates in itself a degree of "musical" expression. Thus both opera and verse-drama, with varying result but working on the same principle, achieve an intensification of expression. It may be admitted that the stylizations of operatic musical form are more radical than those of verse drama, reaching in fact an extreme. From one point of view the music makes the drama more intense; but from another it reduces the flow of events and changing situations, and lengthens the dramatic moment, which imposes a severer conventionalization on the acting and gesture. This produces "operatic" acting, which gives an unnatural and incongruous look to the scene. Hence, though opera may transcend verse-drama in some respects it pays a price in the restriction of the actor's art; in verse-drama the complexity of all the imagery is more naturally and uniformly balanced.

iii. VERSE AND COMEDY

In our general statement about verse in drama we did not discriminate in detail between different types of drama, and it can be admitted that the plainest illustrations for the above observations are to be found in verse tragedy. But the principle applies to drama in general, and to comedy no less than to romantic, historical, and didactic plays. Comedy calls perhaps for a comment not necessary in respect of the latter kinds, because firstly the tone of comedy is more intellectually than emotionally determined and secondly comedy is by tradition "realistic". The idea of a poetic intensification would not be relevant if we meant it only in connexion with emotional meanings. But we do not. The intensification that verse induces applies to all the meanings of a play in relation to its central effect. If this is tragic or otherwise serious the intensification relates to feeling, passion, will, and emotion; if it is comic, the intensification relates to exactly the same things except that they are refracted by the comic intention and therefore make a different effect. The closeness of comedy to tears and sadness has often been remarked, just as, on the other hand, it has been pointed out that the first scene of Lear contains the elements of comedy. A study of the speeches of Arnolphe, the jealous guardian in Molière's *L'École des Femmes*, reveals the language of a genuinely suffering individual, though focused as comic.[4] Similarly the embellished language of characters like Jonson's Volpone or Sir Epicure Mammon is, within the satirical circle drawn round them, poetic and heroic, a more subtle and adequate expression of what as characters they are. And this heightening of the substance induces a heightening of the effect; the more revealing the poetic language, the greater the comic result.

It is not our task here to study in detail the role of verse in comedy, but to indicate how our main principle of poetic intensification applies to this branch of drama. Quite briefly, then, we may say that most of the principal effects of comedy can be enhanced if verse takes the place of prose. Satire, irony, humour, wit, the sardonic, the cynical, mockery, parody, can be expressed with greater liveliness and point, especially when rhyme is used, language, rhythm, and metaphor unfolding their subtler nuances of meaning and tone no less than in tragic plays though they are differently directed. The point is that the idea of heightened expression cannot be confined to the kind of emotional intensity associated with serious drama or lyric poetry.[5]

One need not, however, maintain that verse must always be superior to prose; it is certainly easier to defend this view in the case of serious drama. The example of Restoration Comedy reminds us of a type that calls for prose. The characters here are all of the utmost sophistication, and the intention is to portray manners in a section of society where genuine feeling counts for nothing, and the frivolous cult of egoistic pleasure at the expense of others is the highest good, this embracing every kind of malicious, uncharitable, and cynical attitude expressed in word and gesture. The real core of potential suffering that is apparent in many of Molière's characters in the shadows behind the comic spotlighting is totally absent in Restoration plays; so also is Shakespeare's wide range of comic invention in connexion with character and the situations human beings find themselves in. In Restoration comedy the subject itself, the human subject, is restricted; only a small section of the mind and feelings is in action; and even the exercise of malice and the cult of cynical gallantry, brilliant as they are, are sharply focused on a very restricted area of behaviour. There is nothing here, in consequence, that calls for the verse form.

iv. SYMBOLS AND POETIC INTENSIFICATION IN DRAMA

Symbols are agents of poetic intensification when they function as focal points for feelings, or a group of associated ideas and feelings, the intricacy or density of such symbolism varying greatly. It follows from the main theories of this essay that art and poetry should not be simply equated with "symbols", for of these there are different kinds; but the particular function whereby an image evokes insistently certain feeling-associations or references produces the symbol familiar in poetic contexts. From this point of view there is an element of the symbolic in all art-imagery. In our first chapters, when trying to isolate the "representational" image, we admitted that this never exists in a pure form but always carries with it a charge of expressed feeling. The expressive formula-image, as we called it, is clearly a symbol of feeling. And finally, we referred some of the potency of metaphor to the fact that its effect lies in an image making an immediate feeling-reference. These varying symbolic processes are present in drama as in other literary forms; and so the question at issue is not the absence or presence of features that can be detached, like covers from a chair, and denoted as "symbols"; it is the degree and diversity in the symbolic process. Hence we use the idea of poetic intensification, which takes place between the extremes of simple representation and a density that defeats clarity or dramatic purpose. In this process of intensification what happens is that the symbolic texture is made more intricate, as when verse, to take one example, takes the place of prose, or when metaphor, which includes symbolic substitution, is employed. We do not conceive an addition of symbols, a summation, as an effect of quantity. The law of complex intertexture holds always, its operation here lying in the fine adjustment and co-ordination of all the symbols and the functioning of parts in a whole.

This being the case, the sources of symbolism in drama are numerous, and so long as the symbolism functions within an aesthetic context it enhances poetic quality. We have considered already the symbolism proceeding from plot and character, and referred to the symbolism of myths and dreams; the drama that develops these modes generates some of the effects of poetry or at least catches reflections of the poetic light. What has to be added at this stage is a comment on the deliberate use of chosen and designated symbols that characterizes some styles of drama, as also of poetry and the novel, since the early nineteenth century, the source of this style being either romanticism, or the so-called "symbolist" movement in poetry, or an interest in symbols stimulated by psychology and anthropology, the "new" sciences.

A straightforward example is the cherry orchard in Chekhov's play. It is a complex symbol and owes its force and effectiveness to that. The orchard focuses both the central and the subsidiary meanings of the work; the sale at which it passes into the possession of the self-made man, Lopakhin, is the climax of the whole action. It is the property, a luxury, of the decadent landowning class, who, although in financial need, cling to it to the last moment. It is then transferred to the new dominant social type, the self-made merchant, who knows how to make it financially lucrative and socially useful by cutting down the trees, building bungalows for summer visitors, and enriching himself. The orchard has symbolical and emotional meaning for both parties to this drama of social change, but also for Trofimov the student, who, although outside the immediate clash of interests, is full of premonitions of the progress of humanity, and finally for the spectator, whom Chekhov guides through his whole vision by means of this image. For Madame Ranevsky the orchard means her house and property, her ancestry, the traditions of her class, her style of life, but also her childhood, her youth and happiness. For Lopakhin it is the sign of the slavery in which his father and grandfather lived and his purchase of it represents to him his liberation and a triumphant sense of retribution, of paying off a score on behalf of his downtrodden ancestors, as well as of a blow struck for the "new life" of his grandsons and great-grandsons. For Trofimov it is the symbol of the tortured social past of Russia, which must be expiated so that life can begin anew:

'. . . Think only, Anya, your grandfather, and great-grandfather, and all your ancestors were slave-owners—the owners of living souls—and from every cherry in the orchard, from every leaf, from every trunk there are human creatures looking at you. Cannot you hear their voices? Oh, it is awful! Your orchard is a fearful thing, and when in the evening or at night one walks about the orchard, the old bark on the trees glimmers dimly in the dusk, and the old cherry trees seem to be dreaming of centuries gone by and tortured by fearful visions. Yes! We are at least two hundred years behind, we have really gained nothing yet, we have no definite attitude to the past, we do nothing but theorize or complain of depression or drink vodka. It is clear that to begin to live in the present we must first expiate our past, we must break with it; and we can expiate it only by suffering, by extra-ordinary unceasing labour. Understand that, Anya.'

Finally, whilst the orchard is a symbol of varying emotional reference for these separate characters it is for the author and his spectators a correspondingly complex but also eminently unitary symbol, both structurally and emotionally, for the meaning of the whole play. A symbol functioning in this way intensifies the quality of an aesthetic context; it creates the density of metaphorical texture characteristic of poetry. But let us not forget to add that it is also dramatic by function, being the pivot of the action.

This kind of symbolism appears frequently in modern prose plays and is perhaps especially familiar from Ibsen. He uses two forms of it; one is the visible symbol, like the wild duck or Solness's pinnacle, or Hedda Gabler's pistols ; the other is a repeated reference, like "ghosts" (that is, the habits and traditions that tyrannize over us), or the "white horses" of Rosmersholm. A good example of the intensifying effect of such symbolism on an otherwise plain realistic style is found in Lenormand's *A l'Ombre du Mal*. Here the African jungle, amidst which the action is set and where to the elemental ferocity of nature and the climate are added the primitive practices and magic of natives who are still three quarters savage, is associated in idea and feeling with the primitive, irrational, anti-human ferocity lurking in the nature of civilized man himself, and breaking out uncontrollably against his will and moral sense. The mystery and terror of the physical background are thus not simply superficial dramatic effects, but are equated with the mystery and terror of human nature in the fragility of its best aspirations. The play is enveloped in an emotional atmosphere largely created by this symbolism, whereby a background that might simply have been representational is converted into a powerful expressive image. And again it has dramatic power, being integral to the action.

Contrasted with this uncomplex supporting symbolism are the saturated styles of Maeterlinck and Yeats. In these authors we observe certainly the high poetic quality of symbolic imagery, whether in prose or verse. We feel the confluence of methods from romantic, mystic and symbolist poetry, for all of which the sensuous image often stood as sign or symbol for supernatural powers and transcendent essences; and also the influence of the musicalized ideal of poetry, for which language functions as the meeting-point of visual and auditory imagery with plain verbal meaning reduced to an echo of the normal. And finally we sense the influence of dream images and what became known later as archetypal images, which also formed part of the romantic heritage. Maeterlinck's early "marionette" or "symbolist" plays, as they are variously named, have the qualities of dreams, nightmares and trances, an imagery expressive of the terror of mortals in their precarious situation, face to face with powers against which they are helpless. Yeats's brief plays present always a situation undoubtedly dramatic but conceived with a varied symbolism that finally expresses with great intensity some particular emotion, as for instance patriotism, in *The Dreaming of the Bones*, or the tragic desire of men to be like the gods, in *At the Hawk's Well*. The style of both these authors is a mixture of dramatic and lyric. It is not true to say their work is *un*dramatic; it is dramatic, but within a sharply restricted scale. It deviates from the characteristic dramatic form at its best, and its symbolist stylizations do tend to dissolve the representational human substance of drama into something more musical and lyrical. Thus, although such plays show how powerfully symbolic images of various kinds help to poeticize drama, they also show the risks involved.

V. DRAMA AND MYTH

Since myths are naturally poetic the plays based on them tend to be poetic too. The early history of drama in Greece shows myth allied to verse (with "music" and "dancing" in support) in an inextricable unity, which, influencing an orthodox conception of a poetic drama through many centuries, really prevented anyone from asking precisely whether myth in itself, apart from its embodiment in a composite structure of art, was poetic. We now know the answer to this question. Myths are a form of symbolism akin to dreams and art. They show symbolic situations; they express terrors and desires, taboos and pieties; they are a mode of catharsis.

Modern dramatists, resorting to myth-making either by recovering old myths or creating new ones, have exploited this natural source of poetry. A myth at the centre of a play helps to create style; it gives resonance and depth. At the same time we have to acknowledge that myths are skeletal outlines requiring support before they can become dramatic art, and in the support they can be realized or marred. They all work with a powerful archetypal kernel but the details of every realization depend on a given cultural situation, to which, moreover, the dramatist himself contributes; Aeschylus, Sophocles, and Euripides have different view of Electra, or of Orestes. The myth is filled out each time with a varying substance of human belief and behaviour.

Thus myth gives an impetus towards poetry which has to be followed up. A most powerful dramatic style emerges from the combination of three features: a mythical centre, a forceful psychological reality of persons, and a subtle formula-imagery. The one provides a vibrating and mysterious centre, situated in the heart of human experience and to which we respond from our own centre of feeling. The second adds a convincing picture of real circumstances, and the third enhances the expression of all the associated feelings throughout the action. Thus the vision of reality and the vision of feeling interfuse and are re-enacted as idea in the art of the play. Where this combination is achieved there is the greatest centralization of metaphor, to which we referred above, because the poetic elaboration is the expansion of a poetic seed. This does not mean that style depends entirely on the use of myth, but only that a most intense style is reached in this way. It helps to establish the poetic superiority of Racine over Corneille, of Goethe over Schiller, and, within Greek drama, of Sophocles over Euripides; and, one might add, of Shakespeare's tragedies over the histories.

Amongst contemporary playwrights two in particular have tried to achieve this combined pattern, and with a great measure of success: Eliot in England and Cocteau in France. The former has linked religious myth with the modern psychological knowledge, a stroke brilliant in its insight and cunning in its hieratic purpose; and these he has immersed in the expressive formula-imagery of verse and poetic diction. In *Murder in the Cathedral* he uses a historical subject as a way into myth; in *The Family Reunion* and *The Cocktail Party* he achieves with a contemporary surface an emergent myth, with supporting features from the ancient myths of Greek drama; in *The Confidential Clerk* he takes as his centre not exactly a myth but something very like it, the image of the orphan, or bastard, or outcast, or the veiled, unfound self, repeated and generalized in several persons.

Cocteau has also put myths at the centre of his plays, has also incorporated in them psychological reality in a modern form, and has created an expressive formula-imagery of an unconventional kind; not verse, but a system of symbolic images "of" the theatre—of scene, décor, costume, as well as of incident. Of his original style we shall say more in the next section. Here I simply want to stress the closeness of his intuitions in the matter of dramatic style to Eliot's; they both develop a myth or myth-like situation with realism and with music. They re-infuse into a mythical scheme the truth of particular human behaviour and circumstances, whilst allowing its archetypal power, stored up in the past, to reverberate through reality; and they envelop the whole with an imagery of feeling.

Other writers, contemporary or of the immediate past, draw on the same sources but not with the same balance of effect. Of the most obvious poets, Yeats and Claudel, the former, in a work like *The Dreaming of the Bones*, comes near to it, but on a very restricted scale. Claudel, generating often a subject of mythical power from contemporary, or historical (i.e. non-legendary) persons, amplifies the third element of music or feeling to such an extent that it swamps the psychologically real human situation, converting the play into hymn or religious rhapsody. Sartre, a quite different type, uses in *Huis Clos* a subtle form of myth, that of the Last Judgement and Hell, which irradiates a vivid realism of motive and moral choice, making it the best of his plays from the point of view of dramatic style. The third element is largely missing; there is neither verse nor any marked form of supporting metaphor.

It is a curious fact that Giraudoux, who is looked on as the initiator on the French stage of the modern tradition of myth-drama, and who is also most often praised for his "poetic fantasy", does not fall into line with the authors mentioned in this matter of dramatic style. From what was said in a previous section it will appear that Giraudoux starts by borrowing a scheme from myth but converts it into a fantasy which is nearer to allegory than myth. Giraudoux neither revives nor re-creates myths. He *uses* them. He appropriates their subjects to give him a framework for his own idealizations of persons and his commentary on moral ideas. He achieves a style and beauty of his own, doubtless, but one deviating from the central intensities of dramatic style. For he is diffuse. His "fantasy" and the brilliances of his prose dialogue are drapings thrown about a large open frame; they are not a natural and economical expansion, in different modes, of the symbolism of the central myth, as in Eliot and Cocteau.

vi. COCTEAU'S "POÉSIE DE THÉÂTRE"

Finally we must devote a comment to a strikingly original achievement of dramatic style in this century, Cocteau's theory and practice of a *poésie de théâtre*, which our own argument and point of view enable us to see not as the eccentricity of an irresponsible imagination but as a profoundly logical outcome of certain tendencies of poetic style since the late nineteenth century. Cocteau's principle of a *poésie de théâtre* derives from the salient feature of romantic, and afterwards symbolist, style which we discussed in chapter nine, the functional power of the image—any image—stripped of its literal reference and used as an analogue of sensuous or supra-sensuous experience, and therefore poetic. It is the evocative power which makes the single image into a vibrant symbol or metaphorical agent and thus a repository not of representational meaning but of the life of a responding sensibility or an imagination reaching out to an inexpressible world of spirit. We observed that it was this principle that first recognized "the poetic" as independent of verse. Cocteau follows the idea to a logical conclusion by conceiving his works in various forms as *poésie de théâtre, poésie de roman, poésie cinématographique*, even *poésie de critique*.

Quite early, in the preface to *Les Mariés de la Tour Eiffel*, he stated simply and precisely the aim of his style; only its unexpectedness and total novelty prevented people for two decades and more from recognizing a serious and profound artistic innovation behind the bewildering surface which resembled too much in their eyes "des farces d'atelier". "L'action de ma pièce est imagée tandis que le texte ne l'est pas. J'essaie donc de substituer une "poésie de théâtre" à la "poésie au théâtre". La poésie au théâtre est une dentelle délicate impossible à voir de loin. La poésie de théâtre serait une grosse dentelle; une dentelle en cordages, un navire sur la mer. LES MARIÉS peuvent avoir l'aspect terrible d'une goutte de poésie au microscope. Les scènes s'emboîtent comme les mots d'un poème." A passage in *Le Rappel à l'Ordre* supplements this statement: "Avec *Les Mariés de la Tour Eiffel* j'ai construit à la poésie un gros appareil de transmission pour les planches. Je me vante d'y avoir montré pour la première fois au milieu d'une incompréhension absolue et même de celle d'admirateurs, une poésie de théâtre . . . Je supprime toute image et toute finesse de langue. Il ne reste que la poésie."

Les Mariés de la Tour Eiffel was the first but not the best example of Cocteau's idea of a poetic theatre form. It shows the discovery of a fruitful idea and the exaggerations of an experiment; for to combine successfully in "une grosse dentelle", and in a larger corpus of compositions, the various techniques of ballet, acrobatics, pantomime, drama, satire, orchestra, and dialogue would be asking rather too much. Moreover, such a type of composition is more ballet than drama, and indeed many modern ballets, by contrast with the "classical" style of the nineteenth century, show Cocteau's combination except for the dialogue, and do represent a *poésie de théâtre* in a general, non-Cocteau-ish sense. The real achievement for a style of drama came when Cocteau created *Orphée* and *La Machine Infernale*, which are not a new kind of composite form, as *Les Mariés* was, but stylistic variants of drama itself. In these plays drama is not displaced by a new form; it is drama in a new mode. It is an old warp with a new weft, an action-and-dialogue cross-woven with vivid and beautiful imagery, through which the feelings and the tragedy reverberate musically as they do through the verse and figures— the "dentelle délicate"—of the more orthodox verse form. This imagery is varied. In *Orphée* it begins with the personifications of the main figures: Orphée as poet, Eurydice as love, Heurtebise as the guardian angel, the 'very beautiful young girl in a pink evening gown and fur coat' as Death, with her attendants in surgeon's uniform with masks and rubber gloves—a vivid erotically toned symbol for Death together with a brilliantly modern symbol for her assistants. To these must be added the Horse as a satanic agent. We observe next the symbolism of the décor, 'un décor *utile* où le moindre détail joue son rôle comme les appareils d'un numéro d'acrobates' (Cocteau's note). In this décor colour is absent, except for the blue sky. Its white box for the white horse, its white tables and chairs, and the few objects on the tables, fruit, plates, glasses, a carafe, 'pareils aux ustensiles en carton des jongleurs', suggest mystery and the supernatural, establishing a place whose inhabitants are on familiar terms with things transcending normal and familiar life. In the midst there is a mirror, the gateway to the realm of death. The tone being set thus, the extraordinary events that follow are, despite appearances sometimes farcical, organic and natural. Their immediate effect, like the diabolical messages of the horse, the startling entry of Death, the beautiful girl in evening gown and fur coat, with her surgeon-clad attendants, the head of Orphée thrown back through the window by the Bacchantes, are electric in the unexpectedness of the imagery, but as the play progresses they fit into an action of the greatest seriousness and touching religious fervour. All these various images of person, object, scene and incident cohere in a precise relationship of feeling. At the end we are not superficially "amused", or mildly entertained, or pleasantly titillated and shocked by these clearly brilliant inventions and effects; we are profoundly moved again by the myth which interweaves so mysteriously the themes of death, love, poetry and the divine.

In *La Machine Infernale* action and incident are strengthened and the persons made more substantial and complex, as was inevitable where the subject as handed down from classical tragedy has firmer outlines and more elaborate detail. Nevertheless Cocteau adheres to the same method of poetic style; there are persons and monsters from myth and fable, a vividly effective and purposeful décor (especially in the ramparts scene and that showing Oedipus with the Sphinx), ghosts and dreams, and objects—like Jocasta's scarf and the brooch with which Oedipus blinds himself—charged with a "part" to play. And there is a presiding image, the infernal machine, the time-bomb. The dream, the symbolic object, the world of gods and myth are here projected in their natural interpenetration, with essentially poetic effect.

Later plays show Cocteau moving away from this beautiful though difficult style and it may be that the sound-film gave him greater opportunities for applying the method.* Yet it still echoes through the more realistic surface of all his plays, especially since he stays on the whole near to myth even though it may be

---

* Altogether the modern sound-film has exploited the convergent expressiveness of visual symbol, "atmosphere" of place and scene, and musical accompaniment more dexterously, perhaps because with fewer difficulties to overcome, than the modern drama, and has in consequence more "poetry" to show.

concealed, as in *Les Parents Terribles*. In this play the "portes qui claquent" are again a dominant symbol, as well as the symbolic opposition of order and disorder in the home of Madeleine and Michel's family-"roulotte". The poetic power generated, as we have noted, by a mythical centre, and by tragedy, sustain this later work, which shows less intense style only because the supporting imagery of feeling, the "music", is not drawn upon as in the earlier plays.

CHAPTER TWELVE

CONCLUSION

THIS INQUIRY WAS DIRECTED to illuminating the nature of dramatic art and its affinities with poetry and other art forms.

Central in our conception has been the idea of the functioning of images; for it is by the role of these in certain contexts that we recognize aesthetic structures as distinct from other kinds of perception and thought. And one of the most striking features of the arts is the interaction of different kinds of images, one example of which is the mingling of auditory and motor imagery with evoked visual images in the language of poetry. These two features are all-important. On the one hand we have the liberation of sensuous images from the context of "reality" and their integration in a total metaphorical process expressing a vision of, together with a feeling about, life. On the other hand, different kinds of image—the auditory and the visual, the scenic and the musical, the rhythmical and the pictorial, and so on—lend themselves to a unified purpose and a harmonious intertexture precisely because they are, though sensuously disparate, functionally allied; they are all, by their function, formulas of sense and feeling. We established at the outset, as an essential preliminary clarification, two main categories of image, the representational and the expressive formula-image, emphasizing at the same time that the pure representational image, which would be a scientific copy-image, does not exist in art; even the *most* representational images are selective, interpretative, constructive, and expressive in some degree. And, analysing the literary figure of metaphor in connexion with these two sets of images, we observed that they both partake of the nature of metaphor insofar as their literal meaning is displaced by a functional meaning deriving from their being analogues of sensation and feeling, contributing to a unified context with a predominant idea or emotion, which they help to clarify and constitute as an aesthetic phenomenon.

Using the idea of metaphor, once the nature of the process is analysed and understood, is more helpful than relying only on the general idea of symbolism, because it is more precise. It is quite true that the images of art are "symbols" but so are many other things, like the letters of the Morse code or the precepts that nowadays we are told are a symbolical representation of the "physical world". Expressive formula-images are symbols of "feelings"; but many things outside aesthetic contexts can be symbols of feelings. To this we may add another complication of the meaning of "symbol", for, most art being a mixture of representational and expressive, its images are "symbolical" in different ways at one and the same time; they symbolize objects of sense-perception and also super-induced feelings. But there is also the further point that, although works of art have integrity, as expounded in chapter seven, they almost invariably offer clues to a meaning that is rational as well as emotional; they do not propagate such rational meanings, or exist for the sole sake of them, but they do incorporate or imply them. This applies even to music, as we tried to show by emphasizing its links with nameable experiences. We observed that the musical style of a composer, say Bach, or Mozart, or Debussy, is essentially the same in both choral and instrumental music, which argues a relationship of meaning in the musical symbols. Moreover, by examining the expressive values of physical gesture in relation to feelings, and comparing them with the character of musical phrases and design, it becomes clear how apparently "pure" formula-images convey precise meanings; just as caricaturists abstract from physical contexts the salient lines, which then carry in their abstractness definable feeling tones. The gestures of a conductor, "feeling himself" into the music, suggest a primitive intermediate form of imagery, whilst the ballet offers the most extensive opportunities for mutually elucidatory systems of images. From these complex relationships our imagination constantly derives, consciously or unconsciously, a mass of information and experience which renders the expressive formula-images of the arts less esoteric and mystifying and makes them familiar and luminous.

Because of this, because of the insistent presence of a kernel of rationalizable meanings, metaphor is a more precise concept than the vaguer and much more general "symbolism" to indicate the nature of aesthetic imagery. Its advantages are, first, that it indicates the process by which images are transferred into newly conceived contexts and endowed with a new function differing from their practical and "normal" one of symbolizing objects in perception. Secondly, it gives support to the idea of an intertexture of imagery, the unity of which lies in the harmonious relations between the images. Thirdly, it reveals, as we remarked in chapter three, the constructive operation of the imagination. And fourthly, arising from this, it enshrines the process of "re-enactment as idea" by means of its ambivalence, since it evokes the sensuous world but in the interest of imagination and idea.

Drama conforms to this principle. Every good play is an elaborate metaphor, using images that draw in some respects on the representational but are trained on the responses of feelings. In the foregoing sections we have examined the nature of the particular intertexture that justifies us in distinguishing a form "drama", and, analysing its details, we have drawn on all the analyses and principles of the earlier parts of this essay. As a form for sight and hearing drama exploits a great range of non-linguistic images, in scene, persons, and gesture. As dialogue it incorporates language, which includes its varied linguistic meanings, and also the pre-linguistic imagery associated with language, in the voice, the sounds and rhythm, in all its evocations, and all its figures of speech, poetic or rhetorical.

All ordered structures, however, depend on subordination, and drama is no exception. Amidst its composite imagery we discern an axis to which everything must be subservient, if the various elements are not to engender chaos. That axis is the *persons acting*; here is what can be called the medium of this art, as language is the medium of narrative or lyric, pigment the medium of painting, or stone and wood the medium of sculpture.

The extraordinary nature of this medium appears in two paradoxical consequences. It is, on the one hand, severely restrictive, in the matter of time, action, and subject-matter, when measured against the immense freedom of some literary forms; though it is true that the resulting formal concentration enhances its power and its immediate effect on the feelings. On the other hand the diversity and richness of its imagery, and its sensuous vividness, flow from the nature of "persons acting", for with persons is given the whole psychology of human beings; not only their character, behaviour, and interests, their special aspirations, their moral idealisms, their human weakness, their misery and failure, but also the various spontaneous modes of expressing emotion and passion. Thus some of the natural impulses that in life outside drama are developed into different art forms re-occur within drama in the representation of its persons. In this way, quite apart from the arts of design, architecture, and painting, which establish the setting for a play, drama contains within its own medium a multifold implicit imagery of other arts, more particularly of mime, dance, and song (music). But their characteristic is that they unfold up to a certain point and stop short of the line where they would establish an independent identity. The mime and gesture in drama never exceeds its allotted part; it is never forced, except in bad acting, to the point of carrying autonomous meanings. Song, or musical undercurrents, are always a potential development, especially in verse drama, but they are kept from overflowing into near-opera. Dance imagery is implicit, too, even if less obviously, for many actors and producers, in working out their movements and situations, think in terms of semi-choreographic expression. The richness and density of dramatic form in its finest realization are created by these implicit imageries which, used but not abused, form a controlled reserve of expressive power.

Finally we must set in relief the three major fields of meaning drawn upon by drama, the picture, the music, and the language; or, in the terminology of this essay, the representational images, the expressive formula-images, and language, which has its own complex relations with images and conceptual meanings. The interaction of these systems of imagery and meaning warns us sufficiently that, on the one side, drama is not just "action" or "theatre", and, on the other, that the poetic quality in a play is not just a matter of the linguistic text. The pictorial and expressive sensuousness of drama is exceedingly vivid. Present images, not the vaguely shifting ones of memory, strike us, and the voices and language affect our feelings with a continuously pursued purpose. The drama, and the poetry, reside not in one or the other of these phenomena but in all of them. And the paradox of all art holds here, too; the meaning—the aesthetic situation in which the play and ourselves are established together—is beyond the sensuous imagery, but the only way into it is through the imagery. We repeat, what moves us in a play is not the words, or any other particular, but the whole situation. We are moved by Lear deserted, of which his ragings, however sublime their language, are but the symptom. We are moved by Macbeth and his wife haunted by remorse and fear; moved by Hamlet desperately trying to see his mother through a murk of sin and disloyalty. The symptoms—the images and the language—have to be vivid, but their vividness, of whatever intensity, still serves the total image and the sense of distilled human reality we see captured in it. By means of its simultaneous creation of picture and language drama reflects a feature of life itself, which is both pre- and post-linguistic. It is lived partly *outside* words, but also partly as words. The two layers interpenetrate, but they do not necessarily coalesce, though the degree of coalescence might be held as an index of culture. These conditions of separation, interpenetration, and coalescence are all felt strongly in the form of drama, contributing depth to its sensuous complexity. It is elemental first, then spiritual, then linguistic. It repeats thus the hierarchy of culture, projecting always the world and existence that are before language, and carrying their power into the world-after-language.

The intertexture of drama differing so markedly from that of poems, we judge its imaginative quality by different criteria, and especially must we avoid the shackling influence of the narrower range of meanings for "poetic" in frequent use since romantic and symbolist styles were created. The poetry of drama is not that of a romantic lyric or symbolist poem. But, as we said in chapter nine, it was these two movements together that first clarified deliberately the image—of whatever sensuous field—as mystic sign and analogue of feeling, which laid bare the essential kinship of all images, representational and non-representational, visual, kinetic, and auditory, in a metaphorical process. Wherever this principle operates the imagination is active, and within the rich complexity of dramatic form there are many places where the poetic light can shine and many ways in which it may do so. In the last chapter we adduced some reasons, based on our theory, why a verse drama, if it fulfils all the conditions of the characteristic intertexture of drama, gives more possibilities of great drama and great poetry together, which can easily be illustrated from the most renowned tragic dramatists. But the exclusive test is not the greatest concentration of poetic images possible; that is sufficiently plain from the very diverse but equally acceptable styles within the verse convention itself. It is the pervasive presence of some degree of metaphor in some of its forms. No dramatist needs all the intensifying factors at once, but every dramatist needs some of them if he is to persuade us that his play has been launched by the imagination, by a need to speak, a vision to tell, and a feeling to be expressed. When these conditions are fulfilled we have the play that is dramatic art and has a style. It is then a picture and a music; a poetic image and a ritual; an illumination and a catharsis; an excitement in life and a serenity above it; a re-enactment in sense and a liberation in idea.

NOTES

CHAPTER II
Pages 5–31

[1] Cf. W. Russell Brain : *Mind, Perception and Science* (Oxford, 1951).

[2] Cf. H. Read, *Icon and Idea*, chap. V (The Illusion of the Real) for a view of the part played in much Renaissance painting by the desire to conform to scientific laws.

[3] For the purposes of my general argument I am only concerned here with basic distinctions useful for a modern point of view. For a discussion of the genesis of art images in the early history of man, and the subsequent evolution of art, see especially H. Read, *Icon and Idea*.

[4] Cf. the following passage by Joyce Cary :

I suspect that the theme, for me, and for most writers, is actually the vital element. And that it is active at both ends of the writer's work, both in the first germ and the development.

That is to say, when I see a face in the street that suggests a character, an attitude, to be recorded in a piece of monologue or dialogue, I may think it pure chance that brought that face before me. Whereas, in fact, some pre-occupation in my mind, more or less unconscious, picked out that face from the crowd because it illustrated a general theme, a general idea, or idea-feeling, about the nature of the world, and the human dilemma in that world.

For I suppose every writer must have such an idea—it canalises all his impressions. Without that he could not disentangle any clear pattern from the chaos of daily events, he would find nothing significant in the muddle of affairs, and so he would have nothing to express. In fact, everyone must have such an idea, more or less specific and conscious, of what is important in events, and what is not, or he would not be able to make any sense of his own existence. It is only the idiot, in the most absolute sense, the complete imbecile, who has no values, no idea of proportion, no sense of form. ("Theme and Impression", *The Author*, Vol. LXIV, p. 85).

Cf. also the quotations from Matisse about his principle of composition and way of painting given by H. Read, *The Meaning of Art*, p. 186—8 (Pelican).

[5] Cf. H. Read, *The Meaning of Art* (Pelican), pp. 131—2.

[6] *Artists on Art*, ed. Robert Goldwater (London 1947), p. 363.

[7] The changes twentieth century physics has brought about in our view of matter make it necessary also for science to use the commonsense world as a point of reference. It is not a question of coming back to "reality" but of maintaining a relationship between kinds of knowledge and kinds of experience.

[8] Cf. what is said in chap. X about psychological realism in Renaissance drama.

[9] These remarks are general. The reader is referred to the subtle analysis of self-portraiture in H. Read, *Icon and Idea*, p. 113 ff.

[10] Cf. Bertrand Russell: 'Sensation, perception and memory are essentially pre-verbal experiences.' (*Human Knowledge*, p. 441).

[11] The nature and influence of the medium, and also the question of the artist's progressive creation, or "discovery", of his work, will be discussed later.

CHAPTER III

Pages 32–50

[1] The subject has been admirably expounded by Helmuth Plessner in *Die Einheit der Sinne* (Bonn, 1923).

[2] For example the descending chords in the accompaniment of the aria 'The Saviour falleth low'; the choruses 'Have lightnings and thunders in clouds disappeared?', 'He is guilty of death', 'O tell us, thou Christ, who now smote Thee?' 'Let Him be crucified', and others equally dramatic; the Evangelist's recitative narrating Peter's betrayal ('and He went out and wept bitterly'); the recitative accompaniment to 'And behold the veil of the Temple was rent in twain', and the following chorus 'Truly this was the Son of God', etc., etc.

[3] Cf. Arnold Schering, *Das Symbol in der Musik*, Leipzig, 1941, especially chap. 2, II.

[4] This would apply, in my view, to those subjects of Mozart that Tovey calls "formulae". He always insists on Mozart's remarkable power of developing wonderful music from the barest and most conventional "formulae". I do not think this idea invalidates my argument. Such "formulae" contain, or imply, dynamic and emotional patterns, just as much as other subjects do. Moreover, I think that Tovey's use of the word "formulae" has the curious effect of denuding the themes he refers to, because by implying the absolute minimum of expressiveness it *attributes* this minimum to themes that do not deserve the reproach as much as all that.

[5] Cf. H. Read, *Icon and Idea*, p. 100–101.

[6] Ballet, as the art of dance, shows the body's movements transformed from a real pattern of physical behaviour into an ideal analogue of feelings. Like music, with its real stimulation of vaso-motor reactions, it is firmly linked with physical reality (especially for the performer). But the feelings and sensations are transmuted into physical movements that are either perfected types of gesture, or symbolic suggestions, or invented rhythmic symbols. The refinement of muscular power and sensation in performers shows the physical controlled in order to convert it into idea, in the aesthetic result.

[7] See in particular *Aspects of Form*, ed. by L. L. Whyte (London, 1951).

[8] For an introductory discussion of problems connected with metaphors and their meaning see I. A. Richards, *Philosophy of Rhetoric*.

[9] The passages are from Keats, Shakespeare, Patmore (*Wind and Wave*, in *Selected Poems*, Phoenix Library, London, 1931), Goethe (*Willkommen und Abschied*), and Kathleen Raine (*Passion*, in *Stone and Flower*, London, 1943).

[10] This is a weakness, I think, of Susanne Langer's remarkable and important book *Philosophy in a New Key*, and of her term 'presentational symbolism', insofar as she refers to aesthetic.

[11] Cf. the further analysis in chapter IX.

[12] Juan Gris comments on a related phenomenon (non-realistic images of art): 'Negro sculptures provide a striking proof of the possibilities of an *anti-idealistic* art. Inspired by a religious spirit, they offer a varied and precise representation of great principles and universal ideas. How can one deny the name of art to a creative process which produces on this basis individualistic representations of universal ideas, each time in a different way? It is the reverse of Greek art, which started from the individual and *attempted to suggest* an ideal type.' (Quoted by D. H. Kahnweiler, *Juan Gris*, London, 1947, p. 137).

NOTES

CHAPTER IV
Pages 51–55

[1] Cf. H. Read, *Icon and Idea*, (London, 1955), chapter II.

CHAPTER V
Pages 56–61

Cf. Bertrand Russell, *Human Knowledge*, especially Part IV.
[2] *Biographia Literaria*, chap. XV. It occurs in the passage quoted in chap. IX of this essay, p. 124.

CHAPTER VI
Pages 62–65

[1] Cf. T. Munro, *The Arts and their Interrelations*, (New York, 1949), p. 251, where reference is made to a theory of medium as 'presented sensory images'.

CHAPTER VII
Pages 66–94

[1] Cf. W. H. Auden: 'The artist is occupied in his profession in converting this subjective material (i.e. 'the personal and the existential which are his subject matter') into an a-historical objective form, its actual disorder into one possible order among others' (*Partisan*, Feb. 1950).

[2] Cf. also Edward J. Dent's *Mozart* (Proc. Brit. Acad. XXXIX, 1953, p. 181–195), in which he adduces evidence for extensive preparatory technical work in Mozart's methods, contrary to the romantic view of his sheer naive inspiration.

In this connexion it is also worth mentioning that the *child* prodigy is a phenomenon of executants, and not of creative artists. And even in the remarkable Mozart it is not difficult to feel the experience and maturity of the great piano concertos as against the violin concertos written when he was nineteen, beautiful as they are.

[3] Cf. J.-P. Sartre, *The Psychology of Imagination*, pp. 211–217.

[4] I am not here ignoring, still less rejecting, *Gestalt* theories about immediate awareness of configurations in perception. *Gestalt* theory is important for aesthetic. As in the case of organic natural forms, however, the specific contribution of art lies beyond the processes which *Gestalt* theories illumine. This and related aspects of aesthetic are fully dealt with in H. Osborne's excellent *Theory of Beauty* (London, 1952).

[5] André Malraux, in *La Psychologie de l'Art*, overstates the view that artists are inspired by art rather than by life. They feed on both.

[6] Cf. the thesis of H. Read's *Icon and Idea*, London, 1955.

[7] Cf. William Empson, *The Verbal Analysis*, in *My Credo*, a symposium of Critics. Kenyon Review, XII, 4, 1950.

[8] Cf. the general argument of W. Worringer, *Abstraktion und Einfuhlung*, Müchen, 1908.

This idea does not justify propaganda art. Art may be used as, or degraded into, propaganda, but it has then become less than art in sacrificing its wholeness and honesty of sensibility to a principle of moral (or immoral) will and action. We recognize propaganda in the falsification of probability, which occurs whenever the subject is forced into a mould and made to fit a purpose, theory, dogma, or prejudice. It is then unconvincing because partial and deliberately evasive.

NOTES

9 *Note appended to Chapter VII.* Art may be recognized in the balanced relation between several features:

(1) A unified meaning (idea, emotion), presented in sensuous terms. (Excludes mere " ideas").

(2) A human interest, either objective or subjective. (Excludes mere "pattern").

(3) Novelty; art presents a statement, with a personal quality, not made before. (Excludes imitation).

(4) Powers of reason and sensibility which suggest "philosophical" awareness though not technical philosophy. (Excludes the commonplace and the trivial).

(5) Desire and catharsis. (Excludes the insincere and the calculated artefact).

(6) Technical ability, i.e. the "gift" or "genius" plus practice and virtuosity. (Excludes the incapable and the simple " dreamer").

CHAPTER VIII
Pages 95–119

1 Cf. the views of Croce, in his *Aesthetic.* His position was simple; art is always intuition, and intuitions always unique and individual, making classification a purely external matter.

The chapter on kinds and genres in R. Wellek and A. Warren, *Theory of Literature,* gives an excellent review of the problem.

2 The same principle applies to the use of stanza form. Here a single metrical form is repeated with different words throughout one single poem. Clearly the same metrical scheme appears with contents and meanings varying very considerably from stanza to stanza, which makes it difficult, especially in long poems, to maintain the extreme dogma that 'every content requires its own form'. In such cases the relations between words and metre are governed by the predominant idea or mood of the whole poem. One function of the metre is to maintain the sense of this ideal unity throughout a varying content. But the metre admits of elastic treatment in connexion with the words of the different stanzas. This subtle interchange between unity and variety, between the *general* expressiveness of the metre and the particular expressiveness of each word-rhythm pattern stanza by stanza, might be defined as a relatively constant imagery of one kind, used in complexity that varies from stanza to stanza.

3 Trying to be aesthetically exact leads to inelegant terms. I do not think that any terms precise enough to satisfy theory have much chance of being adopted for the common uses of criticism. One need not be unduly depressed by this because it is not necessary. "Kinds" and "forms", even the not entirely domiciled "genres", will continue to be used; they are useful classifications, and clear enough in a clear context. Like scientists, who in their stricter moments think of objects as systems of particles in movement, or as electronic patterns, but continue to use commonsense language, we can respond to the necessity for precise analytical terms without depriving ourselves of convenient and simple ones.

CHAPTER IX
Pages 120–156

1 Professor Mansell Jones, to whom I am indebted for reading through this chapter, suggested that a more explicit reference to Verlaine, especially to his poem *L'Art Poétique,* might be helpful, since he represents so strikingly the love of music as the "indefinite" art, the ethereal art of nuance and delicate suggestiveness, and the desire that poetry should cultivate a similar ideal. It was a view adopted in opposition to the pictorial and plastic style of the *Parnassiens,* and brings Verlaine into the proximity of Poe's ideals. In his introduction to *Modern French Verse. An Anthology* (Manchester

University Press, 1954), pp. 12–26, Professor Mansell Jones has discussed Verlaine in relation to Poe, Tennyson, Mallarmé and others; the reader is referred to this most illuminating account.

² Cf. the analysis in chapter III.

³ We remember also the words of Poe that were to be so often quoted : 'It is in Music, perhaps, that the soul most nearly attains the great end for which, when inspired by the Poetic Sentiment, it struggles—the creation of supernal Beauty." (The Poetic Principle, 1850). Cf. also this fragment of Novalis: 'Wenn man manche Gedichte in Musik setzt, warum setzt man Sie nicht in Poesie? ' (Novalis, *Werke*, Bd. III, p. 205 (Ed. Kluckhohn, Bibl. Inst., Leipzig)).

⁴ Quoted in Michaud, *La Doctrine Symboliste (Documents)* p.88 (Paris, 1947).

⁵ Cf. C. Soula, *Gloses sur Mallarmé* (Paris, 1945), for an analysis lending support to this view.

CHAPTER X

Pages 157–213

¹ For the connexion of early drama and ritual see H. Read, *Icon and Idea*, p. 57, and his reference (p. 144). to Jane Harrison's remarks on *dromenon* and *drama* in *Ancient Art and Ritual*.

² It is true, of course, that in baroque style this symbolism is elaborated in connexion with a religious attitude, the theatre becoming a symbol of the illusionary nature of mortal life.

³ A comparable feature in music is when fine performance enhances trivial music, though the effect is more restricted.

⁴ The richness of Shakespeare's poetic evocations makes realistic scenery and effects often more suitable than symbolic ones, giving a better balance. Certain features of the recent production of *King Lear*, with the décor and costumes of the Japanese artist Noguchi demonstrated this. The stylized tempest on the heath, for instance, was a cold play of intellect which failed to reinforce the drama. What is wanted here is the most direct sense of nature, a sharp naturalistic image of the forces Lear pits his strength against.

⁵ Cf. the reference to ancient writers on Sanskrit drama, and their theory of the principal "impressions" aroused by drama, in A. Nicoll, *The Theory of Drama*, p. 57.

⁶ A brilliant modern example is the second act of Cocteau's *Les Parents Terribles*, where Madeleine, receiving Michel's family in her flat, is still unaware that she is the mistress of both Georges and his son Michel.

⁷ In connexion with this problem cf. the account given by Madeleine Doran in *Endeavors of Art* (Madison, University of Wisconsin Press, 1954) about the Renaissance doctrine of decorum, character types, and "verisimilitude", p. 77 ff. and p. 216 ff.

⁸ The ambiguities (often cross-references for the *spectators*) in dialogue fulfil an important function here. Cf. W. Empson, *Seven Types of Ambiguity*, and W. Clemen, *The Development of Shakespeare's Imagery*, p. 90 f.

⁹ On this problem cf. J. I. M. Stewart, *Character and Motive in Shakespeare* (London, 1949), and criticisms of his views by A. Sewell, in *Character and Society in Shakespeare* (Oxford, 1951).

¹⁰ Giraudoux is reminiscent of Goethe in his treatment of persons in relation to ideas. Goethe's persons (Iphigenie, Tasso, Faust, etc.), whilst endowed with a measure of psychological reality, also develop symbolically into focal points or images for values or kinds of ethical sensibility. Cf. my essay *Goethe's Version of Poetic Drama*, Publications of the English Goethe Society, New Series, Vol. XVI, 1947.

¹¹ For a fuller analysis of the methods of Giraudoux and Eliot see my paper '*Public and Private Problems in Modern Drama*', Bulletin of the John Rylands Library, Vol. 36, No. 1, 1953.

NOTES

CHAPTER XI

Pages 214–240

[1] The criterion referred to here probably corresponds to Mr. T. S. Eliot's 'degree of form', with which he indicates the difference between prosaic and poetic plays.

[2] J. Middleton Murry has dealt with this problem in his *Shakespeare*, chap. XII. His solution is ingenious but it depends on using an identical motive for "poetic" expression in both fictive person and real poet, a parallel which my view of dramatic imagery excludes.

[3] Cf. for instance M. Doran, *Endeavors of Art*, esp. chap. 2.

[4] Cf. *L'École des Femmes*, Acte III, scène V :

Arnolphe, seul

Comme il faut devant lui que je me mortifie !
Quelle peine à cacher mon déplaisir cuisant !
Quoi ! pour une innocente un esprit si présent !
Elle a feint d'être telle à mes yeux, la traîtresse,
Ou le diable à son âme a soufflé cette adresse.
Enfin me voilà mort par ce funeste écrit.
Je vois qu'il a, le traître, empaumé son esprit,
Qu'à ma suppression il s'est ancré chez elle;
Et c'est mon désespoir et ma peine mortelle.
Je souffre doublement dans le vol de son coeur
Et l'amour y pâtit aussi bien que l'honneur.
J'enrage de trouver cette place usurpée,
Et j'enrage de voir ma prudence trompée.
Je sais que pour punir son amour libertin
Je n'ai qu'à laisser faire à son mauvais destin,
Que je serai vengé d'elle par elle-même;
Mais il est bien fâcheux de perdre ce qu'on aime.
Ciel ! puisque pour un choix j'ai tant philosophé,
Faut-il de ses appas m'être si fort coiffé !
Elle n'a ni parents, ni supports, ni richesse;
Elle trahit mes soins, mes bontés, ma tendresse :
Et cependant je l'aime, après ce lâche tour,
Jusqu'à ne me pouvoir passer de cet amour.
Sot, n'as-tu point de honte ? Ah! je crève, j'enrage,
Et je souffletterois mille fois mon visage.

[5] The Dionysian merriment of Aristophanes is a case apart.

BIBLIOGRAPHY

Lascelles Abercrombie, *The Idea of Great Poetry* (London, 1935).
The Theory of Poetry (London, 1924).
Richard Alewyn, *Der Geist des Barocktheaters*. In: *Weltliteratur*, Festgabe für Fritz Strich (Bern, 1952).
William Archer, *The Old Drama and the New* (London, 1923).
Aristotle, *Aristotle's Theory of Poetry and Fine Art, with a Critical Text and a translation of the Poetics*, by S. H. Butcher (London, 1895).
Charles Bally, *Précis de Stylistique* (Geneva, 1905).
Willi Baumeister, *Das Unbekannte in der Kunst*.
Eric Bentley, *The Modern Theatre* (London, 1948. American edition entitled 'The Playwright as Thinker').
R. P. Blackmur, *Language as Gesture* (London, 1954).
L. Bloomfield, *Language* (London, 1935).
P. Böckmann, *Formgeschichte der deutschen Dichtung* (Hamburg, 1949).
Maud Bodkin, *Archetypal Patterns in Poetry* (London, 1948).
M. C. Bradbrook, *Themes and Conventions of Elizabethan Tragedy* (Cambridge, 1935).
Elizabethan Stage Conditions (Cambridge, 1932).
A. C. Bradley, *Shakespearian Tragedy* (London, 1904).
Oxford Lectures on Poetry (London, 1909).
W. Russell Brain, *Mind, Perception and Science* (Oxford, 1951).
Cleanth Brooks, *The Well Wrought Urn* (London, 1949).
E. Bullough, 'Mind and Medium in Art' (*British Journal of Psychology*, Vol. XI, Part 1, 1920-21).
' "Psychical" Distance as a factor in art and an aesthetic principle', *ibid.*, Vol. V, 2, 1912-13).
M. W. Bundy, *The theory of imagination in classical and mediaeval thought* (Illinois, 1927).
Kenneth Burke, *A Grammar of Motives* (New York, 1945).
Ernst Cassirer, *Philosophie der symbolischen Formen* (Berlin, 1923-1929).
Sir Kenneth Clark, *Landscape into Art* (London, 1949).
S. T. Coleridge, *Lectures and notes on Shakespeare and other dramatists* (London, 1883).
Biographia Literaria (London, 1817).
R. G. Collingwood, *The Principles of Art* (Oxford, 1938).
E. Gordon Craig, *On the Art of the Theatre* (London, 1929).
Marcel Cressot, *Le Style et ses Techniques* (Paris, 1951).
Henri Delacroix, *Psychologie de l'Art* (Paris, 1927).

E. J. Dent, *Foundations of English Opera* (Cambridge, 1928).
  Opera (Penguin Special, London, 1940).
John Dewey, *Art as Experience* (London, 1934).
Madeleine Doran, *Endeavors of Art: A Study of Form in Elizabethan Drama*
  (Madison, Wisc., 1954).
G. Du Genet, *Jean Giraudoux* (Paris, 1945).
Anton Ehrenzweig, *The Psycho-analysis of artistic vision and hearing* (London,
  1953).
T. S. Eliot, *Poetry and Drama* (London, 1951).
  Selected Essays 1917-32 (London, 1932).
  Dramatis Personae (*Criterion*, vol. I, 1923).
  'The Duchess of Malfi and Poetic Drama', in *Art and Letters* (Winter
  1920).
Una Ellis-Fermor, *The Frontiers of Drama* (London, 1948).
Dorothy Emmett, *The Nature of Metaphysical Thinking* (London, 1945).
William Empson, *Seven Types of Ambiguity* (London, 1947).
  The Structure of Complex Words (London, 1951).
  Some Versions of Pastoral (London, 1950).
English Institute Essays 1949, edited by Alan S. Downer (New York, 1950)
Essays on Language and Literature by Proust, Valéry, Sartre, Paulhan,
  Ponge, Parain. Edited by J. L. Hevesi (London, 1947).
Francis Fergusson, *The Idea of a Theater* (Princeton University Press, 1949).
Henri Focillon, *La Vie des Formes* (Paris, 1947).
Katharine E. Gilbert and Helmut Kuhn, *A History of Esthetics* (New
  York, 1939).
H. Goldschmidt, *Die Musikaesthetik des* 18. *Jahrhunderts* und ihre Begiehun-
  gen zu sei nem Kunstschaffen (Zürich und Leipzig, 1915).
Robert Graves, *The Common Asphodel* (London, 1949).
Jane Harrison, *Ancient Art and Ritual* (London, 1913).
Robert Hartl, *Versuch einer psychologischen Grundlegung der Dichtungs-
  gattungen* (Wien, 1924).
Phyllis Hartnoll (ed.), *The Oxford Companion to the Theatre* (London, 1951).
Artur Henkel, *Die Spekulative Musikanschauung des Novalis* (unpublished
  Dr. phil. dissertation, Graz, 1941, kindly lent by the author).
T. R. Henn, *The Apple and the Spectroscope* (London, 1951).
Werner Hilbert, *Die Musikaesthetik der Frühromantik* (Remscheid, 1910).
Gunnar Høst, *L'oeuvre de Jean Giraudoux* (Oslo, 1942).
Humphrey House, *Coleridge*. The Clark Lectures, 1951-52 (London,
  1953).
Erich Rudolf Jaensch, *Eidetic Imagery and typological methods of investigation*
  (London, 1930).
D. G. James, *Scepticism and poetry* (London, 1937).
P. Mansell Jones, *The Background to Modern French Poetry* (Cambridge, 1951).
  Baudelaire (Cambridge, 1952).
Wolfgang Kayser, *Das sprachliche Kunstwerk* (Bern, 1948).
Paul Kluckhohn, *Die Arten des Dramas*, in *Deutsche Vierteljahrsschrift
  für Geistesgeschichte und Literaturwissenschaft* (Vol. XIX, 1941).
G. Wilson Knight, *The Wheel of Fire* (London, 1930).
L. C. Knights, *Explorations* (London, 1946).

BIBLIOGRAPHY

Susanne Langer, *Philosophy in a New Key* (Cambridge, Mass., 1942).
  Feeling and Form (London, 1953).
James Laver, *Drama—its costume and décor* (London, 1951).
Harry Levin, *The Overreacher* (London, 1954).
C. Day Lewis, *The Poetic Image*. The Clark Lectures, 1946 (London, 1947).
C. S. Lewis, *Variation in Shakespeare and others* (in *Rehabilitations*, London, 1939).
Sir Desmond MacCarthy, *Drama* (London, 1940).
Charles Mauron, *Mallarmé l'Obscur* (Paris, 1941).
  Aesthetics and Psychology (London, 1935).
Kathi Meyer, *Bedeutung und Wesen der Musik* (Leipzig, Strasbourg, Zürich, 1932).
Guy Michaud, *Message poétique du symbolisme*, vols. I-III (Paris, 1947).
  La Doctrine symboliste (Paris, 1947).
  Mallarmé (Paris, 1953).
R. Müller-Freienfels, *Psychologie der Musik* (Berlin, 1936).
Thomas Munro, *The Arts and their Interrelations* (New York, 1950).
J. Middleton Murry, *The Problem of Style* (London, 1922).
  Shakespeare (London, 1936).
Walter Muschg, *Tragische Literaturgeschichte* (Bern, 1948).
Eric Newton, *The Meaning of Beauty* (London, 1950).
Allardyce Nicoll, *The Theory of Drama* (London, 1931).
Friedrich Nietzsche, *Die Geburt der Tragödie aus dem Geiste der Musik*.
E. Noulet, *L'oeuvre poétique de Stéphane Mallarmé* (Paris, 1940).
H. Osborne, *Theory of Beauty* (London, 1952).
Brice Parain, *Recherches sur la Nature et les Fonctions du Langage* (Paris, 1942).
A. F. Robert Petsch, *Wesen und Formen des Dramas* (Halle, 1945).
Jean Piaget, *Play, Dreams and Imitation in Childhood* (London, 1951).
John Press, *The Fire and the Fountain* (London, 1955).
H. H. Price, *Perception* (London, 1932).
  Thinking and Experience (London, 1953).
Moody E. Prior, *The Language of Tragedy* (New York, 1947).
Herbert Read, *The Meaning of Art* (London, 1931. Pelican edition, 1949).
  Art and Society (London, 1937, 1945).
  'The Dynamics of Art', *Eranos Jahrbuch*, xxi, 1952).
  The True Voice of Feeling (London, 1953).
  Icon and Idea (London, 1955).
Ernest Reynolds, *Modern English Drama* (London, 1949).
Théodule Armand Ribot, *Essai sur l'imagination créatrice* (Paris, 1900).
I. A. Richards, *Principles of Literary Criticism* (London, 1924).
  Science and Poetry (London, 1926).
  Practical Criticism (London, 1930).
  The Philosophy of Rhetoric (New York, 1936).
Bertrand Russell, *Human Knowledge* (London, 1948).
J.-P. Sartre, *Situations I-III* (Paris, 1947).
  L'Imagination (Paris, 1948).
  The Psychology of Imagination (London, 1950).
R. A. Sayce, *Style in French Prose* (Oxford, 1953).

BIBLIOGRAPHY

Arnold Schering, *Beethoven und die Dichtung* (Berlin, 1936).
Das Symbol in der Musik (Leipzig, 1941).
Friedrich Schiller, *Ueber Matthissons Gedichte.*
A. Sewell, *Character and Society in Shakespeare* (Oxford, 1951).
C. Spearman, *Creative Mind* (London, 1930).
Emil Staiger, *Grundbegriffe der Poetik* (Zürich, 1943).
J. I. M. Stewart, *Character and Motive in Shakespeare* (London, 1949).
Adrian Stokes, *Art and Science* (London, 1949).
J. M. Thorburn, *Art and the Unconscious* (London, 1925).
The Times Music Critic, Various articles on general problems of music
and aesthetic, published from time to time in recent years.
D. F. Tovey, *A Musician Talks* (1) *The Integrity of Music* (2) *Musical
Textures* (Oxford, 1941).
Lionel Trilling, *The Liberal Imagination* (New York, 1951).
R. Wellek & Austin Warren, *Theory of Literature* (London, 1949).
George Whalley, *Poetic Process* (London, 1953).
Wilhelm Worringer, *Abstraktion und Einfühlung* (Munich, 1908). (English
translation—*Abstraction and Empathy*, London, 1953).

INDEX

DATE DUE
DATE DE RETOUR

LOWE-MARTIN No. 1137